Till Death Don't Us Part

A True Story of Awakening to Love After Life

Till Death Don't Us Part

A True Story of Awakening to Love After Life

Karen Frances McCarthy

www.whitecrowbooks.com

Praise for *Till Death Don't Us Part*

~

"A beautiful and candid account of Karen Frances McCarthy's personal experience of falling in love and how her world is torn apart by her fiancé's sudden death. The shock of loss and the madness of grief are vividly expressed in writing that is full of light and darkness, sadness, and despair. Then, confronted by a series of curious incidences, she opens her mind to a challenging possibility and takes the reader along on her fascinating journey of discovery and ultimately hope. A gripping modern love story that transcends all boundaries."

~ **Juanita Wilson**, Writer/Director & Academy Award® Nominee

"I saw Karen go through the experiences described in *Till Death Don't Us Part*. At first, we both thought she was crazy, but it quickly became obvious that something was going on. That strange journey is captured in this riveting story of her being forced to accept what that "something" was. This story blends her inquisitive nature with her dry, Irish humor, and reminds me once again that her experiences made me believe in things I never thought I could believe in."

~ **Alexandra Lipsitz**, Filmmaker & Peabody Award Winner

"A news reporter and former diehard skeptic, McCarthy gives us an entertaining, impeccably researched, and brilliantly written page-turner about continuing love after life, that will move, amaze, and provide deep comfort with its glorious, inspiring, and deafening ring of truth."

~ **Jennifer Belle**, bestselling author of
Going Down and *High Maintenance*

"Karen Frances McCarthy blends journalistic rigor with the heartfelt pain over losing the love of her life in *Till Death Don't Us Part*. It's a fascinating transformational journey that challenges all our assumptions about death."

~ **Susan Shapiro**, *New York Times* bestselling author of
Five Men Who Broke My Heart & Byline Bible

"This beautifully crafted book addresses one of the major questions in life: 'What happens when we die?' Karen starts her journey like many people, from a point of skepticism, but after the pain and grief of losing the man she loved, she provides the reader an insight into her journey to a new reality which helped heal her pain and bring a new dimension to her life through which she could help others. She shows how the message of Spiritualism is transformational to the lives of many thousands of people as they come to understand from an evidence-based approach that death is not the end but rather the gateway to a whole new world."

~ **Minister David R Bruton** MBA, President Spiritualists' National
Union & Principal of the Arthur Findlay College

"Whether skeptic or believer, readers of this absorbing memoir will not easily put it down. A riveting read, Karen Frances McCarthy's memoir lifts the veil off reality hidden from many of us and exposes the larger dimensions of life, love, and the appearance of death. In dialogue with science, psychology, and world religions, her memoir restores faith in the old biblical adage that "love is strong as death." Readers will come away heartened and fortified for whatever lies ahead and will feel themselves changed by the end of the story, but then part of the author's point is that there really is no end, only beginnings."

~ **Professor Ernest Rubinstein**, Adjunct Assistant Professor of
Humanities, NYU School of Professional Studies

"This book's flowing narrative style makes it hard to put down. As you read her experiences in this easily read page turner, you find out what made a pragmatic, atheistic, skeptical war correspondent become a true believer in life after death. She shows satisfactorily that indeed consciousness continues and that an individual can communicate with those still on Earth, bringing comfort and a sense of joy that they have survived."

~ **Tricia J. Robertson**, Author of *Things You Can Do When You're Dead* & Former President of the Scottish Society for Psychical Research

"Karen Frances McCarthy is an extraordinary writer. In *Till Death Don't Us Part* she tells a love story with a difference. She has a way of capturing your attention and making small moments memorable with an exquisite turn of phrase. This is a book we can wholeheartedly recommend to the newly-bereaved as well as to the seasoned afterlife researcher. It is guaranteed to make you see so many things in new ways."

~ **Victor and Wendy Zammit**, Co-authors of *A Lawyer Presents the Evidence for the Afterlife* and the *Friday Afterlife Report*

"Karen's journey is an important read for all who seek answers and solace after the loss of a loved one. Karen was a complete skeptic in regard to the phenomena she began experiencing after the death of her beloved fiancé. Even so, with the eye of a journalist, she began to explore widely divergent possibilities about their cause, including scientific ones, religious, and spiritual. Her colorful way with words makes this book even more inviting and inspirational to those searching for hope and a belief that our loved ones can communicate with us even after death."

~ **Nancy Eubel**, Author of *Mindwalking, Rewrite Your Past to Create Your Future* & former co-executive director of Edgar Cayce's Association for Research and Enlightenment

Published in the United States of America and the United Kingdom by
White Crow Books; an imprint of White Crow Productions Ltd.

For information, contact White Crow Books by e-mail: info@whitecrowbooks.com.

Cover Design by Astrid@Astridpaints.com
Interior design by Velin@Perseus-Design.com

Library of Congress Control Number: 2020907221

A CIP catalogue record for this book is available from the British Library

Paperback ISBN: 978-1-78677-129-2
eBook ISBN: 978-1-78677-130-8

Non-Fiction / Body, Mind & Spirit / Memoir / Death & Dying

www.whitecrowbooks.com

Contents

Preface

The end turned out to be the beginning. The beginning turned out to be an excruciating but ultimately enlightening journey to come to terms with the overwhelming evidence that my beloved not only survived death but was communicating from the hereafter.

It wasn't an easy paradigm shift to make. As a former political journalist, war correspondent, atheist, and sceptic, I needed facts, evidence, something so compelling that I would be left with no option but to accept that we don't die, that consciousness is not an emergent property of the brain, that love endures, and that we are never alone. In the shrinking of self that accompanied my grief and in my distrust of my own senses, I found myself torn between the desire to believe and my need not to be desperate or delusional. Yet, strange occurrences meant the questions persisted: What is life? Is reality simply sensory information or is it something more? My search for answers involved a challenging personal and spiritual transformation that demanded I not only learn to trust in a power greater than me but that I also learn to trust myself.

The message in this book therefore is not one that describes life *in* the hereafter. It's a message about how awakening to the continuity of life after death not only helps us fully experience love but also enriches our understanding of the complexity of existence. To paraphrase Confucius — to know death, we must first know life. This is a story therefore about how death affirms life, about awakening to the magnificence of life and to the feeling of ultimate oneness that can only be called *home*. It's a story of how accepting our connection to all beings gifts us with an open mind, an open heart, and the ability to heal. It's a story of how a willingness to receive the compassion shared with us from loved ones in the spirit form can fill our lives with joy and purpose.

As my wise friend, Professor Ernest Rubinstein said, this is "a story that doesn't just save us from our fear of death but also from the vague uneasiness and sense of disconnection that sometimes infect a life." This gift was offered to me from my beloved, and I now offer it to you. I hope that my journey shows how magnificent is both life and life after life. I hope it inspires you to contemplate the biggest and most unanswerable questions because it's in striving to understand that we are part of something greater that we understand that we are truly spiritual beings. Above all, for those grieving, I hope these pages bring you the comfort of knowing you are eternally loved and that your loved ones walk with you, always.

Karen Frances McCarthy
June 5, 2020

Acknowledgements

Most of the names in the following pages have been changed to protect individuals' privacy, but the teachers, spiritual figures, and healers who were influential on my path appear by name. To all those who helped me on this journey, named or pseudo-named, I offer my heartfelt thanks. I would not be where I am without you.

I also extend my utmost gratitude to the members of my writer's group, led by fabulous writer and writing coach, Jennifer Belle, who offered constructive criticism as I wrote this book. Your contribution helped enrich and clarify the events as they poured onto the page. Thank you to my friends who read early drafts and offered feedback and encouragement, and to those who in one way or another helped me along the way: Victoria Johnson, Ernest Rubinstein, Juanita Wilson, Lisa Hagan, Tricia Robertson, and a special thanks to Karen Rupert Toliver who, over coffee and pastries in the East Village some years ago, encouraged me to write these words. Many thanks, of course, to Jonathan Beecher at White Crow Books who believed in the story.

Finally, to my parents—both of whom passed on to new adventures since this story began—thank you for a lifetime of love and inspiration. And to my beloved, thank you for filling my life with magic.

The End

'We'll be Friends Forever, won't we, Pooh?' asked Piglet.
'Even longer,' Pooh answered.

A.A. Milne

I was starving when I got back from the army base at Fayetteville, North Carolina. I ordered lunch and called Johann from my motel room. We'd only been engaged four weeks, and I'd spent two of them stuck in the sweltering South, writing a follow-up story about a Colonel I'd met in Iraq. I thought I'd never get back to New York and away from fast food, lousy motels, and the exponential aging that comes with being called ma'am by soldiers half my age. Mainly, I wanted to get back to him. There was no answer. I dialed again. Voicemail. He was probably off with James on their usual weekend bike ride up the Hudson River and out of the city. "Food for his soul" he would have called it had he believed in a soul.

"Call me," I texted. "I miss you."

I was eating a veggie burger and pouring over my notes when the phone rang.

"James is trying to reach you." It was my friend Roisin. She was anxious.

"Why?"

"He's at St. Luke's Hospital with Johann."

"What happened? Was he in an accident?" I asked.

"I don't know," she said.

1

"I'll call James."

I dialed quickly and walked to the window for better reception.

"He just collapsed," James said. "We'd cycled out to Jersey and went by Riverside Park on the way back. He said he wasn't feeling well, so we stopped to rest. He was holding his arm and then he fell off the bench and smashed his head on the ground."

James's words heaved from his mouth.

"His heart?" I said. "It's okay. He'll be fine. He's only forty-one. You're at St. Luke's! That's only twenty blocks from the park. He'll be fine. Did someone give him CPR?"

"Some woman tried, and then a parks department guy took over."

"Okay, that's good. He'll be fine."

I was saying "he'll be fine" like a mantra that would make it true.

"Was it vigorous?" I added.

"Not really," he said. "They didn't breathe into his mouth because his face was covered in blood."

A chill crept up my spine.

"I think he's dead," he said.

"No!" I was shrill. "He'll be fine, I'm telling you he'll be fine."

"Hang on," James said. "Cops are here. I'll call you back."

"Don't ..."

He hung up.

I frenzy dialed him for ten minutes until he answered.

"He's dead," he said.

Night fell over Fayetteville. My cold, half-eaten veggie burger sat on the tacky motel table. Life gutted between two bites. My back ached from the lumpy motel armchair into which I'd slumped from dusk into darkness. It never occurred to me to turn on the light. My mind accepted James's words in fragments for fear it be overwhelmed by their assault. My capacity to make the most basic decision was absurdly diminished. I sat. I lay. I stood. I paced. Catatonic one hour and panicked the next. Wasn't there something I could do? Surely something would make me feel less lost, less adrift.

I'd given James the number for Johann's ex that afternoon to pass along to the hospital administrators. It felt like an important thing to do, although she may have been listed as his emergency contact since she was the mother of Tommy, their ten-year-old son and next of kin. What next? His family in Germany? He'd all but lost touch with them since he left East Berlin a few years after the wall came down. I had a number for his step-mother, but she didn't speak English, and I'd no information for his estranged biological mother. I shifted around the room, picking up my phone and putting it down. I didn't even know if I should call. Was it up to me? Or his ex? Or the hospital? Why hadn't I learned German? Why was I so useless?

Later that night, when all competence and comprehension had withered from my shrunken mind, his ex called me. She and Johann had lived separate lives for so many years that she didn't know who else to call. In my haze, I heard her say she spoke German. I heard myself give her what numbers I had since she was better equipped to break the news to his family. She'd arrange a quick and private funeral, I heard her say. Whatever the acrimony between her and Johann had been, her only concern now was protecting Tommy, she said. He needed the support of his family and friends, so a private mourning for him was the only way, she said. He was all that mattered now, she said. She was moving from one pithy statement to the next before I'd absorbed the meaning of the first. I just heard myself punctuating each sentence with, "I understand" like an echo that denied my needs or rights. It didn't occur to me to ask to come to the funeral, and she didn't extend an invite. It didn't occur to me until later that I'd also need the ritual and the gathering of supportive friends. Such was the shriveling of self I experienced in the darkness of his death.

For the next two days, the curtains remained drawn and the "do not disturb" sign hung on my door. Every so often, I'd hear the charwomen pushing their trolley down the hall. I'd stick my head out for more coffee and decline room service. *Leave the mess and death,* my expression said. *Nothing bright or fresh belongs in here.* I didn't belong there either, but I couldn't face New York. I belonged nowhere.

On the third day, a friend persuaded me to caretake a house in the Chesapeake Bay area for the homeowner she knew who was traveling for a couple of months. Where that was, I neither knew nor cared, but anything was better than going home.

I picked up a beat-up red Mustang convertible in Fayetteville for $1200. The Ford decals were missing, and the creaking door had to be lifted to close. I was pretty sure it had been in an accident, then dragged out of a salvage yard, slapped together with some spit and spray paint, and rolled back onto the road. Much like me. That day, we were two wrecks on a blistering hot mountainous drive to nowhere.

I followed my GPS off the interstate onto a narrow road that fed into a tiny town organized into geometric streets lined with brightly painted houses that watched over the hum and swish of sprinklers hydrating perfectly landscaped gardens. The place was deserted and the heat oppressive. I pulled up in front of a hulking forest-green house partially hidden behind tall pine trees that housed hundreds, maybe thousands, of cicada that screeched through my throbbing brain. In some quirk of bad taste, the owner had given the house a dark pink trim and decked out the porch in chimes and lamps that were now covered in cobwebs. I dragged my bags up the steps under the watchful eye of a suspicious cat. A curtain twitched opposite, probably someone horrified at the jalopy I'd parked in their perfect neighborhood. I didn't care. I wasn't there to make friends. I was there to hide. Talking exhausted me. Not talking exhausted me. Sleeping exhausted me.

As instructed, I retrieved the key from a shed in the overgrown garden along with the house manual for feeding Busker the cat, watering the plants, using the cleaning supplies, scraping the lint out of the dryer, and another ten pages of stick-up-her-arse instructions. I'd been angry and bereft and anxious about Johann for five hundred miles. We were supposed to be eloping and adventuring in South America; instead, I was walking into the triviality of a stranger's world order.

Inside, this place looked less like a house and more like a mausoleum with mahogany stairs, doors, and floors. I hated mahogany. The half-pulled blinds let in just enough light for the gasping plants to survive, and the stagnant smell of mildew made me heave. I filled Busker's bowls and hauled my bags up two flights of stairs to the sparse attic apartment that was to be my home for the next two months. It had a bed, a makeshift table with a gaudy brass lamp, and an old chest of drawers. The bedding was clean at least, white, not muddied like everything else in this place.

I lay on the bed, in the cool air streaming from the attic fan, staring at the dust particles floating in the shafts of sunlight that limped through the small window in the sloping ceiling. Tears came again. I didn't want to cry. For hundreds of miles, I'd dripped tears and snot, until my head throbbed and throat was raw. My heart raced and pain pinched my breath as it had been doing for three days now. I didn't unpack, or eat, or shower. I just lay on the bed, scrolling through old photos of Johann on my phone. I knew that was a bad idea. I knew better than to scratch at moments that had been sculpted in another time, but I did, compulsively, in an absurd attempt to cling to the life we had and

4

the promise he'd made to be with me till the end of days. There he was on my tiny screen, handsome in a German Roger Moore sort of way, smiling across the dinner table the night he proposed. I couldn't take my eyes off him then. But now? Now, that memory hurt my heart.

I tossed my phone aside and sank deeper into the pillows on a stranger's bed in an ugly house at the end of nowhere, falling asleep watching leaves dance in fading sunbeams as dusk murdered the day.

It was late afternoon when I woke again. Pain fractured my brain. I dragged myself downstairs and brewed the last grains of some bitter coffee I found in the pantry, and then went into the garden to drink it in the shade of pine trees. Busker curled up at my feet. They say animals can sense a person's distress. I didn't know if Busker did, but the warmth of his tiny body on my feet was the only comfort I knew that day.

The sky was so blue here, unblemished by the clouds that usually offer protection from the throbbing sun. It sapped the last of my feeble energy reserves and forced me back up the creaking old stairs and into bed. Twenty hours later, I woke again with a splitting headache and a furry mouth. I told myself to get up, find my toothbrush, and dig up some coffee, but I couldn't move. For twenty hours, I'd been oblivious, and now I was back. I wished the world would die.

Something caught my eye.

Something was moving on the bed — small, round indentations were tip-toeing up the duvet like the imprints of invisible animal paws. I lay still, straining to see if something were casting shadows, but the sunlight created linear streaks not circles across the bed. I couldn't understand how these depressions were being made. They approached steadily and stopped close to my head. I waited, but they didn't start again. Finally, I dismissed the imprints as a trick of the light playing on my eyes and rolled over, desperate to escape into the oblivion of sleep.

My phone beeped with a text from my friend Sara in LA.

"I know you feel like shit. Shower. Get dressed. Sometimes that's all we can do."

I did stink. I didn't care, but I needed coffee and Busker needed cat food, so I showered, dragged my wet hair into a ponytail, put on fresh clothes and dark sunglasses, and drove to a drugstore I passed on the way into town. It was a real drugstore, like the ones I'd only seen in American movies when I was growing up in Ireland. It was selling pop and ice cream across a Formica bar to a couple of kids sitting on silver stools. I picked up cat food, a large bottle of Advil, and vacuum-packed

Bustelo. I needed food too but hadn't the energy to cook. I found a stack of cup noodles. "Just add water," the package said. That would do.

"Betty, this is the last time I'm letting you off, okay?" the red-faced cashier said to a humped, old woman in front of me in the queue who didn't have enough money to pay for her groceries. The cashier stuffed Betty's few purchases into a plastic bag with mutters and tuts. She apologized to me for the delay. I shrugged. Betty looked bewildered, or maybe she was humiliated. I really wasn't paying much attention.

I was halfway up the mausoleum steps with my grocery bags when I met the middle-aged man next door.

"Hello," he said. "I'm Gerry. Welcome to the Bay."

"Thanks," I said. I might have smiled. I'd been disconnected here, and glad to be, until Gerry. I had to get away. I slipped back inside, for once glad to go back to the brooding mahogany and the musty smell that lingered inside on the dead air.

At sunset, seeing the street was clear of neighbors and the danger of small talk, I ventured the half-mile to the seafront with the cat trotting after me until he got fed up and went home. On the strand, parents were packing up their kids' beach toys and ushering them homeward. Some people were still fishing off a pier. Other than that, I was alone. I stepped into the cool water, digging my toes into the sand. It was fresh here and salty, not like New York. I thought there'd be nothing here to remind me of Johann. But there was the sun. Always the sun. We often sat on the East River at dusk, watching it set and the lights of the Manhattan skyline come on.

Our first sunset hadn't been on the river's edge exactly. It was at a summer party on the rooftop of an industrial building turned into artist lofts overlooking the waterfront. Sara was in town and invited me along. Her friend Hans, an East German arthouse filmmaker, was known for throwing the building open to the local artists and writers and most of its barflies. I was new to the neighborhood and knew no one. We weren't long at the party when Sara and Hans started getting cozy in the corner. I leaned against the low wall around the roof, the only sober person in a sea of booze and a cloud of weed, watching beautiful people drift and flit and hug and kiss while they shared beer and vodka and spliffs.

The sun was setting when a tall, blonde guy I'd seen in passing at a Polish café a week before arrived with a handful of Europeans — French and German by the sound of them. I didn't know him as Johann then. Their small group trickled into the larger one on the rooftop like rivulets of art and sophistication. I watched him. I couldn't take my eyes off him to be honest. He was surrounded by chattering people who were getting drunk and high. He was listening to them, that much I could tell, and every so often he'd say something I couldn't hear, and they'd all laugh. He was the center of that group but detached somehow, as if he were entertained by the drama of people offloading drunken secrets that tomorrow they'd be ashamed of sharing. He seemed private, saying little and revealing nothing. We were both alone, I thought, me by myself and him in a crowd.

After dark, an awful arthouse movie that Hans had made was projected onto a makeshift screen. I was sidling toward the door when Johann intercepted me with two bottles of Pilsner.

"You look lost," he said in a crisp German accent. He offered me a bottle.

"Thanks, but I don't drink," I said.

"Then both for me," he said.

"You like German beer?" I asked.

"As often as possible," he smiled. He had a shy smile, which made this gorgeous social animal even more alluring.

"Johann, we're leaving," someone shouted. The Europeans were packing up and getting out. "Gustave invited us back for eats."

Johann took a card out of his pocket and scribbled something on the back.

"My address. Brunch at eleven at my place tomorrow. They'll be there," he said, tilting his head back toward the crowd, "but don't let that stop you."

He glanced back before disappearing out the door in the midst of the group. I'd spoken to him for less than five minutes, but my heart fluttered when he looked at me.

The palpitations I'd had since the day he died were pinching my heart again. I left the empty strand and slouched back to the mausoleum where I found Busker crying on the deck beside empty bowls. I opened a tin of cat food while he meowed and danced under my feet in his eagerness to get to his dinner. The mausoleum manual said to feed him in the sunroom because he sprayed the furniture, but the sunroom was like a greenhouse; it was always hot as hell in there. I guess the owner preferred to bake the creature than have stinky furniture. I preferred she have stinky furniture, so I fed him in the cooler kitchen, brewed some more coffee, and watched this little cat devour his dinner. He was scrawny but cute, a little prickly, but there was something sweet about him all the same. While he ate, I watered the wilting plants and raised the blinds so some light could get in before everything in this house was dead. Johann said once that he was afraid of getting old and not being needed or useful. I understood him now — caring for a cat and a handful of plants was all I had to hold onto.

I climbed up to attic with Busker on my heels. Shafts of moonlight limped through the window. Hopper's "Moonlight Interior" came to mind. I always thought the woman in that painting was deliciously liberated, unabashedly naked in front of an open window, and about to share sexual delights with her secret lover who's out of frame; but that night, as I crawled back into bed, its shades of yellow and brown only reminded me of piss and shit.

A strange knocking came from inside the house. It was a rhythmic knock, slow and steady, not like a knocking at the door. I was trying to localize it when it started banging in rapid fire like a machine gun.

Pop. Pop. Pop. Pop. Pop.

It reverberated through the house. Disorienting. Unnatural. What the hell was it? An animal? Had an animal gotten into the house?

I forced myself out of the attic and into the stairwell, clutching the banister tightly, while the knocking got louder and faster. Step after reluctant step I took with a pounding heart and stifled breath.

It stopped. I waited. Silence. I pried my hand off the banister and watched my sweaty imprint evaporate. I crept down to the second floor, peaking under the beds from a distance, and then to the first floor, timidly looking around and under the glut of mahogany tables and chairs, but there was nothing there that I could see. Nothing I could hear except for the distant hum of a generator. I felt disturbed and then ridiculous — paranoid from moping alone in this dark place. There had to be an explanation, but I had neither the energy nor interest to give it more thought. I hadn't the energy or interest in anything then, not without my love.

It was love at first sight, although it took me some time to realize this. I heard someone say once that if we're not transformed by love, we haven't loved enough. No one could accuse Johann and me of that. Our story didn't evolve from love at first sight into a perfect relationship and perfect life. It took four years of hell and heaven and love and tears, hewing and chipping each other's edges until we polished ourselves into a congruous form. Whoever said life with the love of your life would be easy never knew love; it wasn't perfect, but goodness, was it glorious.

Johann was a smart man with a wry sense of humor, but as his friend Peter said later, the funniest people are usually the most sad. On the outside, he was witty and sociable, but inside, suffering had turned optimism to criticism, humor to sarcasm, and the need to be loved to the need to self-soothe in unhealthy ways. He was kind, but to a select few, engaging, but emotionally distant, and if he loved you, well, you better strap in for a maelstrom of love, desire, devotion, and self-loathing.

The truth was, he wasn't joking that night on the rooftop when he said he loved to drink. On the weekends that he didn't have Tommy, he indulged his every impulse. It's hard for a sober person to maintain a relationship with someone who's acting out. It's hard for someone who's acting out to maintain a relationship at all. We'd be inseparable, then he'd retreat into himself for days. "You wouldn't benefit from my company today," he'd simply say. We cycled between the peaks and valleys of devotion and remorse, while his lifestyle turned mine into one of emotional unpredictability and secrecy and arguments that I didn't begin and the cause of which I rarely understood. It was impossible to know what to expect in those crazy days before neither of us could take any more of the way things were.

"Maybe I should give up drinking," he said one evening when we were curled up on the sofa watching a movie, him playing with my hair as he often did when he was in a good mood.

"Maybe?" I asked.

"Maybe is a baby-step in the right direction given my fear of commitment," he replied.

"Do you think you'll be happy on the wagon?" I'd asked.

"Life will be a Shirley Temple with two cherries," he said. "Who wouldn't be happy?"

"Seriously," I said.

"Hope so," he replied. "I want to go to AA meetings. How would working 12-steps work for me? I'm not a fan of sharing. I don't really have anything interesting to share since I'm an extremely well-behaved drunk, and I don't want to go to a meeting in a depressing moldy church basement. Is there a meeting in a nicer setting?"

"What a snob you are!" I said. "Deal with the moldy setting."

He groaned.

"And don't think for a minute that you're a well-behaved drunk."

I was relieved when he stopped drinking, but sobriety is hard work. There's nothing like it to spotlight the wounds that alcohol medicates. At first, Johann complained about how boring life had become. I worried if a sober life would be enough, and given how much he loved the attention of women and how much of that he got, I wondered if I'd be enough.

"Will you be happy with monogamy and me?" I asked, when he'd counted thirty days of sobriety.

"I'm already happy," he said, squeezing me. "Don't worry. Everything will be fine."

I wasn't entirely sure which one of us he was trying to convince, until a week later when he dispelled my lingering insecurities with a few little words that I knew to be true. We were sitting in an almost empty movie theater eating chocolate cherries and watching *The Lives of Others*. The film was set in communist East Berlin in the mid-eighties when artists were heavily censored. It tells the story of a couple, a writer and an actress, who are under surveillance by the Stasi on suspicion of compromising state security. The poor Stasi agent tasked with spying on them becomes secretly sympathetic and covers for them to prevent their arrest. The agent, a solitary character without any life of his own, reports for work each day in the drabness of East Berlin, harboring unexpressed sympathies for art and theater and yearning for freedom within the regime he perpetuates.

"*Ich bin jetzt ganz bei dir. Ganz egal was,*" Johann whispered.

"What?"

"That's what Christa just said. Aren't you listening?"

"It's a German movie," I whispered. "I'm reading subtitles. I'm not listening."

Except for rustling chocolate cherries out of the cellophane bag, Johann was silent throughout the movie. This was the world in which he grew up, the son of an artist who had spent almost a year in jail on the orders of the new communist party. After going to live with his father after his parent's divorce, his stepmother packed him off to boarding school as a teen. He was forced voluntarily like everyone else his age into Honecker's Free German Youth before doing his eighteen-month military service for the *Sekretär für Agitation und Propaganda*. He said he was a pencil pusher, but his whole life had been steeped in secrecy and lies and manipulation, something he loathed but mastered in his own way to protect himself.

He offered me the last chocolate cherry and slipped his arm around my shoulders.

"She said '*Ich bin jetzt ganz bei dir. Ganz egal, was*,'" he repeated. He kissed my forehead and both my eyelids, which he often did. "It means 'I'm with you now no matter what.'"

I woke to the smell of cigarette smoke hanging on the attic air. Dawn had broken over the bay. I inhaled the smell deeply, the way I secondhand smoked Johann's Lucky Strikes after I quit. It reminded me of him, but this was different. It was stronger, much stronger, as if someone was smoking right beside the bed. I dragged myself up and checked the attic window. It was closed, firmly. I wrenched it open and stuck my head out to see if a neighbor was down below charcoaling a lung. No one. I went down a flight of stairs, and the smell faded. When I got back to the attic, there was just the usual faint smell of furniture polish and must.

I pulled on a t-shirt and shorts and slipped out onto the deck for some air to check my messages over morning coffee. It was an old habit of constantly checking for the little texts he sent throughout the day, the steady stream of trivia in a hundred or so characters that really said "I'm here" or "I'm thinking about you" as we weaved each other into the tiny details of our lives.

Before I'd even clicked the messaging app, the cell phone's speakers hissed and screeched as if it had been shocked by an energy surge. I tried to turn it off, but it wouldn't shut down. I yanked out the battery which killed the sound. When I put the battery back in, it started up normally. That had never happened before.

I'd no messages, of course. It was a stupid impulse to check for his texts now.

"Hi honey, I'm home," I'd text when I landed at JFK after being away on an assignment. We'd reached a new level of honesty and intimacy in sobriety, and I missed him terribly when I traveled. We rotated around each other like satellites in each other's gravity well, normal people doing normal things, catching a movie, taking in a play, linking arms on a long walk, checking in for no particular reason throughout the day, showing up for each other when things were good and bad, when one was sick or stressed or wanted to celebrate, or simply because we just wanted to be together and nowhere else.

"Love you too babe," he'd text back.

"Why do you only ever write that," I asked, when he was cooking dinner one night. "Why do you never say it?"

"You'll know why when we've been married five years," he said.

I stopped setting the table.

"We're getting married?" I asked. "When?"

"When you stop hunting around for some imaginary Prince Charming."

He was peeling and slicing artichokes. Then he simmered salt and herbs in a pan. He blended miso and soy and drizzled oil as if he'd said nothing. I waited for him to make a joke of it, after all, everyone who knew him heard him say he'd never marry again, and he was stubborn when it came to such absolutisms. He was also dreadful when it came to expressing his feelings, but that night he looked uncomfortable, the way he often did when he felt vulnerable.

"You're waiting on me?" I asked.

"Yes, you."

"But I already know you're my Prince Charming," I said.

He stopped dicing and turned to face me.

"So, we'll do it?" he asked.

"Sure," I answered.

We laughed at how casually we made the big decision in the end. It was an odd proposal as far as proposals go, but it wasn't just a proposal. It was an epiphany that brought the strangest feeling, but not a feeling, a visceral reminder of something I was born knowing but somehow forgot—I was always meant to be with him.

Two weeks later, I packed for a two-month research trip to the Southern states.

A week after that, his texts and calls trailed off.

"Where have you been?" I asked when he finally answered his phone. "I thought you'd run off with another woman."

"The only women in my life are you and my mother," he said. "Sorry. I've just been working. I billed forty-eight hours in the last three days. I had to move several piles of money just to find my phone to answer you."

In truth, this workload was normal for him. He was an architectural designer with many high-end clients in the Emirates. He'd obsess when inspired and stress when a deadline loomed and he'd nothing but a blank screen to show for his shillings.

"How's your sobriety?" I asked.

"It's so boring."

"Have you been hanging out in bars?"

"No. I'm at the Green Street Café, waiting for Gustave."

"What are you doing for sex?" I asked.

"Imagining it," he answered.

"With me?"

"Of course with you."

"How often?"

Silence.

"How often?"

"Let's say more than ten times and less than a thousand."

"What are you imagining?" I asked

Silence. For someone so sexually liberated, he could be bemusedly shy.

"Based on your enthusiasm, I'm guessing we're doing it through a hole in a sheet like the Hasids," I said.

"Ah, you're into role play now?"

"Well, I don't think Hasidic porn is flying off the video shelves," I said.

"I'll try anything twice."

"We can do better than that," I said.

"Careful," he said. "You're getting hopes and other things raised."

"Really?"

"Yeah."

"You're serious."

"I am. You want a photo?"

"Sure."

"Better not," he said. "Gustave just sat down. He wouldn't appreciate it."

I went to bed that evening with my iPad and scrolled for something on Netflix to distract me from the past.

A floorboard creaked. A shiver ran up my spine. I peered into the hallway with the uncomfortable feeling that someone was lurking in the shadows, but there was no one there.

Later, having watched a few minutes of everything and all of nothing, I drifted off. My iPad must have continued to pour faint flickers of light into the room until the battery died and the world fell to silence broken only by the burp of a bullfrog, the hoot of an owl, and the heavy breathing of me sleeping.

Creak.

I jolted awake. The bedframe was groaning under a great weight. My heart raced. Someone had sat on the bed behind me. Someone big. Someone silent.

Turn around! I told myself.

I couldn't move.

Turn around for fuck's sake! On three. One, two, three.

I flipped around. No one. I scrambled up, got tangled in the sheet, fell over, whacked my face on the windowsill, and bounced back onto the floor. Pain scorched my head.

Get up!

My hands were shaking. I fumbled with the switch of the gaudy lamp. It flipped on. No one was there. No one could have gotten down the stairs that fast and without a sound. I fumbled on the table for my phone to call 911, then remembered it was in the kitchen.

Shit!

I picked up a glass Saratoga Spring bottle by the neck and crept down the stairs, peering into the dark, listening for any creek or rustle. No one could move in this house without the floors creaking. Except for the faint chirp of crickets and my own stressed breath, there was silence in every room and every stairwell the whole way down to the kitchen where I found the windows closed and the doors locked. No one could have gotten out; then again, no one could have gotten in.

I slipped out onto the front porch and sat on the steps in a T-shirt and boy shorts, clutching the bottleneck with white knuckles, hearing nothing but the normal sounds of the night. After an hour of sitting out there in the dark, I decided that I'd imagined the whole thing and went back inside. Still, I stood in the hallway for a few minutes, afraid to move, listening, hearing nothing and no one.

This was so stupid. Four years earlier, I spent the summer crawling around in Iraq as an embedded journalist with the Stryker Division out of Washington and the 2/10 Mountain Division out of New York, washing with baby wipes, and eating MREs to get the worms-eye view of the war. I waded through shit-filled creeks and hunkered down with the guys during rocket attacks in Sadr City. I walked in the footsteps of the soldiers in front of me as we navigated IED terrain. I'd been crammed into Humvees in 120 pounds of body armor in 130-degree heat as we rolled outside the wire to bullets pinging off the metal and the gunner spinning his M2 in every direction. Now, here I was, in rural Virginia with a bruise on my forehead from imaginings in the night.

Stupid or not, I didn't have the courage to go back upstairs. I wandered into the library, the smallest and most defensible room in the house, and picked out a book called *Classic American Decorating*. I curled up in the throw blanket on the chaise and flipped mindlessly through the pictures. It was almost dawn before I was calm enough to sleep. As I began to doze, the air around me seemed to change somehow, growing warmer or softer maybe. A feather-like sensation brushed my forehead and then both my eyelids like little kisses that felt strangely familiar, but I couldn't quite remember why.

I woke to a hissing catfight. I flung open the back door to see a feral cat staking a claim to the dry food I'd left on the deck for Busker. Little Busker conceded. With his back hunched and fur standing on end, he was too small, not vicious enough and no match for the bully. I yelled, and the stray took off. Busker's little body trembled as he walked between my ankles.

"It's okay, little guy," I said, "nothing to be ashamed of."

This was more than I could say for myself. I stood at the bottom of the stairs, clutching my coffee, and feeling pretty embarrassed in the light of day.

I marched up those stairs and back into the attic. I charged my phone and iPad, hung up my clothes, tidied the mess of sheets and pillows, and opened the window to let in some light and air. Down below, I saw a small water feature in the corner of the garden that I hadn't noticed before. With Busker on my heels, I went out to investigate.

A couple of frogs were hopping about a nasty slime-covered pond. The water wasn't moving. I followed a cable and found the pump was unplugged. I powered it on, and it started to hum. The frogs hopped off. While the water bubbled and the slime cleared, Busker and I sat under a pine tree, him napping and me berating myself for missing Johann's last days, for leaving, for not staying in Brooklyn. I should have stayed. Maybe he wouldn't have gone cycling that day. I should have stayed. Maybe I would have noticed that the deep vein thrombosis he had four years prior wasn't gone and that he needed to see a doctor. I should have stayed. Maybe I could have done CPR and saved him when he collapsed. I should ... My old 12-step sponsor would say, "Stop shoulding on yourself," because the quickest way off the wagon was to beat yourself to a pulp and then crawl back to your drug of choice to soothe the tattered remains of your self-esteem. I hadn't been this

15

self-critical for years, but now I was back and feeling angry, powerless, and useless. Tears started to sting again. I leaned my head against the tree trunk to hold them back. I was sick of convulsions.

"You said you were with me now no matter what," I whispered as if he could hear me, as if my accusation would guilt him into coming back.

Something tugged lightly on my hair. Two tugs. Stop. Two more tugs. Stop. I must have gotten caught on a twig. I shuffled to get unstuck. But it started again. Two tugs. Stop.

It reminded me of how Johann used to play with my hair on lazy afternoons.

We had been looking out of my bedroom window, anticipating a downpour, and enjoying the lull before a storm when the canopy of clouds invites introspection. "Irish weather" I called it. It was our favorite.

I'd been upset that day. I'd been hoping for an assignment in Afghanistan, but my editor had emailed to say he gave the beat to a staffer in Pakistan.

"You just came back from Iraq," Johann said, lightly tugging my hair.

"That was ages ago," I said.

"Forget Afghanistan," he said. "Take a dozen freshly printed twenties and attach them to your forehead with a rubber band. Put on your tiniest mini-skirt and go for an evening stroll in Brooklyn's lovely Brownsville. That will be far more eventful than an occasional roadside bomb."

I laughed.

"I'm serious," I said. "If I stay here, I'll end up covering the financial crisis, which doesn't interest me at all."

"Stay, *meine Süße*," he said, pulling the duvet over us and slipping his hands around my waist. "There are more things to investigate than the bankers' meltdown."

I clambered up from beneath the pine tree. I needed to move. I needed to stop thinking. Every tiny thing sparked a memory of him. I needed to eat something. My stomach was stripped.

I shook out my hair to get rid of whatever was stuck there that I couldn't see and went into the kitchen to forage for snacks. There were slim pickings except for a few oranges in the fridge. I took a couple, shut the door, and swung around to come face-to-face with a large, two-dimensional, solid-black figure standing in the doorway.

I froze.

It looked like a black hole I'd seen on TV with a perfectly crisp edge that delineated its dense dark form from the event horizon surrounding it. But this wasn't a black hole. It was crudely outlined and had no neck so that the shoulders and head were fused like a gorilla. But this wasn't a gorilla. It was a tall, broad man, six-foot easily, silent, and unmoving. It wasn't just blocking the doorway; it had been lurking behind me while I rummaged in the fridge.

It disappeared.

Tap. Tap. Tap.

Juice was dripping onto my feet and all over the floor. I'd gripped the oranges so hard I punctured the skin. My breath was shallow and my heart was still racing. I scanned the kitchen for an explanation. Billions of times a day my brain created three-dimensional constructs out of the two-dimensional images impinging on my retina. Neurons in my visual cortex made the third dimension appear, but not this time. The kitchen was bright, so it wasn't a trick of the light. I couldn't blame it on peripheral vision where floaters or fleeting black flashes often appear in tired eyes. This, whatever it was, was solid, stationary, in full-frontal vision, and by no means fleeting.

I must have been losing my mind. I must have been having some sort of breakdown. I needed Johann. It hurt to think about him, but it hurt not to think about him. In some alcove of my mind I was pleading: *whatever I've done to deserve this, I've done my penance, I've learned my lesson, send him back.* I'd no idea who I was bargaining with — the god of my childhood, perhaps — but no amount of atonement would make this right.

I crawled up the stairs, flopped onto the bed, and buried my face in the pillow. My head throbbed and my shoulders and neck were knotted and painful, and I couldn't relax enough to ease the pain. Gradually, heat built between my shoulder blades, heat that felt familiar like the *warmflasche* he'd given me months earlier when I pulled a muscle and tried to microwave a couple of gel packs. I exploded them one after the other and ended up with gobs of gel dripping everywhere. I'd texted Johann at his office to whine.

"You are supposed to microwave those packs between ten and thirty seconds depending on size. Maybe you boiled them too long? It isn't corned beef," he said, never missing a chance to make a jab at Irish food. "A warmflasche might do the trick. They are made from rubber and can be filled with hot water. They make them for kids and they are sitting inside teddy bears."

He showed up that evening with a warmflasche, which turned out to be a hot water bottle in a furry toy. He filled it and put it between my shoulder blades, and it made me feel better, just like this heat sensation was doing now. But this wasn't the product of a warmflasche; it was something else I couldn't explain.

Panic rose again. What was wrong with me? Or was there something wrong with this house? No, that was too stupid. No, something much worse was probably happening. I was stressed and anxious. My heart palpitated and my head hurt constantly. I was isolated and disconnected and morose. I looked like shit and was barely functioning. Was this a nervous breakdown? Surely not. Surely there was a rational explanation. Then again, people who lose their minds are often convinced of their sanity. No, there was no way I was having a breakdown. It was just stress. Let's face it, stress can cause all sorts of imaginings like something sitting on the bed, or touching my forehead, or tugging my hair, warming my skin, or manifesting as a gorilla-shaped black hole.

Make it stop. Please make it stop.

I didn't know who I was begging, but the sensation faded, and my world returned to just me in pain, grieving alone in a stranger's home.

It was pitch dark. The tops of the fifty or so circus sideshow tents were just about visible from the strings of fairy lights that hung around the edges of their sidewalls. They were old sun-bleached canvas tents with a nauseating smell of mold. Johann walked into the circus village. I pushed through the crowd in that direction. With each piece of ground I covered, new landscapes were added: a Ferris wheel, a merry-go-round of rodents and sideshow exhibits of a half man half bat, a hermaphrodite and a woman with a face on each side of her face. The harder I tried to reach him, the denser and louder the crowd became until it was impenetrable. He was gone. I sank exhausted onto the ground behind a small tent. Someone approached. The dim light highlighted the contour of his body. I could see his shape, but not his face. He didn't speak, but I heard his thoughts.

I am here.

The anxiety of my waking life was corroding the sleep that had once been my refuge. I wasn't entirely surprised that my nightmare took the form of a circus-scape. My first two years in the States were spent as a general roustabout with a travelling circus that played up and down the Eastern seaboard. Each week, seventy-two trucks emblazoned with red scrolls and Playbill font pulled onto a lot, and we'd pile out, drive stakes, roll out the big top, and build the stables and the concessions stands. We'd carve out the arrivals walkway and decorate it with lights and place a cheerful yellow fence around us — our boundary with the world. Inside, we'd run electricity and water into trailers and sewage pipes out of them. Our former trapeze artist turned alcoholic cook churned out slop on a daily basis, and the porta-potties stank of shit, especially in the summer. The circus was a world of smiles painted onto faces, but on the interior, it was a self-contained subculture that pushed its way into people's lives so circus folk, who couldn't or wouldn't function in the real world, could entertain by day, and get into drunken fights by night. At the end of each week, the big top and picket fence were loaded onto trucks and sent down the road to the next town, and we scattered onto interstates and sped along behind it in our various vehicles like seventy-two anxious ants trying to find their way back to a moving anthill. It's an ephemeral world the circus — two-faced, disconnected, otherworldly, and belonging nowhere. No, considering how I felt these days, I wasn't surprised that I was dreaming about the circus.

Grief has many faces. It doesn't come like a single shockwave; it creeps along in pieces, a thought here, a realization there, fragments sniffing around the edges of a numbness that serves to protect us from a fracture that would obliterate our fragile hearts and minds. One day I was stunned, as if my mind knew there was an earthquake at sea and was waiting for a tsunami. On another, I wailed like a starving baby until my face was swollen and my head hurt. Next, I was depressed and withdrawn, not eating, not sleeping, not engaging. Then, I'd wake angry with the world and myself. I'd lumber along with each day differing from the next, so I hadn't even the comfort of consistency. I'd think I was progressing, like being about to get out of bed or not cry for a day, but then I'd wake up stunned again or find myself in tears or imagining ridiculous events.

I'd arrived at the first worst of those days — the first holiday. As adopted Americans, the Fourth of July was a borrowed holiday for Johann and me, so it shouldn't have mattered, but the sounds of family members arriving and the neighbors' children squealing dragged me out of the comfort I'd found in isolation and reminded me that I was one half of holiday togetherness, which amounted to the whole of nothing.

Holidays are a scab picked off torment.

I could hide inside, microwave dinner, read a book, and try to ignore the life outside that kept moving forward when I was screaming at it to stop its worthless, pointless celebrations because that which was most vital was gone. Gerry was setting up his BBQ, and kids were already setting off fireworks, and every bang ricocheted around my sore head, reminding me that this day refused to be ignored. But I had to go outside. There was nothing to eat in the mausoleum. I was losing weight. My clothes were hanging off me, and an aged face I didn't know looked back at me from mirrors. I was a lamentable character. Miss Havisham skulking mad in a hulking house in the rags of a wedding dress. I didn't care, but Busker did. He was out of food too.

I drove my wretched Mustang back to the supermarket before the neighborhood descended on it for hotdogs and soda and whatever Americans eat on the Fourth.

Old, hunched over Betty was dragging her cart around again, and the same cashier who had humiliated her earlier was at the register. I tossed two weeks' worth of cat food into a basket and loaded up on cheap salad bar stuff that I wouldn't have to cook. It was a far cry from Wholefoods, but I didn't care. I headed for the check out. While the cashier was scanning my groceries, I watched Betty check each label and count her change again as if it had multiplied in her scrawny fist. *It must be lousy to be that old and alone, counting your pennies,* I thought. But it was more than lousy. It sparked fear in me, as if I were watching myself decades from now: old, alone, weak, and half mad.

"Does she have any help?" I asked the cashier.

"She gets social welfare."

"Does anyone look in on her?"

"I don't know ma'am. Will that be all?" The Southern accent I'd once thought charming grated on my nerves. I handed her my credit card and twenty in cash.

"Here," I said. "That's to cover whatever she's short."

One of my first stories as a journalist was on New York's homeless. Most of the people I met weren't psychologically fit to take care of themselves or had too much pride or fear to go into a shelter. I couldn't blame them. While they slept, thieves would relieve them of their meagre possessions. Those places were ruthless. If a modicum of pride was keeping Betty going, that cashier had no business taking it away.

I was halfway up the mausoleum steps when Gerry spotted me.

"Come on over, we have cans of Guinness," he beamed, as if that's all it took to lure us Irish to a party. Still, it was decent of him to be neighborly on this day of days, and sanity demanded that I get out of that mausoleum and into the land of the living, even for an hour.

In the kitchen, I did my best to create an edible looking dish from my supermarket salad bar containers, covered it with cling film I found in the pantry, fed Busker, and went next door to hide in the background. Gerry, to give him his due, made a point of prying me off the wall where I leaned like a spare bed.

"Meet Karen," he said to a small group. "She's from Ireland. She was a journalist in Iraq."

I had only mentioned journalism and Iraq in passing one day, so he'd no idea what kind of stories I had, but it was a safe to assume I had some. This piqued the interest of a few guests. I never liked talking about Iraq, the paranoia, the cheapness of life, the stink of death, the hostility and the piles of rotting garbage that lined the streets, but Gerry had set me up. He forced me to engage. He plucked me from piteousness and temporarily restored me to personhood. Then, he pushed a cold can of Guinness into my hand. Slivers of ice slid down its sides and along my arms. It was wonderfully cool. I wanted to pull back the ring and hear the sensual hiss of the can decompressing. I wanted to pour it slowly down the inside of a tilted glass, filling it and straightening it until a thick creamy head formed in contrast to the bitterness of the stout. It would be colder than we'd drink it in Ireland but a welcome chill in the heat of the Virginia sun. Each sip would slide down my throat, fill my empty stomach and take the edge off this day — then make tomorrow even worse. There was nothing so bad that booze couldn't make worse.

"Thanks, but I don't drink," I said, handing it back.

"What? You're Irish and you don't drink?" He laughed, as people do when they roll out that old chestnut.

"No." I smiled.

"Okay, there's juice and soda in the cooler. Is that okay?"

"Perfect," I said.

Gerry meandered off to entertain. From time to time, loud laughter erupted from some corner or other as Gerry inflicted his predictable sense of humor on his unfortunate guests, like the bad comedians that showed up one night at TBD, our local bar and event venue in Brooklyn.

"I got a big, noisy, annoying reminder from Roisin to call in tonight for a party at Kent's bar," Johann had said when he called from the office that afternoon. "They listed a couple of standups, which I assume are the only difference to a regular drinking day at Kent's. It will take a big whiskey and your best cleavage shirt to get me there."

"I've a deadline for a story on the primaries," I said. "And a long way to go to meet it. Definitely not a cleavage night tonight."

A couple of hours later, finding me not there, he called.

"I'm sitting here and trying to limit the pain caused by horrible wannabe-comedians with overpriced shots of whiskey," he said. "I don't think this event will draw more than twenty-five people. Only Roisin and Des and the host that's counting the incoming shekels and the lonely musician who lives on Chair 5 and possibly carpet-sales-guy trying to hide from wife and kids are here. When are you coming?"

"I can't come, I told you already," I said.

"I made it out of the office early despite a big pile of work on my desk to go to an event you asked me to go with you to repeatedly, and you don't show with the excuse that you have too much work to do?"

"I didn't ask you to go," I said.

"Ten lame points for you," he said. "And you are penciled in for a spanking."

I didn't go. Back then, I didn't want to be at a bar with cheap beer and bad jokes any more than I wanted to be at Gerry's party now. But what I wouldn't give to have that night back. Who cared about cheap beer and drunken crowds or deadlines? He had been there — that mattered — but I'd squandered precious moments on things that didn't matter at all.

Gerry's guests gathered around to watch the fireworks that started just after dark. There was a good view from his garden, but it was a small display, dwarfed by the Macy's Fourth of July fireworks that Johann and I used to watch on East River barges. That had always been a good day. The neighborhood's pale-faced artists, expat Europeans, mostly German, French, and Irish, would throw parties on the rooftops of their lofts that overlooked the East River. We'd swan about drinking and eating and watching the fireworks and then wander from studio to studio, bumping into people, as the whole building became one large meandering party that lasted until morning. On Franklin Street at dawn, he'd put his hands in his pockets and stick out his elbow so I could hook my arm in his on the tired walk home.

The End

This display was small but sweet, the big effort of a small town to celebrate what it meant to be American. Color burst into the night sky, lighting up the eager faces of kids, the parents who held them, and the couples who dreamt of their own. They had included me in their group, and I'd tried to be sociable, but I wasn't one of them. I never would be. The skin had been flayed from my body, and pain stung my frayed nerves. I wanted Johann's chest to lean into or his smell to inhale or his arms around me.

I slipped out of the party and sidled along the side of the house. Busker sprinted from under the porch steps to join me. His little body was trembling with fright from the fireworks. He didn't like to be picked up, so I stood still to let him lean into my legs, which seemed to give him comfort. We weren't moving, but the motion sensitive exterior light popped on. Something had turned it on, but I didn't know what.

In the yellow glow of the security light, something glittering caught my eye. About three feet above my head, a pine needle was spinning rhythmically in midair, reflecting the light, and twinkling like a golden bauble on a Christmas tree. It couldn't have been hanging on a cobweb because the pine trees along that pathway were thirty feet high, and there was no branch directly overhead from which a cobweb could hang. How it was suspended in midair, spinning perfectly, I didn't know. It looked like an invisible person was dangling it there just for me. That was silly of course, but for once, I didn't berate myself for absurd imaginings. I just reveled in this delightful trifle that was more captivating than the fireworks had been.

While Busker and I stood there enjoying our own private Fourth of July display, the air around me began to change, much like it had done that night in the library: getting softer, wrapping around me like a deep, familiar hug, then flowing through me as if it were filling the holes, soothing the hurt, and plumping up my shriveled self. The enchanting display lasted only minutes before the light popped off. The pine needle disappeared into the dark, and the air current surrounding me faded. I didn't understand what had happened or how. All I knew was that the more I surrendered to the sensation, the less alone I felt in the world.

Awakening

*But ultimately you come to the truth of the adage that
'love is stronger than death.'*

Ram Dass

The Victorian drawing room was covered in green flock wallpaper. I was alone. Rows of empty chairs were arranged before a low stage with black curtains. Center stage, a floodlight shone through a one-foot gap in the drapes. I was about to pull back the curtains when Johann stepped into the light between them. He was blonder than he'd been in life. He wore a long, black coat and his favorite black shirt. I rushed toward him, but he stopped me.

Sssh, he whispered, putting his finger to his mouth. *It's okay. I'm here.*

The room flooded with early morning sunshine and the promise of a scorching day. As usual, I woke with bright light searing my eyelids, a sick stomach, and a grinding headache. I knew I had to get up. The pretty pine needle and the comfort I experienced on the Fourth of July had offered a moment's respite from my desire to mope and avoid the world, but this misery was feeding a creeping fear that I was succumbing to dark imaginings that were part of a mental strain that could break my mind. I'd rather be dead than mad. Truth be told, I'd rather be dead than anything.

I threw on some clothes and wandered the empty roads of this tiny town to get some air before the day got too hot. I did my best to focus on the little houses and the occasional neighbor who emerged from them, but I quickly fell into an oblivious fog.

A bell roused me from my haze. I found myself standing on a street I'd never been, in front of a Catholic church that I'd never seen. It was a small, wooden building with a flight of steps up to a bright red oak door. According to its noticeboard, 8:00 a.m. Mass was about to start.

"In the name of the Father, and of the Son, and of the Holy Spirit," the priest said as I slipped into a pew at the back.

"Amen," came the chorus of parishioners.

"The grace of our Lord Jesus Christ and the love of God and the fellowship of the Holy Spirit be with you all."

"And also with you."

I'd heard those words thousands of times before I reached seventeen and graduated from a high school run by Catholic nuns. On that last day of school, I swore, to my holy and observant mother's dismay, that I would never set foot in Mass again. That god was a menace. The guilt heaped upon the child, as in, "you're a bad child, you'll make baby Jesus cry," and the bargaining that resulted in, "God, if you help me pass my math test, I promise to give my allowance to the starving babies in Africa for a whole month," gave way to the teenager's prostrations, flagellation, and daily mantra of "I am not worthy." Eventually, this became the adult's detestation of the Church's power and whatever created us to punish us, if there were a creator.

Today, however, I felt safe in the familiarity of the words and the ritual. They brought me back to school days when we made sets and costumes and put on Nativity plays at Christmas, when there was nothing in the world so bad that my father couldn't make it better.

An old man shuffled to the altar.

"Our reading today is from First Corinthians," he said, fixing his glasses. "Love is patient, love is kind. It does not envy, it does not boast, it is not proud. It does not dishonor others, it is not self-seeking, it is not easily angered, it keeps no record of wrongs. Love does not delight in evil but rejoices with the truth. It always protects, always trusts, always hopes, always perseveres. Love never fails."

Sun poured through the stained-glass windows creating pretty shafts of colored light. Ceiling fans circulated cool air, refreshing after the hot morning outside. I closed my eyes and listened to the rhythmic whir blending with the hum of the invocation and response.

"Lord have mercy."

"Lord have mercy."

"Christ have mercy."

"Christ have mercy."

That place, with its light and warmth and sound, seemed outside time. The first few bars of "Ave Maria" were tapped out on a piano, and a tenor began to sing in Latin with such gentleness and power that the twisted muscles in my eyes and shoulders relaxed. I didn't care that I was basking in the light in a small country church with a group of strangers, offering up space and time for the glory of a god I didn't believe in. For the first time since that day, I realized that it was okay to be in this much pain. It was okay to grieve. It was okay to be afraid. It was okay to allow the tears to fall from my eyes.

After the blessing, Father Peter walked down the aisle and stood outside on the steps to wish each parishioner a farewell and a nice day as they left. A tight-knit group they seemed to be, all well dressed for the morning service, except for me. The chatter from the lingerers outside was painful after the peace inside. I waited until they had all gone to slip away, only to bump into Father Peter still standing on the steps.

"Morning," he smiled. "You're new to our community."

I was caught off guard by his gentle face and the honesty in his pale blue eyes. Tears welled in my eyes and then poured down my cheeks. He put his hand on my arm and gently ushered me into the rectory.

"Rose, would you make some tea?" he said to his housekeeper.

Rose nodded and disappeared into the kitchen as if wreckage washing up on the church steps was business as usual. Father Peter motioned me to one armchair and sat in another, presumably waiting patiently for me to stop sobbing and tell him what was going on. Rose returned with a tray of tea and cookies. I fixated on the bright red tulip pattern on both cup and saucer and tried to stop them from clattering in my shaking hands. Finally, I spoke.

"My fiancé, Father," I said, "is dead."

Tea splashed onto the saucer.

"And I'm seeing things and feeling things, like feathers brushing my face when there's no one there, and I'm smelling things and hearing noises. I'm scared," I admitted. "I think I'm having a breakdown."

"Not at all," he said with a smile. "These things are common in bereavement. It's our loved ones letting us know they're okay. A few of our parishioners have had those experiences you know. I had one too."

What had he said?

"After my father's funeral," he went on, "we went to my mother's house for tea and the grandfather clock in the hall started to chime.

He wound it every week for fifty-five years, but by the time he died, it hadn't worked for ages, so when it started chiming after his funeral, my mother said, 'That's your father letting us know he's okay.'"

"Had someone fixed it?" I asked.

"No," Father Peter said. "It hasn't worked since. Never chimed again. It's boxed up in the attic up those stairs now."

I followed his glance up the stairs. Somehow, in that rectory on that morning, I found comfort in the story of a magical clock.

"Do you remember your St. Dominic?" he asked.

I nodded, lying, not wanting to admit to being a lousy Catholic when I was taking his time and drinking his tea.

"Well, there you go. Take refuge in St. Dominic. As for the grief, that will ease in time," he said. "Get out and talk to people, and remember, you're always welcome here."

I finished my tea, thanked him, got directions home, and promised to return.

I mulled over his magical clock the whole way back to the mausoleum, wanting to believe that the spirits of the dearly departed continued in the ether and could manipulate objects, which oddly enough sat easier with me than having a fractured mind. But who was I fooling? Wasn't this just a bedside story told to appease the bereaved?

For all my cynicism, I climbed the stairs and googled St. Dominic. I came across a copy of a London *Observer* article from 1999 with the headline: "Dialogue with the dead is feasible, Vatican spokesman says." It went on, "One of the most authoritative spokesmen of the Roman Catholic Church has raised eyebrows among the faithful by declaring that the Church believes in the feasibility of communication with the dead." The spokesman, the Reverend Gino Concetti, took pains to emphasize that he wasn't advocating raising the dead, whatever that meant, but went on to say, "It may even be that God lets our loved ones send us messages to guide us at certain moments in our life."

That was a lot to take in from the Vatican. Although, I shouldn't have been so surprised. The Church always encouraged us to pray to the saints. As a kid, I had prayed to St. Anthony when I lost something, St. Brigid when I was sick and St. Francis for whom I was named when my dog wasn't well. Saints were once normal people walking the earth. If we could talk to them, why not regular people?

I scrolled to the bottom and came across a quote from St. Dominic: "Do not weep, for I shall be more useful to you after my death and I shall help you then more effectively than during my life."

I went downstairs, poured hot water over cup noodles, and watched them steep.

If an institution as conservative as the Catholic Church was prepared to recognize this possibility — the possibility that our loved ones could help us after they died, could I?

What was I thinking? This was lunacy. They said energy couldn't be destroyed, but this was a far cry from atoms organizing to make clocks chime. Besides, even if I did place credence in the Vatican, the story could have been fake. It was posted on a third-party website, not the London *Observer* Service website, although I wasn't sure if the service had a website in 1999 when the story was written. I needed a source. I found an email address for John Hooper, the Rome correspondent who apparently wrote the article and emailed him asking if he remembered that interview and had in fact written the story.

The next morning, an email from John Hooper awaited. Yes, he did remember the interview and had written that story.

I dragged my MacBook downstairs, fed Busker, brewed a pot of coffee, and went out onto the deck to research the mysterious encounters out in the world of which Father Peter spoke. An Amazon search returned a book called *Love Lives On* by former State University of New York Professor Louis LaGrand. I downloaded the Kindle version to learn that the professor had done a twenty-five-year investigation into what he called "extraordinary encounters," which were signs from deceased loved ones. They "come in a variety of forms and colors, from visions and apparitions to sensing the presence or hearing their voice," he wrote, "and touch, smell." They were supposed to bring healing and an expanded consciousness and were not, he stressed, the products of magical thinking. I read story after story of people who had asked for and received these encounters with deceased loved ones. There were stories from skeptics like myself who didn't ask for them but got them anyway. Seventy million cases were documented apparently, although he didn't say by whom. In each case, he wrote, the recipient knew it was a loved one or an intelligent power communicating.

I wanted to believe. I really did. The professor's belief offered a twisted comfort by suggesting that not only had my distressed mind not cracked and generated the supposed external encounters I'd been experiencing, but Johann may have survived in some form.

I sat with this for a long time, rapidly cycling between excitement, fear, hope, and apprehension. I poured more coffee, walked around the garden, stared into the sky, watched the toads hop, the birds flit, Busker nap. Could the professor be right—something survives when all of this dies? What is that something?

As much as I tried, I couldn't convince myself that a disembodied loved one was floating about trying to communicate by manipulating external events in the physical world.

I climbed back up the stairs to the deck and read on. Admittedly, some of the "communications" he reported were extraordinary, such as clear apparitions or objects moving, but a lot of them were subjective and sounded more like the magical thinking of the bereft clinging to a survival myth. Yet, the professor was claiming, based on thousands of stories, that death was not the end and that our loved ones are with us now no matter what.

That reminded me of a promise Johann had once made.

It was mid-afternoon when I finished reading Professor LeGrand's book. My Irish skin had turned decidedly pink, and my energy was drained from the sunshine. I went upstairs to sleep through the afternoon heat. My laptop was low on juice, so I expended the last of my patience unknotting the power cord to charge it up. My GPS was lying dead next to it. That was fine. I didn't need it. I wasn't going anywhere. It was a small GPS and not the easiest to manage. I bought it to help me find a remote Pentecostal church where I was to interview a snake handling pastor for a story I was doing on politics and religion in America. After about an hour of fruitlessly trying to preprogram some obscure rural addresses, I'd pleaded with Johann for help, since he was as technically proficient as I was inept. He had been working all day to meet a deadline, but he took the GPS and tried to plug in addresses for me. Unfortunately, its keys were too tiny for his big hands.

"*Scheisse*," he said. I lost count of the number of German swear words he used while backspacing to correct typos. He rummaged in a drawer for a pack of Lucky Strikes.

"I thought you were quitting."

"I was."

"You said it's unhealthy, expensive, and embarrassing."

"Not now."

Since I was the cause of his stress, I shut up. The sun was about to rise in Abu Dhabi, and he had a lot of work to send over before it did, so he resorted to getting coordinates on Google maps and plugging those in instead.

"Will that work?" I asked.

"No reason why it shouldn't," he said.

A week later, I was lost in Appalachia.

I slept lightly that afternoon. I dreamt Johann was lying beside me, his arm lying across my waist, his breath on my neck the way he always lay. It felt so real, and he felt so present that it didn't feel like a dream. I couldn't remember feeling happier.

Sometime later, in the twilight between waking and sleeping, the letters *CIS* floated into my field of vision like a colorful prism floating on a soap bubble — crisp and vibrant and drifting slowly from side to side of their own accord. I opened my eyes to find it still there. I couldn't control its movement, which I could have done had I, for some inexplicable reason, imagined it. I couldn't understand how I was seeing it or why. It was as if someone had hijacked the electrical impulses in my brain and inserted an image between my optic nerve and occipital cortex.

Pop.

It was gone.

I hopped up to the keyboard to search for "optic nerve hallucinations" but found nothing of interest in the results. A search of the term "CIS" produced nothing relevant. Then it occurred to me that if I could entertain just for a moment that extraordinary encounters were possible and that this could be one—even though it was an internal image not an external event as the professor described—then CIS could be German. I searched Google Deutschland, which listed CIS as a European notation for the musical note C-sharp. I searched for an MP3 of C-sharp and clicked play. The second it sounded, the GPS crackled to life and announced loudly, "You have reached your destination."

I leapt off my chair and backed away from the desk. A few minutes later, with no further incident, I inched back to find the GPS had powered on and was lying there as if entirely pleased with itself for having done a good job.

I slipped into my flip-flops and ran out of the house.

Down at the strand, I sat on a bench trying to bring the CIS image back into my mind, but no matter how hard I focused, I couldn't come near to replicating its brightness or crispness, nor could I see it in the same place as before, wherever that was. I was probably being stupid. It was probably just a coincidence. It hadn't felt random, but I couldn't explain the visceral feeling I had about it. The professor would probably call it a meaningful coincidence or a synchronicity—a term Carl Jung attributed to events that occur with no causal relationship yet seem to be meaningfully related. But this wasn't like the accounts the professor described. It wasn't two seemingly unrelated external events, like a meaningful song playing on the radio just when you turn it on or a rainbow appearing shortly after someone asked for a sign from a departed loved one. This started inside my head and that internal image prompted me to take an action. This was an internal cause that prompted an external event. No, this wasn't what the professor described.

An old woman I'd seen at Father Peter's church interrupted my thoughts.

"Hello," she said in a tiny voice. "I'm Millie."

"Karen," I said, taking her outstretched hand. "Nice to meet you."

"Do you mind if I join you. The sun will be setting soon."

I didn't want company, but I couldn't say no.

"I heard you talking to Father Peter in the rectory the other day," she said. "I hope you don't think I'm interfering, but I had one of those signs from my sister after she died, you know. I don't really talk about it because a lot of people would think I'm a silly fool. Not Father Peter, thank God," she whispered. "But I didn't summon her you understand."

"I'm sorry, I don't understand."

"Call her up."

I still didn't understand.

"Do you remember King Saul's story in the Old Testament?"

I shook my head.

"He went to the Witch of Endor because he needed advice about a battle against the Philistines. He asked her to call up Samuel from the dead, but that was forbidden."

"What happened?"

"He lost the battle the next day and committed suicide."

That didn't surprise me. If there was anything predictable in the bible it was swift and merciless retribution for wrongdoing.

"The Spiritualists do it you know."

"Do what?" I asked.

"Call up the dead."

"What are Spiritualists?"

"A sect I think," she said. "They have a church across the bay. I've heard that they summon the dead twice on Sundays."

I laughed, but she was serious.

How I ended up sharing a sunset with a woman with whom I'd nothing in common, I didn't know. I figured it was safe to assume we had polar opposite worldviews. She was rural and religious and probably politically conservative. She probably learned to drive in a Cadillac at sixteen, never rode a subway, and married her high school boyfriend. The sixties probably passed her by. She seemed the type to shy away from activism — innocent, sheltered, obliging. How far had she ventured from this town? Not far, I bet.

From the corner of my eye, I noticed her making very slight movements and her thin face and delicate features straining from a discomfort she was trying to hide. She focused her gaze out over the water, but she was clearly in more pain than she was letting on. "Longsuffering" my grandmother would have called her. She was wearing a gold band on a thin, arthritic finger, and so, in an uncharacteristic fit of sociability, I asked after her husband.

"Oh, he died five years ago," she said. "We used to come down here and watch the sunset on summer evenings. I still do it."

I reddened. She wouldn't have known why, but I felt thoroughly ashamed of myself for heaping judgment on this old woman who'd shown me kindness. We were from different generations and different countries, but we were raised Catholic, and, while I wasn't observant and didn't share her religious beliefs, we shared a culture. We shared memories of evenings watching the sunset with our beloveds, one over Manhattan and the other over this bay. We shared the pain of love lost. We were two crumbs of people marking time on the crust of a ball rotating around the sun. We were like Vladimir and Estragon in *Waiting for Godot*. The sun would go down and come up again. We would sleep, eat, walk, talk, and do a hundred other things to fill our days. We'd do this over and over until we died.

I remembered an old lady who lived near us in Dublin. Her husband died many years before her, and her children had emigrated. When she died, movers came in with a large dumpster and tossed in everything she owned. On top of a pile of broken teapots and Wedgwood were carelessly tossed photo albums that had fallen open to show carefully affixed black and white photos of loved ones standing in little studios in their Sunday best, husbands and wives and children from generations past, once full of life and excited to be in the studio; special people on special occasions now all consigned to a rubbish heap — the grand finale of her life.

Would that be my life now?

The sun went down and the sky turned from orange to purple and then to indigo.

"It was lovely seeing you again Millie," I said. "Thanks for the chat."

"Good night dear. See you on Sunday."

I sat under the light of the gaudy brass lamp long into the night. I searched for "Spiritualist church Virginia" and found an amateurish website for the church across the bay, which claimed to be a "common sense religion." From what I'd been told, I expected to find pentagrams and the Temple of Set, but this just offered a short description of spiritual healing, which sounded like some sort of faith healing and mediumship or direct communicating with the spirit world, which, frankly, sounded better than summoning the dead. It had a short reading list of afterlife communication experiments done by a professor at the University of Arizona, Gary E. Schwartz. I added these to my Amazon list and went searching for information about Spiritualism, which returned a surprising list of sympathizers. On the top of the list was one name I didn't expect to see: the indubitable creator of Sherlock Holmes, the master of logic. Why would Sir Arthur Conan Doyle, the man who could think with the hyper-rationality of Sherlock be part of a group that made leaps of faith into the afterlife? Alfred Russel Wallace, a giant of nineteenth-century intellectualism, the man who conceived of the theory of evolution independently of Charles Darwin, appeared on the list. Wallace's reputation eclipsed Darwin's during his lifetime and was only overtaken by him afterwards. What I didn't know until now was that Wallace believed that human consciousness couldn't be explained by the mechanics of evolution alone, a belief that hurt his credibility in the scientific community in the end. The list of supporters went on and included mathematicians, scientists, and social reformers. The physicist, Sir Oliver Lodge, had written, "I know how weighty the word 'fact' is in science and I say without hesitation that individual personal continuance is to me a demonstrated fact." Even the work of Carl Jung was heavily influenced by the Spiritualist belief system, and one of my favorite journalists, W. T. Stead, father of investigative journalism, turned out to be a Spiritualist. That "knocked me into a tall hat," as my mother would say. In fairness to my ignorance, it looked like the religion reached the peak of popularity in the late nineteenth century but went into decline after frauds preyed on the bereaved.

Whether I believed anything Spiritualism stood for or not, and I was still leaning toward not, I decided it warranted further investigation. The church had a lyceum, which sounded a little archaic, but I emailed the contact, Rev. Cutler for more information. Then I emailed Professor LaGrand, introducing myself as a journalist who may have had some of his extraordinary encounters, and asked if he'd be interested in talking.

I closed my MacBook and was about to turn out the light when I smelled the rich aroma of fresh burning tobacco again, much more pleasant than it had been the previous week. Again, the window was closed, and I didn't know how the smell was getting in. I didn't care. It echoed of a happier time, and I inhaled it deeply.

Next morning, after a shot of Bustelo, a bowl of Whiskas, and a watering and spritzing of plants, we mausoleum occupants were ready for the day. I felt a bit better that morning. For once, my head didn't hurt and my stomach wasn't in ribbons.

It was cool outside, so I went for a walk. I felt like a geriatric. I hadn't done a yoga practice for so long that if I tried to do a standing forward bend, I'd probably grind my joints and tear my sinews. A walk was a more sensible alternative. On my dawdle, I happened upon a farmer's market. For the first time in a while, I had a yearning for unprocessed food, real food, something tasty and rich with substance that would make me feel better. I loaded up with fruits and greens, breads, and some pre-made vegetarian dishes. I even made an effort to be sociable. I nodded and smiled and said "good morning" and "thank you," but before long I was back at the farmer's market in Brooklyn where Johann and I had gone on Saturday mornings, and a wave of sadness pushed me to tears. Grief catches you like that, pulling the rug out just when you've just tottered onto your feet, reducing your capacity to function, and undermining your shriveled self-esteem. I rummaged for cash in my pockets to the pitying glances of the seller and customers and then retreated into the solitude of the mausoleum, berating myself for being hopeful and gullible enough to believe that this crappy life might be a fairytale, where an immortal beloved could influence us or orchestrate events to help us when we need help most.

I was putting the food in the fridge when my phone beeped with an email from Rev. Cutler.

"Dear Karen, We would be delighted to have you join us at our lyceum tomorrow evening at 7:00 p.m. Bring a notebook and pen. We look forward to meeting you."

I decided not to go — I was done with this foolishness.

The next evening, I sat in the old Mustang for some time, then I started the engine and drove across the bay. After all, I reasoned, I'd nothing else to do and nothing left to lose.

Rev. Cutler's church was larger than I expected and more benign for a place that rumor held was into the dark arts and necromancy. Except for its lack of a bell tower and crucifixes, it looked like any small-town church—more *Little House on the Prairie* than Notre Dame Cathedral. It was a bit disappointing really. I'd been looking forward to the drama of pentagrams and a great gothic structure, but it was just a wooden church with white cladding, a small steeple, and a few steps up to a very average door.

Inside was a different story. It felt brooding and oppressive with light limping through the heavy stained-glass windows to die in the darkness of a mahogany pulpit and walnut pews. More awful mahogany. Candles stood on little wooden tables under dull neoclassical paintings that languished on the walls in weighty frames. Something was itching around in my mind, a memory that was trying to get free, but I couldn't get to it.

I slipped into the back row just as three people on a low altar-like stage started singing a cappella. Everyone else stood with hymnbook in hand. They were clearly a community of believers, but they seemed like a gathering of individuals in one place with no connection. Or maybe I was projecting my disconnection onto them.

After the songs, they sat in silence for a few minutes to send healing to those in need. I wasn't really sure what this meant or how to do it, so I just sat still and hoped nobody would notice me not doing whatever it was I was supposed to be doing. Afterwards, one of the singers read an excerpt from a book I'd never heard of called *The Four Agreements*. "What you are seeing and hearing now is nothing but a dream," she read. "You are dreaming right now in this moment. You are dreaming with the brain awake."

I wished I were dreaming. How glorious it would have been to wake up and find myself back at the bar on Valentine's night, where Johann and I had retreated after a less than stellar dining experience at a new restaurant on Franklin Street. I couldn't remember the name of the place, but it didn't matter because, unsurprisingly, it went out of business shortly afterward. Johann had ordered fish that arrived like a decaying carcass floating in watery tomato broth. He pushed it around and said, "Are you ready?" He was a terrific food snob. I wasn't bothered, but I wasn't going to argue. Something was off with him that night. I didn't know what.

"You okay?"

"Yeah, why?"

"You seem distant. Are you worried about something?"

"I'm fine," he said, putting his hands in his pockets and jutting out his elbow so we could link arms on our walk to the neighborhood Irish bar. There, we met his close and somewhat eccentric friend Daniella whom he likened to a brother. He'd just ordered two Kalibers when I got a work call and stepped outside. When I came back, he slipped his arm around me as if I'd been gone for a month.

"I love her," he said to Daniella, who was as surprised as me at this public burst of emotional expression.

"I love her accent. I love her breasts. I love ..."

I cut him off before he went further.

"I have to go," I said. "I have to make changes to a story."

"Don't go," he pleaded. "If you go, who will I talk to?"

"Who am I?" Daniella asked.

"See, Daniella will keep you company," I said.

I'd played that night over and over in my head since he died. I could see his pale eyes brim with sadness, as if somewhere he knew badness was brewing and was reaching for help. He couldn't have known that — not consciously — and neither did I back then, but I didn't reach back; I left him to idle chatter and neighborhood gossip. In retrospect, I may have been layering in a narrative that hadn't been, but it didn't matter now. No matter how many times I replayed that night, the ending wouldn't change.

Yes Pastor, I thought. *I wish I were dreaming.*

"We learn how to behave in society," the pastor went on. "What to believe and what not to believe; what is acceptable; what is good and what is bad; what is beautiful and what is ugly; what is right and what is wrong."

She put her book down and gave a speech about questioning and freethinking and breaking out of the bonds of acceptable concepts and conventions, but all I could see was Johann's face that night at the bar, his hand slipping off my waist as I turned to leave.

On the platform, the pastor started, supposedly, getting information from the dead. I tried to be open-minded. I wanted this to be something other than a debacle of cold reading and fraudulence.

"I have a man here with me who is the father of someone here. He has gold fillings and a limp. Who understands this man please?"

A woman put up her hand. The pastor kept talking, giving her more details, all entirely meaningless to me, but I kept looking at the woman sitting there on the other side of the church, saying "yes" to each detail. It meant something to her, but she was so dispassionate that I hardly felt the presence of the living in this place, never mind the dead.

After few more songs and a collection tray, the service ended, and a small group of people gathered in a room beside the church for the lyceum or class. I followed the herd and introduced myself to Rev. Cutler and then took a seat around a large table with nine or ten other people who had been going there for some time. She introduced me to polite nods and explained that they were reading from *The Four Agreements.*

"Do you have a copy?"

Why would I have a copy?

"No, I don't, sorry."

"Here, you can borrow one from the church. We're reading 'Chapter 3: Don't Make Assumptions.'"

The cover described it as a Toltec wisdom book. I thought the Toltec culture was a South or Central American mythological culture, in which case, I wasn't convinced it was their wisdom in this little book, but I thought it best to start by heeding the prescribed reading and, well, not make any assumptions.

After reading some excerpts, they did some exercises, and while I protested that I was only there for research and observation, Rev. Cutler persuaded me to try a thing called psychometry, a psychic exercise in which everyone put an object into a basket, passed it around, took an object belonging to someone else out of the basket, and sat with it in hand until impressions started to come to mind. An odd little exercise, but I picked a ring out of the basket and gave it a shot so as not to be rude.

"Thoughts and memories are imprinted on metals," Rev. Cutler said, "Have you ever walked into an empty room and felt like there'd been an argument in there?"

I nodded. Hadn't everyone?

"That's because energy leaves imprints," she said. "It's the same idea here. You can get impressions from the energy imprinted on an object.

Don't try to see or sense anything. Let whatever wants to come to you come and write it down."

I wrote down a description of some stranger's personality, someone who liked to help people but was passive and taken advantage of as a result, someone who was single but surrounded by females, someone who lacked confidence and had an issue with boundaries. That was about it for me, and I was sure it was either rubbish or obvious.

I had put my engagement ring in the basket, and the person who pulled it out said something like "this woman is in a committed relationship," which of course didn't convince me that it was divinely inspired. When it came to my turn, I was a little embarrassed to share my paltry bit of psychobabble, but as it turned out, the ring belonged to the woman sitting opposite who lived with her sister and was working with her therapist to set healthy boundaries.

"Have you done this before?" Karl, a guy beside me whispered. He looked a bit like Clark Kent with loveable puppy eyes that were magnified by his thick, black-rimmed glasses.

"You kidding?" I whispered back. "I've no idea what I'm doing."

"Are there psychics in your family? Extrasensory perception often runs in families."

"Not my family," I said.

I thought back over the character description I gave. I wasn't convinced that was embedded in a ring. It was pretty generic and probably could have applied to half of the people in the room. But more to the point, even if this were true — and I could see some validity to the concept — it had no bearing on or relevance to the claim that the dead lived.

"One more exercise tonight," Rev. Cutler said. "I spoke to a woman this week who's moving. Her name is Marcy. I want you to tell me where she is moving to? Tune in and ask your guides for help."

I didn't know what guides were, something like the guardian angel children have presumably. If that were the case, mine had long since taken off. A basket of oranges hopped into my mind.

"Karen, what do you have?"

"Florida," I said. I'd no idea. Oranges and Florida. That would have to do.

"Yes, she is moving to Florida, well done," Rev. Cutler said. Had the oranges not popped into my head, I would have said a lucky guess, but who knew what was going on in that room.

"Okay, before we wrap it up, does anyone have anything you want to share this week?" she asked.

One guy shared that he had a craniosacral session and felt more relaxed. Another had been listening to music to develop his clairaudience, whatever that was. Another had seen a black two-dimensional figure again.

"Davy's still trying," Karl said.

"Yep," the first student said.

"What is it?" I asked.

"When someone isn't long in the spirit world, sometimes they will try to manifest, but they haven't learned how to do it yet so they look like a black figure. This has been happening since his brother passed to spirit," Karl said.

"A black figure is a someone trying to manifest?" I asked.

"Yes," Karl said. "It's not that common, but it's nothing to be afraid of. It's usually someone we know."

Someone we know?

"Okay, before we go, I want everyone to give Karen a message," Rev. Cutler interrupted. "We do this for new folks, Karen. Just say 'yes' if you understand the message and 'no' if you don't."

After a few minutes of presumably communing with their guides, one said, "I'm picking up a J name."

"Yes."

"I feel a man with an artistic nature."

"Yes."

"I am seeing a man with a bicycle," said another.

"Yes."

"There is a young man standing behind you," Rev. Cutler added. "He's tall, over six-feet, blonde, and very protective of you, and he's not long in the spirit world. Do you know him?"

Did I know him? Of course, I knew him. I desperately wanted to spin around and see who or what was behind me. Instead, I stared at her, poker-faced, at least I thought I did, but I was likely gaping. I'd told her nothing except my first name and that I was a visiting journalist.

"Yes," I said. "I do. He died recently."

"He hasn't died," Rev. Cutler smiled. "Only his body has died. You'll understand that sooner or later."

He hadn't died? I looped on that the whole way back along the twenty-three miles of dips and curves of the Chesapeake Bay Bridge-Tunnel that separated the mausoleum from the church. I mulled over her description of him standing behind me and the rest of the details the students shared, but by the time I pulled up outside the house, my willingness to be swayed had been replaced, not by the thought that Johann had really been there giving them information, but by a single question: *How the hell did they know all that?*

I was a passenger in someone's car. I didn't know whose. I didn't know where we were going or why. The world outside passed by like a streak of beige. My phone beeped with a text from James, "Johann is back." I grabbed my phone and scrolled frantically through my contact list to reply. It was full of people I didn't recognize, and no matter how hard I tried, I couldn't find his contact. I was finally struck by the obvious — type in his number. "Where RU?" I wrote. The message failed. I tried again. Failed. I tried dialing, but it wouldn't ring. I was panicking, hyperventilating, and woke up gasping.

I dragged myself downstairs, made coffee, and went outside for air.

Busker curled up under my deckchair. I sipped an espresso, which was tearing strips off my empty stomach, and scrolled through old texts from Johann, which tore strips off my heart.

"When we get married, can we get a dog?" I'd written.

"Sure, why not?"

"I could really use an iPad, but I don't want to spend $400 on one."

"Then you don't want it bad enough. Wait for one to show up on fleabay."

"My friend is in an off-off-Broadway play. I have to go. Please come."

"It will take your best cleavage to get me there," he'd replied.

"How was the party last night?" I'd asked.

"The usual drunks. Linda fell over. Watching Phil trying to pick her up was worth the trip."

And on and on, text messages back and forth all day every day, the lightest touch of little thoughts on the other's mind about nothing in particular, just us humming along, spinning around like two ends of a string, sharing trifles and showing up, never realizing that we were building a shrine out of character strings that I'd end up rereading alone in a hulking house in the blistering heat of rural Virginia. I'd have given anything for my phone to beep with another message from him.

My phone beeped with an email from Professor LaGrand.

"I am free at 4:00 p.m. Friday. If that's a good time for you, call me at the number below."

Is that a good time? I had lots of time, but none of it good.

"Yes, 4:00 p.m. is good," I replied. "Look forward to speaking to you."

I had just pressed send when someone squeezed my right shoulder. I jumped out of the deck chair and spun around. No one was there. I rotated my shoulder joint in case it was my T-shirt blowing in the wind, but there was barely a breeze. I squeezed my shoulder with my left hand to see how hard it would have to have been to feel that amount of pressure. Pretty substantial, definitely not the wind.

Rev. Cutler's image of him standing behind me sprang to mind.

Could it ...?

No, that was ridiculous!

Wasn't it?

The truth was, if I were honest with myself, that I wanted to believe both her and Father Peter that he was alive in some form, but I'd no idea how that could be, and so I kept coming back to the belief that the odd incidents in the last couple of weeks could have been, and most likely were, delusions wrought by my frayed nerves at best or a nervous breakdown at worst. This Spiritualist church could at best be a bunch of misguided do-gooders or at worst tricksters preying on the vulnerability of the bereaved. I rejected the latter. I didn't know what was going on here, but I knew it wasn't trickery. The students seemed to be an average cross-section of small-town America, and Rev. Cutler wasn't asking people to max out their credit cards for her enrichment or the glory of God. The Sunday service, like any Sunday service, asked for a donation, and the class afterwards was only ten dollars. No, they weren't con-artists trying to relieve the bereaved of their cash, of that I was certain.

I rambled around the garden. Busker whined indignantly at being deprived of the shade that the deckchair and I had provided him. The pond pump was worthless. The water had slimed over again and stank. I raked the surface and slathered the bushes with pond scum.

Despite my fear of going soft in the head, the tiniest sense of optimism was creeping into my being. Was it Sherlock Holmes who said, "Once you eliminate the impossible, whatever remains, no matter how improbable, must be the truth"?

I went inside to make some tea and toast to ease my sore stomach. I watered the mausoleum plants while waiting for the kettle to boil. The white bird-of-paradise wasn't doing well. The owner had put it in a corner as if it were on a time-out for bad behavior. I moved it in front of a window hoping more light would revive its limp leaves.

My brain was itching for answers. It didn't like uncertainty. I had been pushed into the outer reaches of my knowledge and experience. How on earth could there be such a thing as discarnate consciousness? I had read quite a bit about energy and matter the previous year when I wrote a series of articles about Irish physicists, Ernest Walton and John Bell, and the Austrian-Irish citizen Erwin Schrödinger. Then, as if physics contained the answer to the ultimate nature of reality, my mind decided to deliver up its tome of scientific knowledge with the pride of a cat presenting its owner with a dead mouse.

Schrodinger had spent seventeen years heading up the Dublin Institute of Advanced Studies in a cold, creaking Georgian house that overlooked Merrion Square in wartime Dublin. He loved Dublin. It was a refuge from the Führer that allowed him to mix and mingle in the city's literary circles and cycle along the seafront from Clontarf to the square each day. Ironically, Dublin wasn't moral enough to object to his polygamous relationship, as universities in other cities had been, or religious enough to frown upon his interest in Vedanta, the Hindu philosophy that addresses the fundamental questions of life and reality. Dublin in those days was an unexpected destination for one of the fathers of quantum mechanics, but, as I'd just discovered, life could land us places we never imagined we'd be, asking questions we never imagined we'd ponder.

My mind was still scratching about in Merrion Square when the kettle started whistling and smoke started billowing from the toaster. I scraped the burned crust off the bread and headed upstairs with breakfast in hand and Busker underfoot. I remembered the Danish physicist Niels Bohr said, "Everything we call real is made of things that cannot be regarded as real." I remembered the particles in atoms, the tiniest building blocks of existence, can quantum tunnel through a barrier, much like Busker and me getting from Virginia to New York by passing effortlessly through an Appalachian mountain. I remembered particles exist as waves of probability in all places at once and only take on individual existence when measured or observed, which suggested that reality is inextricable from our observation of it. Even the very atoms we're made of are more than 99.9 percent empty space—so much for a solid, physical world. If all the atoms in the room decompiled, would Busker and I fall through the floor? Of course not, I realized—there'd be no floor, no house, no planet, no human, and no cat. All of this begged the question: What is real? And what of quantum entanglement, where two particles could be strewn across space and yet the behavior of one instantaneously affected the behavior of the other. If a scientist spun one particle on Earth in one direction, its twin on Pluto would spin the other direction simultaneously, as if the first were directing the second instantaneously, faster than the speed of light, as if they were separated in space but not in time. No one knew how. Einstein called it "spooky action." Pseudo-scientific articles alluded to telepathy. All that seemed certain in the weird world of quantum on which our physical world is predicated is that all is uncertain.

If no one really understood what was happening in this world, what hope was there of understanding anything of the next—if there were a next?

And what of consciousness? I vaguely remembered Schrodinger had said something about this. I searched and found it in an old interview he gave the London *Observer*: "Although I think that life may be the result of an accident," he said. "I do not think that of consciousness. Consciousness cannot be accounted for in physical terms." Such was the elusive, non-material nature of the thing.

All things considered, I wasn't surprised that Schrödinger had turned to Vedanta, one of the six schools of Hindu philosophy, for answers to the ultimate nature of reality when he reached a mental impasse where the intellect was exhausted and the whole world was a mass of doubt and questioning. Much like being tortured by a Zen koan.

I'd found my way into the Zen center that was a few blocks from my apartment when I lived in downtown Brooklyn a decade earlier. That first Sunday morning, I stood outside a small red brick building with large, perfectly lacquered doors that had once been a funeral parlor, wondering if I should go in. A couple of people stood outside in the cold with their hands stuffed into the sleeves of their grey robes, taking them out only to place them in prayer position and bow each time someone arrived. People approached in silence, bowed, and entered in reverence. One of the robed people smiled at me and motioned with her hand for me to pass through the open door. I nodded rather than feel like a hack doing a phony bow.

My life had sounded like a feedback loop for a long time. I'd grown sick of covering politics. It was the same old stories being spun by different politicians, and nothing ever changing in any meaningful way. I gorged on a daily diet of lies, self-interest, power struggles, unjust wars, and unrelenting greed. I was knowledgeable but impotent, observing and recording the futility of our existence but helping no one. We were just rolling about on the planet, specks on a speck in the grand scheme of the universe, petty, power hungry and abusive. Thirteen billion years of evolution and the best the universe could do was spit us up.

"Do you ever wonder why we're here, like what's the point of us?" I'd asked my friend Sara who was visiting from LA.

"I think we're here to love each other," she replied. She had a new boyfriend and was feeling very hemp and granola.

"For what?"

"I dunno. So, we can spend our lives with someone we love," she said.

"For what?"

"Are you trying to be difficult?" she asked.

"No. I'm just curious. We are born, we find someone to love, we breed so they can find someone to love, and on it goes. Meanwhile, we're turning the world to shit. And then we die."

"Maybe we're supposed to learn to love everyone," she said.

"For what?"

"Maybe you need Prozac," she said.

I needed something. I knew very little about Zen, but this center was convenient and seemed as good a place as any to start looking for whatever I was missing.

The Zen monks in black robes were sitting perfectly still on the floor beneath a low-rise stage in a fairly large room called the Zendo, which was reserved for meditation and talks about the dharma or Buddhist philosophy. There were candles, incense and bowls of water, and a simple brass statue of the Buddha on a platform at one end. Eighty or so people sat in rows in front of them, each person sitting in lotus position on round black cushions on top of thick black mats.

Interesting, I thought. *The Buddha is on the platform but monks sit on the floor at the same level as the people.*

I followed their lead by slipping off my shoes in the hallway and walking into the Zendo to find an empty cushion. The marble floor was freezing under my feet. People were bowing to the Buddha and then to their mats before sitting down. I found an empty mat and made a half-assed bow before cracking my knees into a cross-legged position. Everyone on every mat was absolutely still, no twitching, no swallowing, not even blinking.

Five minutes later, someone started banging drums at the back of the Zendo. Everyone stood up, which was a relief because I already had pins and needles in my feet. Someone in a grey robe whizzed down the aisle handing out little books. As if I were a child, the person beside me opened my book to a particular page, and the group started chanting the Heart Sutra. There was no melody to the cacophonous chant, but it was easy to follow, and I eventually joined in. "Form does not differ from emptiness. Emptiness does not differ from form." And on it went, making no sense to me. Afterward, everyone got comfortable on their cushions again and settled into perfect stillness. I'd been told to sit still, count my breath, allow thoughts arise and then let them go without judgment and return quite simply to counting the breath. Next, the bell rang, indicating meditation was about to begin. For the next forty minutes, the only noise was the whirring of ceiling fans blowing cool air overhead and the faint sound of car horns as Brooklyn went on about its day outside. Inside, was mental and physical torture. My legs ached, my face itched, and my mind was terrorized by having nothing to do. I started counting my breaths.

One. A siren screeched outside. That sounds like an ambulance. I'm thinking, let that go and start again. One. My feet are getting numb. Maybe I can move without anyone noticing. Shit, the fabric is dragging on the mat. Dammit. I'm thinking again. One.

I learned in my effort to practice zazen that something can be simple and impossible at the same time.

A half an hour later, came dharma talk, the part of the service where one of the monks gave a sermon on Buddhism and how it relates to our lives. It was a lovely dharma talk. I expected some sort of dogma, but he just talked in deceptively simple terms about how times challenge us to take in a world of recurring tragedy, destruction, and loss yet still have faith in wholeness and original perfection.

I grew to love that sangha and the monks. I loved the harmony I experienced from sitting on the black cushions on a marble floor each week, counting my breath as the fans whispered overhead. Its godlessness and the absence of dogma, reincarnation, or retribution in an afterlife appealed to me. I loved the intuitive nature of the dharma talk and the way the monks could take complex and even distressing situations and change how we perceived them.

After a year or so, one of the monks gave me a koan to work with, one of those paradoxical riddles for which Zen is famous, such as "what is the sound of one hand clapping?" They were designed to be confounding apparently, and working with them was supposed to help us achieve enlightenment, although I didn't know how.

"Koans are dark to the mind and radiant to the heart," he said.

He explained that the only way to work with a koan is to release the ego's need to understand.

"Your koan this week is 'the coin lost in the river is found in the river.' Don't work on the koan; allow the koan to work on you. We'll meet again next week."

I spent the week meditating on this, churning it over in my head and getting frustrated because I couldn't figure out the answer. I came back the next week with some sort of analytical answer that missed the point completely.

"You lack compassion," he said and sent me away.

This I couldn't understand either. I went away again and made myself suffer more because I couldn't grasp the answer. Then I noticed I was creating my own suffering by grasping. After that, I watched my mind treat everything in my day as a problem to be solved or as an answer to be discovered. I realized I was creating my own suffering by chasing thoughts around and trying to control the outcome. I was doing this to myself. I was lacking self-compassion by chasing endless coins around endless rivers.

I came back the next week and offered this up as the answer.

"No," he said, "the answer is before speech, before thinking."

I gave up. Maybe there was no coin, maybe there was no river, or maybe the coin wasn't lost because it was in the river, or maybe I could just afford to let the coin go.

One thing I didn't experience in my Zen practice was the sense of oneness with each other and the universe that we are said to be capable of reaching when we let ego fall away. I understood the laws of cause and effect. I understood that we couldn't exist as physical beings separate from the universe, so intellectually I could see that we were all interconnected. But I never experienced it. I never glimpsed what Chinese Buddhist teacher Zhiyi described as the "three thousand realms in a single moment of life." I never had the experience of being part of the one, seamless, ever-changing landscape that Zen Master Thich Nhat Hanh called "interbeing."

Each Sunday, I showed up in the Zendo and chanted the Heart Sutra and sat down on my cushion. On a good day, I got as far as two or even three before a thought rose, and I let it go. I did feel peaceful in the Zen center and probably calmer in life, but I couldn't shake my compulsion to look outside and want to do something. The world was a disaster, and I didn't understand how me meditating would make a difference.

"We don't meditate for ourselves," the monk said, "we meditate for others."

I probably would have understood that had I taken the time to sit with it, but I didn't. Many of us on that marble floor were trying to be more than our insignificant selves. Our attachment to our desire to be or do more was causing us to suffer. We were holding and grasping and suffering because we didn't understand where to look.

A couple of years later, someone brought bed bugs to our building in downtown Brooklyn. I cleared out and left almost everything behind. I moved to the Greenpoint neighborhood in north Brooklyn for a fresh start with a few boxes of books and a suitcase of freshly laundered clothes. Unfortunately, the eleven stops on the G train between my new apartment and the Zen center might as well have been eleven hundred. The G train was notoriously unreliable, especially on Sundays, and many weeks I arrived after zazen had started and couldn't go in. If I wasn't late, it was because I wasn't there at all; I was sitting on the platform at Greenpoint Avenue waiting for a train that never came. Eventually, I stopped going.

On my way back from one of those mornings on the subway platform, I stopped into Peter Pan, the Polish bakery on Manhattan Avenue, for coffee and a bagel. A tall blonde man was sitting at the counter with his young son eating muffins and drinking coffee. I could just hear his voice and the trace of a German accent. I looked back at him on my way out the door and saw him looking after me. We smiled, a little embarrassed perhaps to be caught checking each other out. At least I was. The door swung closed behind me, and I continued out into the morning sun, pondering over what, in the absence of Zen, could be my new path.

Busker napped contentedly under a shaft of sunlight pouring through the attic window. I lay on the bed staring at the ceiling in a state of discontent. I'd been doing intellectual gymnastics for hours, trying to make sense of patterns I couldn't see. I couldn't understand how Zen or Vedanta or quantum physics or anything I knew could begin to explain an invisible force squeezing my shoulder on a Thursday morning on a deck in Virginia or any of the other events of late. If there were any semblance of truth in Rev. Cutler's comments, if my experiences were in fact supernatural, I still didn't have the faintest understanding of what was happening or why or how. How particles could remain entangled after death to such a degree that the complex matrix of consciousness was preserved, I didn't know. I didn't even know if I were asking the right question.

I know nothing.

As that simple statement arose in my mind, I felt the monkey — the ego's need to revel in its own perceived power — slide off my back, as if I were only now realizing beginner's mind, as if I'd finally touched the essence of a koan by simply being here now, accepting uncertainty, accepting that nothing was as I perceived it to be.

I called the professor at 4:00 p.m.

"Hello." The professor's small voice was unexpected.

"Hello, Professor. This is Karen. Thanks for taking the time to talk to me."

"You're very welcome."

"I enjoyed your book," I said.

"Thank you," he said. "It took a lot of work over a lot of years to collect all those stories. Are you doing an article on extraordinary encounters?"

He was sincere about his work and humble in attitude.

"Possibly," I lied. "I'm actually wondering if I've been having extraordinary encounters of my own."

"Ah," he said. "How so?"

I told him about Johann, about the creaking, the smelling, the squeezing, the black gorilla, the CIS image in my mind, and the unexpected events in the back room of a Spiritualist church. Not so long ago, this all added up to crazy. Today, as I sat there in the soft light of the shaded attic window, the world looked different, and I hoped it amounted to something else.

"Am I imagining this, Professor?"

"No, no," he said. "These are all very common."

"And you really think these are signs from the dead?"

"You mean extraordinary encounters? Yes, most likely."

"How do the people know they are extraordinary encounters and not their imagination?"

"Well, sometimes a loved one will appear to them or to a child in the house. It's more common for children to see them because they haven't had time to conform to all the conventions our society puts around death and the afterlife," he said.

"But a lot of the encounters you wrote about were much more subtle than an apparition. I mean some of them were songs just coming on the radio, which could be totally random, and some people sensed a presence, which could just be their imagination."

"It's true. It's hard to quantify, but the key is that the encounter will resonate with the person here. Then they know in their hearts that their loved one has survived death and is sending them a message to let them know they're okay," he said. "Some encounters are more obvious than others. If the loved one smoked, sometimes people smell their pipe or cigarette smoke. Someone else could see a butterfly and know it's their loved one. Or sometimes the message comes as a synchronicity, which happens say when the person who asked for a sign turns on the radio and hears their favorite song playing."

This was beautifully abstract, but it didn't explain how the dead could get a song on the radio. And even though I'd been smelling cigarette smoke, that could just be emanating from the lungs of the living.

"These synchronicities reassure the grieving that there is something beyond this life and that they are part of something bigger," he added, "a larger unknown plan."

"So, the image of CIS I saw in my head that led to me play C-sharp that coincided with the dead GPS springing back to life was a synchronicity?" I asked.

"It could be. It was a meaningful coincidence that you played a note you'd been shown and then your GPS gave you a message."

"But I saw that image in my mind and that prompted the sequence of events. The other stories I read didn't involve any internal images; all the sightings happened externally."

"Yes, that's true. Extraordinary encounters usually happen externally, out in the world."

I couldn't fathom how I was getting information internally in my mind that led me to take actions when everyone else had encounters externally in the physical world. There was a difference in our meaningful coincidences, but I didn't understand why.

"Extraordinary encounters are very common," he said. "If you look back, I'm willing to bet you've had some unexplainable experiences before that you may have dismissed or repressed."

"None spring to mind," I confessed.

"These encounters are possible because of the bond of love that connects two people. That's why I say love lives on," he said. "Think about it, and ask your fiancé for a communication. Maybe he'll send you a butterfly.

"Professor, he was far too sarcastic to send something so delicate. Hijack my GPS maybe, but if I saw a butterfly flutter past me, I'd never associate it with him."

A dial tone started beeping on the phone line, the same seven digits repeating steadily. It sounded like someone else picked up another extension and was dialing out, but it wasn't someone in the mausoleum because I was on my mobile phone.

"I think someone is trying to dial out on another extension in your house," I said through the beeps.

"We don't have another extension," he replied.

The beeps stopped.

"What was I saying? Oh yes, ask him for something that would tell you it's him," the professor offered. "I have visitors here and need to go, but email me if you'd like to set up a time to talk more."

"Sounds good, Professor, I'll do that."

I wandered along the strand that evening, thinking about the professor's question and wondering — if these external extraordinary encounters were real — what single action could I experience that would make me say, "Whoa! That's Johann!" I might have said cigarette smoke, but that was too easily explained, or something electrical since he was tech savvy, but that could just be a surge. I also wondered if I'd had unexplainable experiences before as the professor suggested. Something was scratching around my head, something uncomfortable that I couldn't reach.

I took a wrong turn home on the way back from the strand and happened upon a clothes and household store. It was full of pretty things and brightly colored clothes I'd never wear. I'd been hovering around in black bootcut yoga pants and an assortment of black T-shirts, mostly long-sleeved, my go-to New York City wardrobe. It suited my mood and stopped my skin from burning, but I sweltered daily. The beach had been particularly hot for the last few evenings, and I was tired of the feeble scraps of energy I could muster being siphoned off by the southern heat wave. I had no desire to shop, but I needed to cool down.

I ran my finger across the rows of beachwear: brightly colored beach wraps, yellow linen Palazzo pants, baggy shirts covered in seashells and starfish, clothes no designer would own up to and no woman would wear. Maybe I could find a large sunhat and darker sunglasses so I could swan about town avoiding everyone's gaze and discouraging small talk and the way they had of assuaging their own helplessness when confronted with my grief. The only people who really understood were Father Peter and poor old Millie watching the sunset each evening and waiting for the day it wouldn't rise again for her.

My current sunglasses were nothing special. They were the result of an abortive attempt a few months earlier to buy a summer dress in a new boutique that opened on Meserole Avenue in Brooklyn. After spending a morning gazing vacantly at a blank screen devoid of even a single inspired word, I slipped out for some shopping therapy. The new boutique had some nice but overpriced stock. I tried on a white cotton dress with splotches of color, aqua, and purples with a splash of yellow — uncharacteristically cheerful of me. The shop assistant, obviously on commission, was delighted to help, checking in to make sure it fit, asking if she could get me anything else, and fawning over how beautiful I looked in colors.

"Come down. Need your opinion," I texted Johann.

A few minutes later, he stuck his head through the dressing room curtains.

"It looks like a paint pot exploded on you."

"You hate it?"

"*Hässlich*," he said.

The assistant beamed when I walked out of the dressing room and handed her the dress.

"He hates it."

She scowled at him.

I plucked a pair of shades out of a basket by way of small recompense. Those sunglasses now sat atop my head in Virginia, a relic from a moment forged in time, like off-Broadway ticket stubs, the warmflasche, a turquoise shell box, Johann's old hoody that I borrowed and never gave back, my engagement ring, and a hundred other scraps of our life that I hoarded like a squirrel preparing for a life of winter.

I had to get out of the store. It was like every other place these days, lulling me into the comfort of the past and then spitting me back into the present. I'd be better served doing something more productive, like calling the one person who might know if anyone else in the family had these extraordinary encounters either internally in their mind or externally in the world that the professor described. I would do that first thing in the morning.

"Hi, Mam."

"Oh, Karen, just a minute." She turned volume on the television down to settle in for an unexpected transatlantic chat.

"How are you?" she asked.

I knew my mother well enough to know this was less an invitation to emote and more an assumption that I was bucking up and getting on with it.

"I'm grand. I'm in Virginia."

"What are you doing there?"

"Taking a break."

My mother had a knack for asking a question without asking a question. She could ask about my mental state while tiptoeing around the reason why I might be in a state. Her reluctance to ask about Johann went far beyond the adage of don't speak ill of the dead to don't speak of them at all — unusual considering how well we Irish do death. Traditional Irish wakes are treasured community affairs where, for three days and nights, the living watch over the dead, usually in the parlor of the deceased person's house. The whole town turns up at one point or another to view the body lying there in its Sunday best, to say a little prayer, and offer condolences before being offered tea and biscuits or a pint of the black stuff.

When I was seven, my father's mother died. All I knew of death till then was a puppy my father had brought me that died a week later. He wrapped him in a sack so I couldn't see him, and we had a funeral in the back garden where his little body was laid to rest all alone in the cold and dark. I picked some flowers from my mother's flowerbed to stick in the soil to cheer him up, but they withered. Each week, I placed more, and each week they died. Eventually, my father got me a new puppy, and I stopped bringing flowers to the old one.

When my grandmother died, a steady stream of strange people trampled into her tiny house. I spent a lot of time with Nana as a child. She would get special biscuits for my visits, and my glamorous Auntie Joyce would brush my hair and paint my nails. Nana made my first communion dress of cotton and lace. I wore it with silver rosary beads wrapped round my lace-gloved hands and felt like royalty. She had that way about her — making you feel special. I remembered the string of pearl drops she stitched onto the front of my dress and her making tea in the kitchen and the Bourbon Creams on the plate. This wasn't like my puppy. I couldn't get another Nana.

My mother held my hand as we stood around her coffin in the cramped parlor. I put my hands on the sides and stood on my tiptoes to try to see her face.

"Take a good look," my grandfather laughed. "That's the last you'll see of her."

I burst into tears and buried my head in my mother's belly. She didn't say anything then, but I later heard her tell my father that his father had been appallingly insensitive. I was angry with my granddad and glad my mother criticized him. Maybe it was his way of grieving, but all I remembered was him being frightening and me not being tall enough to see her face.

Unlike my aunt who loved to hear every detail about how someone sickened and died, how many came to the funeral, and who was fighting with whom afterward, my mother didn't dwell on death, except to pray to the beatified dead on a regular basis to intercede with God on her behalf. Distraction was her solution to crisis, so I hadn't talked about Johann since the day he died. We just talked about the weather and my other grandmother's bad hip and a trip to Paris she was planning with the Ladies Club. Better that than an intimate conversation that could result in a meltdown on my end and helpless discomfort on hers.

"Mam, did we have anyone in the family who was good with herbs or healing?"

"What do you mean?"

"Was anyone in our family ever, I dunno, say, a witch?"

"Well my Aunt Mamie could roll up her sleeves and curse like a sailor."

I could hear her moving things around. She'd run her fingers across a surface and saw a speck of dust and was now cleaning. She was always cleaning.

"I don't mean that, I mean, okay, do you think people can talk to the dead?"

"Good Lord. That's all in their heads."

"But you pray to the saints, and they're dead people."

"That's different."

"How."

"Why are you asking about this?"

My mother also had a knack for changing the direction of a conversation to get out of a corner.

"I'm just wondering. You know, you hear stories about people hearing spirits around the house. I was just wondering if anyone in our family did."

"I don't know," she said. "Let me get your father. He's in the garden."

"No! Don't call Dad."

"Billy, Billy, come in. Karen's on the phone," she yelled out the backdoor. I could hear them mumbling and rustling to exchange the phone, her likely telling him I was off my rocker.

"Hi Karen, Dad here. How's it going?"

"Fine, Dad, how are you?"

"No news here. Your mother says you want to know if we have ghosts?"

I could tell by the levity in his voice that he wasn't taking me seriously.

"Well, I was just wondering if anyone in the family had ever said anything about seeing or hearing ghosts or spirits. I mean, people in the country talk about this all the time."

"I think my father used to talk to his mother, if that's what you mean, and Joyce said she saw him in the mirror behind her after he died. She got a fright and ran out into the street. Hang on, your mother wants to say something,"

The phone was passed back.

"Do you not remember the thing that happened on the Girl Guides week? Remember you and Brigid Boyle saw something."

Something was niggling about in my head, something I couldn't drag into focus.

"The Girl Guides week?"

"Remember that house down in Wicklow, the one you all went to and came back with some story about a ghost? Do you not remember?"

I'd forgotten all about that awful Girl Guides house. Our company was sent there when we were twelve or thirteen for a week of campfires, sing songs, hiking, bird watching, and other badge-worthy pursuits. It was one of those old country estates that had long since lost its luster. The paintings and tapestries and furniture from its grand old days had been sold off long ago, so by the time the house was bequeathed to the Girl Guides, the floors were bare, and lumpy mattresses lay on the heavy metal bunk beds that had been donated from some abandoned military barracks. All that was left of its former glory was the mahogany stairs and banisters and the ramshackle wardrobes that couldn't find a buyer when the house was stripped. It was a dark and gloomy house, made worse each night by the banging of window shutter after window shutter as Girl Guides in each room barricaded us into a mahogany tomb for the night.

Our first campfire came after an afternoon hike. Brigid Boyle and I were late getting back. We were running up the stairs to get into our pajamas when everyone else was already assembled downstairs. There were three of those bunk beds in the corners of our dorm and three single beds in the middle. I'd finished changing and was standing by the door waiting for Brigid when my bunk suddenly banged and rattled and violently shook its way out of the corner toward the center of the room. Nothing else moved. The noise was as scary as the shimmying.

I wrestled with the loose doorknob to engage the lock and open the door.

"Wait!" Brigid cried, running after me, with one leg in her pajamas and one pajama leg trailing behind her as we bolted down the stairs and into the room where the campfire was burning. We were shaking. The story twittered through the troop and the captain soon had a panic on her hands.

"Sit down," she thundered. "You two, come with me."

We were hoping for some explanation, like an earthquake maybe, but got a tongue lashing for scaring the other Girl Guides and were then marched back into the room to tell everyone we'd made it up. I felt like a fool. I hated her for making us sound like liars and for not explaining what happened. She was the captain, she was the adult in charge, and she was supposed to know these things. They hated us as much as we hated her. No one would speak to us for the rest of the night, so we were scared, cold, and maligned. We were called Girl Guides in Ireland, not Girl Scouts, for a reason. The boys were scouts; they went on adventures. We were guides; we were supposed to be helpful, and this wasn't helpful.

After the campfire, we had to go back into that dorm room. The bunk was about three feet away from the walls. It would have taken ten grown men to move it. We couldn't have done it. The captain knew it, but she cared more about keeping the troop under control. She just told us to go to bed, which meant I had to get back into that bottom bunk. I pulled the blankets up tight around my chin as if they would afford me some protection. Brigid was in the single bed beside me doing the same.

"What if it comes back?" she whispered.

"I don't know," I whispered.

"Shut up," said my cousin who was in another bunk.

I spent the night looking at the slats in the bunk above me. At one point, I leaned over to look into the gap between the wall and the floorboards to see if something were there. I was terrified it would slither back up through that space. I was far too petrified to look under the bed in case it already had, so there I lay for hours and hours, hiding under a blanket, heart racing, craning to see and hear every creak and movement, while everyone else, including Brigid Boyle, fell asleep.

For the rest of the week, Brigid and I had to scrub the pots and breakfast dishes while the others went hiking.

"What do you think it was?" she asked.

"A ghost, a big ghost," I said.

"A big angry ghost," she added.

"Do you think it's still here somewhere, watching us maybe?" I asked. We looked around the kitchen, scaring ourselves silly.

"I hope not."

"Probably is," I said.

For the rest of the week, lots of small glittery things disappeared: earrings, trinkets, jewelry. The captain said we had a thief in our midst, but I was convinced the angry ghost had taken them. We were told to search the whole house, which meant we had to go into old, cold, dusty rooms where fires hadn't been lit and humans hadn't been for decades. In the corner of one room, I saw an empty mahogany planter that was full of rubbish. While I debated whether I should put my hand in to check for contraband, the rubbish started to move as if something had woken up underneath. I ran out of the room and out of the house and stayed out there in a field until I'd convinced myself that a mouse was in the planter and a magpie was stealing the glittery things. That's what magpies do after all. Later, I decided it was all nonsense and that the bunk was caused by a seismic shift. I forgot about it. But I hated mahogany forever after.

My mother and father were mumbling away from the receiver again. I leaned against the window and looked over the garden while they chatted between themselves on my transatlantic dime. Busker was napping under a tree. The frogs had returned to the pond along with the slime. A monarch butterfly landed on the window. I leaned in close to see its black belly and spindly legs. Up close, they're ugly bugs.

"Mam," I said trying to get her attention as I paced around the bedroom aware of the clock ticking. That strong burning tobacco smell was back and so strong and localized that I thought someone was smoking in the attic, but there was no one there.

"Mam!"

"That was an imaginary friend," my mother was saying to my father.

"There's no harm in telling her," my father said.

"Tell me what?" I asked.

"Well, when we were living in the North Strand" (that was the house we lived in until I was six) "you were in the living room talking to someone out in the hall."

"So?"

"Well it was the middle of the day and we were the only two home, so I thought your Dad had come home from work early and you were talking to him. But when I went to the hall, there was no one there. So I asked you who you were talking to and you pointed to the empty space and said 'I'm talking to that man.'"

I didn't remember that.

"And you used to talk to a woman you said was Nana Murphy with the little silver cross" she said.

"Who's Nana Murphy with the little silver cross?" I asked.

"Your great-grandmother," she said. "She always wore a tiny crucifix on a silver chain, but she died ten years before you were born."

The conversation with my mother awakened memories of other strange childhood encounters. At about six, I remembered waking up to see a man I didn't know looking down at me. His blue eyes reflected light even though there was no light in the room, which made him look lovely, but below the knees, he faded into darkness and so seemed to be suspended in midair. His grey curly hair and layers of grey clothes were like those my grandfather wore: an old-fashioned jacket and a waistcoat over a white shirt. He came a few times. He didn't wake me, but in the middle of the night, I'd open my eyes to see him watching me sleep. He never said anything, and neither did I. He always looked calm. I knew he wasn't alive like I was or my parents were, but I also knew he wasn't dead, or if he were dead, then dead didn't mean what people said it did. I'd go back to sleep, and in the morning, he'd be gone. My mother was in the kitchen with my Auntie Ann the day I told her about him. My aunt blessed herself, and my mother dismissed me as an imaginative child. By the time I reached my teens, I joined their ranks in thinking these encounters were dreams or hallucinations. Eventually, they stopped happening. Now, I wasn't so sure that they had been hallucinations. If not, what were they?

I picked up my phone and emailed the only person I knew who might have some answers.

"Hi, Rev. Cutler, can you recommend some books on psychic phenomena or the survival of consciousness?"

"Go to the Edgar Cayce A.R.E. in Virginia Beach," she wrote back a couple of hours later. "They have a library and a great spa. Pay it a visit if you go."

In the early hours, I was woken by a familiar smell, a faint musky smell with a light hint of sweat. It was so intense and so close that it seemed to seep from my pores. I recognized it immediately. This was Johann's smell, as if he were right beside me. I inhaled as if it were the last oxygen molecule I would ever breathe. Then it was gone.

I was startled, not just by how strong it was or how clearly I remembered it, but that it happened at all. Smells trigger memories; memories don't trigger smells. I sniffed around the room again, but there was nothing. I gave up and went back to bed, but as I drifted off, I felt warmth behind me, like a body pressed up against mine and then the lightest pressure across my waist like an arm resting there. The way Johann used to lie.

Maybe it was the weight of the duvet.

I woke up sweating. It promised to be a blistering day. I spritzed and doused the plants, filled Busker's bowls, and took my espresso and laptop out onto the deck. I felt happy. Maybe it was because I'd had a solid few hours of calm and comforting sleep. Or maybe it was something else. I dared not believe what I'd been told by the priest, the pastor, and the professor, but somewhere in me, despite myself and my skepticism, there was hope that there may be something more to life than what we can physically perceive.

An orange butterfly was sitting on the arm of the deckchair. I slipped gently into the chair expecting it to flutter off, but it stayed there, its wings standing on end, swaying slightly in the soft breeze.

I opened Safari on my iPad and found the website for The Edgar Cayce Association for Research and Enlightenment in Virginia Beach. It had a nice spa that offered a trademarked Cayce massage and a Japanese healing modality called Reiki that apparently reduced stress by channeling life force energy through the laying on of hands. It sounded like Pentecostal faith healing. I'd always loved the Pentecostal flair for the dramatic; it doesn't get much more theatrical than speaking in tongues and having flames dance over your head. I called the health center and made an appointment for both. Why not make the trek, and if I were going to go that far, I might as well go the whole hog. Johann would have approved of me lying naked on a table and having a full-body massage, but he would have thought energy healing was fodder for the feeble minded, as would I have once, but I really wasn't sure about anything anymore.

I closed my laptop to get ready for my day trip to Virginia Beach. The butterfly was still on the arm of the chair.

"What a brazen little butterfly you are."

I stopped for gas before getting on the bridge.

"Morning," I said to the old Asian man behind the counter.

"*Selamat pagi.* Good morning," he said.

"Arabic?" I asked. It sounded familiar, although not quite Arabic.

"Indonesian," he responded.

"Selamat pagi," I said. "Will you put twenty on number three please?"

I'd heard those words from Johann one morning when he left before I woke up.

"You're an arse. You left without saying good morning," I'd texted.

"Good morning," he texted back.

"You could have woken me."

A few minutes later, I got another text, "*Bon dia.*"

Thirty minutes later, I got "*Bon matin*," and thirty minutes after that, "*Selamat pagi.*"

"Okay, I get it," I wrote back.

At lunchtime, I got "*Aloha*" and mid-afternoon, "*Buongiorno.*"

"Stop!"

"*Buenos días.*"

"STOP!"

Silence.

"*Guten morgen.*"

I was secretly hoping the Edgar Cayce A.R.E. library held proof of the survival of consciousness. I hoped the Holy Grail of the afterlife was stashed on the dusty shelves of that library to tell me beyond a doubt that Johann had survived death, that we all survive, and that consciousness exists independently of the body. I needed proof beyond the continued existence of residual energy. I needed proof of thinking, talking, communicating spirits, not the silent apparitions of my childhood. Energy can't be destroyed, granted, but recompiling atoms is entirely different from the survival of an actual personality.

After a glorious drive over the bridge, along the coast, and into the grounds, I came upon a New England-style mansion standing on an elevation looking down on the world. I parked my car, climbed the steps, and crossed a large paved circle designed like a labyrinth, pausing just long enough to make out two dolphins forming a blue yin and yang symbol at its center. I then made a beeline for the visitor's center in search of the library. Outside, people quietly wandered about in the gardens. Inside, people bustled. I followed an arrow pointing up winding stairs to the library, expecting something colorful and unusual and worthy of America's most famous psychic. Instead, I got an underwhelming room with low ceilings, fluorescent lighting, a slightly dusty smell, and stacks of ordinary wooden bookshelves lined with hundreds of uniform brown binders. It was disappointingly bland.

Walking up and down the aisles, I noticed thousands of transcripts bound and stacked here that recorded the treatment of illness, philosophy and reincarnation, dreams and dream interpretation, ESP and psychic phenomena, spiritual growth, and meditation and prayer. A woman at the desk told me that he was called the "sleeping prophet" because he did all of these readings while in trance, many for people who weren't in the same room or even the same state. She pointed me to some background information and clucked off like a mother hen to greet and repeat this information to another epistemophiliac who wandered into her Cayce paradise.

I opened a hardback from the 1940s with an illegible gold embossed title and read that Cayce was born in 1877 and raised on a backwoods farm in Hopkinsville, Kentucky. He had an eighth-grade education because his family couldn't afford a ninth. As a child, he saw and spoke to his late grandfather's spirit and played with other spirits, although people said they were imaginary friends. That sounded familiar. I pulled up a chair at a large, round table in the middle of the aisle and read on. In 1889, at the age of twelve, he was reading in his hut in the woods, when a woman with wings appeared and asked him what he wanted most of all. He said he wanted to help sick children, but he hadn't the knowledge or know-how to do so and was a terrible student. She said she'd help. After that, he discovered that if he slept on his books, he could absorb all the knowledge within them before he awoke. Ten or so years later, Cayce met a traveling stage hypnotist and ventured into diagnosing medical conditions when in a hypnotic trance. Fame brought him Woodrow Wilson, Thomas Edison, Irving Berlin, and George Gershwin along with a variety of unscrupulous men who waited until he was in a trance to ask where treasures could be found or the outcome of a horse race. Eventually, Cayce was advised by one of his voices to move to Virginia Beach and set up a hospital of sorts there. A New York stock trader bought him the house and he set about checking his remedies and producing a compendium of his remedies and medical profession.

I was surprised I'd never heard of him. He was the most documented psychic of all time. Three hundred books had been written about him, and he'd been featured in the *New York Times* and *Washington Post*. The media was also replete with skeptics who were out in force. Admittedly, he had some out-there ideas. He talked about Atlantis as the dwelling place of aliens and made predictions that didn't come true. Catnip to a skeptic. They called him a quack and a fraud who got his information not in a trance but from voracious reading and his own imagination.

Once, I would have agreed, but too many things were happening that I couldn't explain. It's easy to be cynical. Much of the time, it's a shrill voice that offers not intelligence but sloven intellectualism. It's easier to discredit than apply the intellectual rigor needed to understand. It's often easier to define ourselves not by what we stand for but by what we stand against. It's easier to surround ourselves, politically, religiously, and socially, with friends and colleagues and media sources that confirm our biases rather than be agitated by a worldview incongruous to our own. It's easier to dismiss someone like Cayce than try to understand.

How could there be an honest investigation when we hold fast to what we think is true? I knew there were beliefs and prejudices so deeply embedded in my thinking, driving my perceptions, that they were affecting how I interpreted all my experiences. I was growing tired of the pessimism of belittlers, including my own. If I were going to understand what was happening, it was time to retire limiting attitudes and be open to new experiences.

It was almost noon. I left the library and went to the spa.

The spa was a different world after the heavy brownness of the library. The climate was calm and the sea air was crisp. I understood why Cayce believed this location would have healing properties. It was still and peaceful here, as any spa should be, but this one whispered simplicity not luxury. Everything about it was understated: a gurgle from a water cooler filled with cucumber slices, the imperceptible hum of air conditioning, and the trace of peppermint lingering in the air. Occasionally, clients and practitioners passed by, nodding, smiling, and directing each other into small rooms in some wordless language.

My masseuse, a tall man called Robert, came to meet me. He was very white. He was dressed in white, had white hair to the nape of his neck, and a perfectly groomed white goatee. His skin however was sun-kissed and smooth although he must have been fifty. He had the markings of a man who'd spent many moons in India, but now massaged people by day and communed with the universe by night. He lifted his hands to prayer position, made a slight bow and an even slighter smile, and motioned for me to follow his hand in the direction of my room.

"Is there anything troubling you," he asked in mild mannered voice.

"Everything."

"Physically or mentally or emotionally?" he asked.

"All of the above," I said. "My fiancé just died ..." I trailed off.

"I understand," he said. "I'm going to mix some oils. Please undress and lie face down under the sheet. I'll be back in a few moments."

The last massage I got was from Johann, if you could call it a massage. I'd arrived back in Brooklyn after a transatlantic flight with knots so big I could have checked them. We were watching *Wings of Desire*, my favorite Wim Wenders movie about Damiel, an angel in a long, black overcoat who observed humans from the skies over Berlin and came down to listen to their thoughts and talk to Peter Falk. He fell in love with a circus performer and leapt from the heavens to live a mortal life with her. We'd watched it before, but I could never watch it too many times. Since he was German and my first job when I arrived in the States was with a traveling circus, we decided it was our movie. That night, I was watching it with a warmflasche balanced on my neck. It didn't help. Eventually, he removed it and started to knead. It hurt like hell, and I called him a lot of names, but it did the trick in the end.

Robert knocked and came back into the room with a mixture of neroli oil and frankincense, which he explained helped to move through the stress and anxiety of loss in times of grief as well as calm and uplift the spirit.

"It will help strengthen your connection to the Divine," he said, "which can weaken when we lose a loved one."

He assumed I had a connection to the Divine. I supposed most people did who found their way into these rooms.

For the next forty-five minutes, Robert did an agonizing osteopathic massage, which was prefixed by "take a deep breath," four little words I began to dread, as if forewarning me of agony would make it more tolerable. He overestimated my stoicism. He gave me simple explanations of the technique as the session went on, telling me how neuromuscular release would help reset the mental feedback loop I was experiencing. Mostly though, he was silent, carefully working out the pain that infiltrated my body.

He finished with a soothing Swedish massage for which I was grateful, then rubbed some citrus oil onto my temples, which he said would help release me from the dark grip of death to see the light that's still in my life. He put his hands together, bowed, wished me well, and left me to dress.

Bits of me felt better. I didn't have the same physical pain nor did I feel as morose as I had upon arrival. My six-week-old headache was gone, and I could turn my head to the right without straining the cramped muscles in my neck.

Outside the room, a young woman waited.

"I'm Amanda," she said. "I am your Reiki healer."

She led me to another room, asked me if I'd had Reiki before, and proceeded to explain in a soft voice, with just a trace of a southern accent, more or less what I'd read on the website: that it was a form of Japanese energy healing, during which she attuned to the life force or universal energy or Reiki Masters, whichever concept resonated with my belief system (I didn't tell her I had none), and channeled healing from there through her hands to me. She held up perfectly manicured, delicate hands that sported a sparkling solitaire. Once, mine was like that — sparkling. Now, it seemed to lack luster. While she washed her hands, I held mine up to the light. I would probably have to take it off someday, but that day, the only way it was coming off was if my finger went with it.

Amanda asked me to remove my shoes and lie on the table.

"You might feel hot or cold or tingly. That's the healing energy, but even if you don't feel anything, don't worry," she said, drawing out the "o" like she had a strawberry under her tongue. "The healing is still flowing to wherever it's needed most. Is that okay?"

"That's fine, Amanda."

I watched her make signs in the air and then hold her hands a few inches from my head. I closed my eyes. It was pretty boring actually, this Reiki, but after a few minutes, I began to feel pressure on my head. She moved her hands over my forehead, chest, stomach, and at each place I felt terrific heat, then tingles, localized at first to wherever her hands were and then to where they weren't. In the last few minutes, a much more intense feeling tingled up my spine, dancing along raw nerves from my tailbone and shooting up to the top of my head. It was

64

like an electrical impulse, comfortable and uncomfortable at the same time, intensely agitating initially and then calming.

Amanda's little voice brought me back to the room. She gently asked me to open my eyes and sit up slowly when I was ready.

"How do you feel?" she said offering me a glass of water.

"Good," I said. "Relaxed."

"Did you feel any sensations during your session?" she asked.

I told her about the spinal tingling.

"Yes, that's Shakti, primordial cosmic energy."

"In my spine?"

"In everything," she said. "There are some good books on healing in the bookstore if you're interested, although you probably know most of it already."

"No, I don't," I said.

"But you're psychic," she said.

"But I'm not." I said.

"You have the energy field of a psychic. Very sensitive. Aren't you very sensitive?"

Was I sensitive? As a kid, I drove my mother mad for being sensitive. She tried to think of all sorts of ways to "get me out of my shell," enrolling me in summer camps and dance and art classes to make me interact with other kids, which just made me more introverted and her more frustrated. Eventually, sensitivity became a crusty skin of anger and belligerence, as can happen when you get trampled on enough, then go through life expecting to be trampled on, so trample others first. Still, I didn't think this is what Amanda meant.

"Maybe," I said.

"Well, take it easy for the next few days," she said. "You absorbed a lot of healing in this session, so you might feel a little raw for a few days."

More raw to chafe my rawness. Maybe two treatments was overkill. I was feeling a little strange. I didn't know if I wanted to sleep or eat. I wanted to know about Shakti, but I hadn't the brainpower. I'd Google it later. Eat. I needed to eat.

Café 67 was in the same building as the spa. It had white metal chairs, aqua tables, a porch overlooking the ocean, and a menu of healthy salads made from locally sourced ingredients. Except for one woman a few years older than me at the next table, the porch was empty, and I was glad. I was feeling strung-out since the massage and Reiki sessions. This must be what Amanda meant. The clattering of the kitchen seemed amplified, and the sunlight, although diffused by the long filaments of cirrus clouds, was burning my eyes. I needed quiet, the ocean, and comfort food, but this menu wasn't big on comfort.

"Is avocado toast and fried egg good?" I asked a young, inexperienced waitress who clutched her pad as if it were the only thing between her and the welfare office.

"I don't know. I haven't tried it yet," she said.

"It's good," a woman at the next table said.

"I'll take it," I said, handing the waitress back the menu.

"Nancy," the other woman said. "Nice to meet you."

"Karen."

"First time here?"

"Yes," I said.

"What brings you to the A.R.E.?"

I found myself blurting out an outline of events: Johann's death, the ugly house, the strange occurrences, and my search for answers. I was babbling as if I'd been in solitary confinement for a month. I was reclusive over there on the other side of the bay but not isolated. I ran into people all the time and carried on the requisite small talk. Now, I was babbling my life story to a perfect stranger. I looked for a micro-expression to indicate a judgment of lunacy, but there was none. She looked interested. She nodded, listened, turned to her plate every so often to nibble her chopped salad.

"You must think grief has driven me mad," I said in the end.

"Not at all," she said. "I've had those sorts of experiences. My husband died too, and I'm aware of him quite a lot of the time."

"You are?"

She nodded, slicing up her last tomato, putting down the knife, and scooping slices on her fork. She was remarkably calm, calmer than anyone I'd ever met, except maybe the monks at the Zen center.

"How so?" I asked.

"Well, we had an ongoing joke about frogs. Our home was in a rural part of Virginia Beach by a stream. Part of the road to our home used to flood at high tide and Frank would say that he had to dodge frogs the whole way along it after dark. After he died, I started seeing frogs everywhere. I came home one evening, and there was a frog in the toilet. The doors and windows were all closed. Tell me, how did it get in there?" She chuckled.

"I also saw him in India."

"You mean an apparition?" I asked.

"Yes."

"Did you talk to him?" I asked.

"No, he crossed my path twice while I was walking beside the reflecting pool in front of the mausoleum at the Taj Mahal. He looked at me and smiled. It was a meaningful manifestation actually. I was a widow, and I was very apprehensive about going to India. It's not socially acceptable to be a widow there, you see. In the past, Indian widows joined their husbands on the funeral pyre. That's a Hindu custom called *sati*. It's ritual suicide, but I later learned that it was often not by the widow's choice. But I had to go. It was the World Congress for Regression Therapy."

The waitress put a check on Nancy's table, and Nancy slipped cash into it.

"Is that what you do? Regression therapy?"

"Yes," she said.

"What is it?"

"It's a form of hypnosis that allows you to explore past lives so that you can release old patterns," she said. "Think about it this way, if you could go back to a previous life and revisit an event that had a huge impact on your life to understand why it happened, would you?"

Forget past lives, I could think of one impactful event in this life I'd like to understand.

"Understanding why things happened the way they did helps us understand why our life is the way it is," she said, "and this gives us the ability to choose to move in a direction that is more in keeping with our soul's purpose."

This was just a theory, but it made me agitated. It seemed to suggest that Johann died for a reason, like his death might have something to do with my soul's purpose, if I had a soul's purpose, if I had an immortal soul. Whether I did or didn't, there was no way anything I did in this life could justify his death. Anger rose in me. Reacting to old wounds, my sponsor would say. Attached to ego, the Zen monk would say. But I couldn't let the thought go. I wanted to defend his whole, beautiful, independent life, not see it as some purpose in mine or see his death as part of my dharma or our joined dharma. I was confused. I was antsy, restless. I needed to walk, run maybe, run off some nervous energy. I didn't know what was wrong.

An orange butterfly landed on the bush beside my table and sat there, wings up, having a little rest. I ate my egg with shaking hands and clattering silverware. I chewed and watched its wings quiver until I was composed enough to speak.

"I don't believe things happen for a reason," I eventually said. "I believe stuff just happens, and we just deal with it."

"It may seem that way," she said. "But we have a choice in how we respond, and how we respond can take us in the direction of our soul's purpose, or not, depending on what we choose to do."

The waitress picked up her check and scampered away.

"Why do you think your husband appeared?"

"To help me when I needed him in a way only he could help."

She checked her watch, and picked up her bag and jacket to leave.

"Johann may be helping you in a way only he can too. I know it doesn't feel like this now, but I sense you have an interesting path ahead of you."

After Nancy left, I finished my egg and went to the bookstore. It was full of pretty things—crystals, dream catchers, jewelry, candles, ornaments, and oils—set alongside the bookshelves. A book by Andrew Jackson Davis, "the first American prophet and clairvoyant," caught my eye. He allegedly went to the heavens while in a trance state and brought back information about the nature of the afterlife, the process of dying, and all sorts of other scientific information. I bought a copy and headed to the meditation garden.

A couple of people wandered quietly, reverently, out of the mediation garden as I walked in. It was a beautiful place, filled with paving stones and shrubbery and a little wooden bridge over a pond that was replenished by water trickling over a rockery. A thousand times nicer than the mausoleum's pond. A solitary little bench stood in the corner. I sat on it to read. It was incredibly peaceful; the only noise was the occasional swish of wind through the shrubs and the constant trickling of water.

I opened the book and read that Davis grew up largely illiterate in a poor hamlet upstate New York. After experimenting with mesmerism with a local tailor, he went into the first of many trances and began talking about subjects of which, in his waking state, he knew nothing. He called the trance state the "Superior Condition," and it allowed him travel to the heavens and receive information from higher spheres of consciousness about a whole host of subjects, including anatomy, astronomy, social reform, and education. It sounded like what others called an out of body experience. His description of the afterlife, or the Summerland, was a vibrant, soft, and musical place. It consisted of seven spheres of existence, the first being our material world and the other six being increasingly higher and inaccessible to most people. At the moment of death, the spiritual body was freed to go to the Summerland, where it continued to heal and grow and advance through the spheres.

I tried to read more about the Summerland, but I was finding it hard and harder to maintain focus beyond one or two sentences. A couple of butterflies flitted around the garden. I zoned out watching them. This was pointless. I closed the book and then my eyes. I was suddenly exhausted. I wanted to wallow in this tranquility for a moment, in the moment, just me and my breath, letting thoughts arise and go. Resting. I counted to four before a thought arose. Something changed. It were as if the fabric of my clothes had changed to silk, and I was sliding around inside. I felt lightheaded, as if I were looking at the world but not part of it. I needed to get on the road before this got worse.

The rattle of my old Mustang seemed louder than usual as I wound my way along the dips and inclines of the Chesapeake Bay Bridge-Tunnel. I felt pretty rattled myself. The farther across the bridge I got the worse I felt. I knew my hands were on the steering wheel and the wind was blowing through the open window, but I didn't feel present, and this didn't feel real. The harder I tried to focus, the more illusory it became.

I was going to hurl.

I stopped at the first rest stop on the bridge to pull myself together. I leaned over the railings and watched the black Atlantic Ocean swell and heave. The rhythm was soothing, although I never liked dark water because I didn't know what lay beneath. Psychologists say our ego gets paranoid about what we can't see because it can't keep us safe in strange, dark places. My ego was paranoid about black water. As a child, I leaned over the railings of the River Liffey in Dublin. When the tide went out, I saw meters of nasty seaweed clinging to the walls trying to claw its way free of an evil lurking on the riverbed. It was ugly and I hated it, but the tide would come in again and swallow it into darkness, and I pitied it. There was a vibrant ecosystem beneath these Atlantic waves, no doubt, but something sinister could be down there too, like Jaws or Jason Voorhees in Camp Crystal Lake. How hard it is to shake the impressions of formative years; they rattle around in the dark whispering things like "he's still out there" or "this shark, swallow you whole." I was a strong swimmer, but I rarely, if ever, swam in the sea. Nancy might have said I drowned in a past life. She might be right, but I blamed Jason and Quint.

The air wasn't helping and neither was the heaving ocean.

I got back in my car and drove ten more miles until the illusory sensation became the panic that I was withering into emptiness or being sucked backwards into a void. I slowed down, put my hazards on, and tried to keep it together for fear I'd kill myself, or worse, another.

That lousy Reiki must have done this.

I limped back to the mausoleum, went inside and up the stairs before any of the neighbors saw me, and got under the comforter to hide from a visceral conviction that I was about to die. I was glad to die, but it felt so bad, I just wanted the dying to be over. Busker meowed and trotted up the stairs after me, tiptoed gently across the comforter, and curled up behind my legs, while I sank into the most absolute sense of hopelessness I'd ever experienced.

Hours later, I opened my eyes. The sun was low in the sky. I hadn't died. Two butterflies were perched on the windowpane. I wanted to close the curtain to block the light, but I couldn't move.

It was night when I woke again. Busker meowed. He was hungry.

"Five more minutes, okay?"

I woke again to Busker patting my face. The sun was bright in the midday sky. Three butterflies were perched on the hot windowpane.

"Five more minutes," I said.

My throat was painfully dry, my eyes were swollen, and my head pounded, but that didn't stop me falling back to sleep in a pit of despair.

It was dark and hazy, as if I were looking through a fog from another dimension, but I knew where I was. It was back in the Girl Guides house. I was standing on the last step of the winding stairs that led into a dark basement, lined with cots laid out like hospital beds and covered with torn, dusty sheets. I couldn't see them too clearly, but I knew they were all empty, as if their occupants had long since perished.

SLAM!

The trapdoor above that led out of this place slammed shut. It was pitch dark.

THUMP!

Something far into the darkest recess of this basement was awake. Something large, sinister. The rotten smell began to choke the basement and the stairway, filling my lungs with its noxious fumes. I gagged. I tried to feel my way back up the stairs in the dark.

THUMP! THUMP!

Whatever had woken was moving, pounding along the floor, rattling the basement as it picked up speed. I banged frantically on the trapdoor, trying desperately to force the handle, but it wouldn't budge. I was retching from the stench and suffocating in fear. The creature grabbed my ankles with powerful claws, crushing the bones in my feet as it pulled me downward. I held onto the trapdoor handle with all my might. It was pulling me one way, and I the other, and it was winning.

"Help me!" I screamed.

A blinding light appeared overhead, and sunlight powered down the stairs. The quality of the environment changed, the darkness and haze of my dreamscape disappeared and everything became clear, as if I had become lucid, as if I'd woken up in the dream. I glanced back down the stairs, but the creature had disappeared.

Above, a figure emerged from the light—a beautiful, deliriously happy sight.

I began to cry, my whole body wracked with sobs of relief.

Johann! Oh, my God. Johann, it's you. You're here.

There he was, golden and beautiful. He was bright like that old man in my bedroom years ago whose eyes reflected light in the darkness, except Johann's entire body reflected light. He was blonder than he had been, but his body was the same, broad, and firm.

Yes, it's me.

He felt wonderful, present, as if we occupied the same body, mind, and space. It was an intimacy I'd never known — not even with him — a fleeting sense of connection to something far greater than me.

Don't leave, Johann, please.

The room went dark. He was gone.

When I woke again, I was groggy, having slept too heavily for too long. I made my way downstairs and ransacked the pantry where I found some chamomile tea. I rubbed my feet and ankles. They felt fine. It was as if nothing had happened.

Busker came crying into the kitchen.

"I'm sorry, little buddy," I said, putting food in his bowl.

It was just after four in the morning. I sat on the cold tiles beside him drinking my tea, while he ate and then settled down to nap under the crook of my knees.

I couldn't understand what had happened or if it were real. Johann felt intensely real, but if he were real, what was the creature? Why did he need to come save me from something I feared so greatly? By the time

I'd finished my tea, I'd stopped dwelling on the creature and dwelled instead on the feeling of complete, unconditional love with which his appearance filled me.

The first draft of my email to Rev. Cutler was long and filled with too much information that I decided, upon reflection, I didn't need to share. Wasn't it Pascal who said, "I have only made this letter longer because I have not had the time to make it shorter"? I had lots of time. There were two more hours till dawn when normal people rose. I edited and reedited, until all I said was that I'd had Reiki, was feeling sensitive, had a monstrous dream, and saw my dead fiancé glowing in the dark. Was there a reasonable explanation?

I took me so long to write such a short note that dawn was breaking by the time I clicked send. I got a blanket from the sofa and went outside to wait for the sunlight to break over the deck. Busker curled up under my chair. I tried to recapture the fullness of feeling I'd had when Johann appeared but couldn't now that the moment was gone.

I must have dozed because when I woke it was almost seven, and Busker was trying to swat a butterfly as if it were a cat toy. I unfurled from the blanket. The strand would be cool and deserted now. I flip-flopped down the road with Busker following halfway until he got fed up and went home as he always did. A butterfly flew alongside my head most of the way. There was an epidemic of butterflies that week.

I paddled in the cold water almost the length of the beach holding that radiant image of Johann in my mind for as long as I could. I was sitting on the pier when my phone pinged with an email from Rev. Cutler.

"Don't worry," she wrote, "you just popped on like a light bulb, and you may find yourself having all sorts of new experiences. What you experienced could represent a fear you need to face or it could have been a visitation dream—Johann showing that he's trying help you. Remember, fear is negative and has a low vibration, so stay positive. Like attracts like. The spirit world exists on a higher vibration than us so to reach high-vibrational beings there, you have to have a high vibration. Make sure to keep up your development. Focus on your healing and spiritual growth. And don't forget to ask for help," she signed off. "The Spirit World will always help."

I read her email a few times. I still didn't know if apparitions, like the old man in my childhood bedroom or Nancy's husband, were conscious and real, dreamed, or just the non-conscious energy imprints she talked about in class? I didn't know what had just happened in that dream or who or what caused the whispers in my head.

Maybe I was overthinking, but I couldn't get past how consciousness could survive outside the brain: if we, our energy, melted back into the cosmic cauldron, then signs, weird dreams, and energy imprints didn't necessarily mean the survival of an actual individual. What seemed simple to so many people seemed beyond complicated to me. Millions of people had seen the mark of their loved ones in extraordinary encounters out there in the world. I'd been having extraordinary experiences externally and had been receiving sounds and images internally in my mind, yet I hadn't seen evidence of Johann's personality in a way that would say *he* survived. I hadn't experienced the "aha" moment as they had.

A large butterfly crashed into my head.

I ducked.

What's with the bloody butterflies in this place?

"Morning," said a passerby.

"Morning," I said.

Then it clicked: good morning, *guten morgen, bonjour, buenos dias* ... I remembered the professor's butterflies and the beeps on the phone line when I dismissed them. I remembered Johann's dry humor: he wouldn't send me *a* butterfly — he'd send me a hundred.

I sat there for a few minutes, willing myself to ask the question the professor recommended: "Show me a sign so I know it's you." What if I asked and got no reply? Where would that leave me? Robbed of my secret hope that the believers were right. What if I asked and did get a reply? What would that mean?

Finally.

Are you sending me butterflies?

A monarch butterfly fluttered along, landed on my foot, and sat there with wings erect, quivering in the ocean breeze.

I sat there staring at this pretty insect on a beach at dawn in some tiny town where I'd hid and cried and wanted to be dead and searched for meaning and answers and found none. Till now.

It is you! Holy freaking shit!

Searching

Sometimes in all this talk I find a word
With your mark on it
In the blood of love.
And the worlds go quiet.

Jalal-ud-Din Rumi

My journey home was seven hours edging north along the Atlantic coast through small towns and past people driving in air-conditioned SUVs with closed windows that kept the world out and their own irritation in, much the way I had arrived months before. I was grateful to the little town I'd once maligned. Its seclusion had given me space to grieve, and its cast of characters helped me to wake up to the realization that other planes of splendid consciousness existed and that death was far from the end.

I spent my last Sunday watching autumn leaves whip up in funnels and blow away. For one last time, I went to Father Peter's morning Mass and basked in the peace I'd found there; the colored shafts of sunlight pouring from stained glass windows, the agility and lightness in the tenor's voice that eased body and mind as he sang the "Ave Maria," and the compassion of Father Peter, Rose, and Millie and the other parishioners who found me when I was lost. I said goodbye to Gerry, the boisterous neighbor who reached out during the dark times and to Busker, who gave me a reason to get out of bed on those awful early days. Our mornings of breakfast in the kitchen had come to an end. The owner was due back that night.

I sat with the little cat for an hour or so, scratching his cheeks until it got too hot and he retreated under the stairs for shade.

"Bye-bye, little buddy."

I programmed my GPS to take me north to Brooklyn along a route I hadn't traveled before. It would be a longer journey along a smaller road in a bigger world than the one in which I'd arrived. I didn't know what the survival of consciousness actually meant or how the absence of death as we understand it would affect my life or what this would mean for Johann and me. All I knew was that whatever happened from this moment on wouldn't be dull.

Can you hear me Johann? We're going home.

I'm here.

Those two tantalizing words popped into my mind suddenly — crisp and clear — resonating in what felt like some new part of my brain. They left me with a lingering sense of completeness, as if some essential part of me had been soothed. With that feeling, I put my foot on the gas and drove out of town and along the swell and dips of the Chesapeake Bay Bridge for the last time.

I love New York in the fall, but garbage day stinks. When I pulled in that evening, the only available parking spot on my block was by rancid piles of trash outside the Key Food on McGuinness Boulevard. It was a feast for the scurrying rats that made my brain shiver. I dragged my bags down the block to my cheerful apartment with its baby blue, apricot, and salmon pink rooms and wall-to-wall bookcases that I loved. It was stale and dusty from being shut up and abandoned for the summer. I opened the windows, and the living room filled with the exhaust fumes and the sound of trucks rumbling toward I-495. It was once just white noise; now it sounded like jackhammers.

Are you here?

There was no invisible person sitting on the bed or gorilla in the doorway or someone tugging on my hair.

Do you know I'm in New York?

Still nothing. I stuck earplugs in my ears and crashed into the bed.

The next morning, I met James for breakfast at Forest Natural. Johann and I had eaten there often after the waitress mistook him for an obscure German actor and gave him free coffee and pastries. That became our regular hangout until she realized he was just a guy from the neighborhood and cut him off.

It was strange to be looking out the window on our old, familiar neighborhood where our past was written. I expected to hear him tapping away on his computer, or smell the rich aroma of his tobacco burning, or see him walking to the counter to greet the staff — all of whom he knew by name — to order coffee. My stomach lurched again with the sting of his death, the way it had done in the early days. I hadn't expected that.

James arrived late. We hadn't spoken much since our conversation from the hospital on that fateful day. Now, here we were again, months later, this time sitting in a café watching the early morning rush, sharing pleasantries and the usual preamble of two people waiting for the other to start the conversation. James was unpredictable. He was caustic, funny, and sensitive. He'd regale the room with tall tales one minute and rant about the abomination of capitalism the next. His was a volatile combination that gave rise to an intensity that Johann found entertaining, but I found overwhelming. I usually gave him a wide berth, but we had something in common now. Afterlife or not, grief is grief, and we both needed help.

"You know what was weird?" James said, tipping his straw fedora off his forehead. "We used to go to a bike shop in the City, and we got to know the owner. A few weeks before …" James's voice broke. He lit a cigarette and swigged some coffee. "A few weeks before he died, we went into the bicycle shop and found out that the man who owned it had died. He was about fifty, and he used to go for long bike rides by himself on weekends. He got off his bicycle one day and had a massive heart attack. Johann said it was a good way to go because the guy spent his last day doing something he loved."

This story offered a bleak sort of comfort.

"He seemed happy in the end," James said. "Happier than usual."

"We'd decided to get married two months before, just before I left for the South," I said, twisting my ring on my finger.

"I *knew* he was happy about something," he said. "I didn't know why. I asked him about it, and he said he was so happy he could slap himself. I thought it was because he was sober. But he couldn't have been that happy to be off the booze."

We laughed. That Johann didn't share his plans wasn't surprising. James knew how private he was and how he compartmentalized his life so no one could get too close or know too much about him. Johann liked knowing other people's secrets but was militant about keeping his own counsel.

I was itching to ask if James had had any extraordinary encounters but was afraid of finding myself on the receiving end of his ridicule.

Eventually, I spit it out. "Do you believe in an afterlife?"

"No," he said.

"What about the things people say they see? You know, ghosts, stuff like that."

"Schizophrenia," he said.

That was quintessentially James. Nothing I could say would convince him otherwise, which meant there was nothing more for us to do besides share a few more memories, allow the conversation to run its course, finish our coffee, and move on.

After a few days without outward signs from Johann, I had the idea that a little pilgrimage through our old Brooklyn hangouts might help me sense him. I made my way toward the river. Every street, every storefront, every café was a place we'd been together. I went into St. Anthony's church, where, despite our atheism, he'd come to buy a Mass card with me for a Catholic neighbor who died. He loved the large macabre cards on display, the kind normally covered in flowers or cartoons for Valentine's Day or children's birthdays but were here covered in lilies and misery. I went to the Pencil Factory where we spent our last Valentine's night. I passed the corner where I bought a dog-eared copy of the *Tao of Pooh* from a guy selling used books and then to the stationary store where he bought me a Pooh Bear notebook.

"Here's one for you," I'd read the day we bought the *Tao*. "By the time it came to the edge of the Forest, the stream had grown up, so that it was almost a river, and, being grown-up, it did not run and jump and sparkle along as it used to when it was younger, but moved more slowly. For it knew now where it was going, and it said to itself, 'There is no hurry. We shall get there some day.'"

"I never ran and jumped and sparkled," he said, tossing away the butt of a Lucky. "Give it to me."

He flicked through the pages.

"Here's you. 'Gon Out. Backson. Bisy Backson," he read. "Always going somewhere, anywhere but where he is."

"That's not me."

"It says Bisy Backsons burn their toast a lot."

"It does not."

"It does."

It did. I was always burning toast.

I walked to the riverfront along Franklin Street, past his old apartment, which was kitty-corner to where I lived with my ex-boyfriend in the spring of '98. I'd just spent a freezing winter in Berlin and needed a place to crash while I looked for a new apartment. A few months later, I found a small place in South Brooklyn and moved out. Eight years later, I was driven out of there by bedbugs and moved back to Greenpoint, to the other side of the neighborhood. At that point, Johann's short-lived marriage had ended, and he left the Franklin Street apartment for one three blocks from my new place. We pieced our movements together later. We'd both been in Berlin that same winter and hadn't met, then lived on opposite sides of an intersection for three months and hadn't met, then lived a few blocks from each other and hadn't met. We'd been missing each other for eight years until we crossed paths that morning at the Peter Pan bakery.

With still no signs from him, I left the water and took the subway to Riverside Park. If I couldn't sense him where he lived, maybe I could sense him where he died.

It was a surprisingly hot day for autumn. People were stinking, irritated, and crammed onto the platform. At West 14th Street, I switched to the 2 Uptown. Even the Jamaican guy playing steel drums there was hard on the ears that day. By the time I got off at West 86th, the noise and crowds of the New York City subway had drained me. People's bad breath and perspiration were intense. Their voices were too loud, and the lights were so bright my eyes stung. Being jostled by people and their bad humors overwhelmed me. I got off the train in a stinking mood and walked to the place James told me Johann fell.

Time had erased his parting from that place. Now, parents were playing with toddlers, older children ran around with skateboards, and smaller children rode tricycles. I thought about his young son, Tommy. The last time I saw him, he was upset because his tricycle had a flat. Johann was working, so I took him to the local gas station where we pried the tire back onto the rim and filled it with air. My phone beeped with an email from the news desk asking for edits to an article I'd filed, so we went back to my apartment, him squealing and racing ahead, excited by the speed of his tricycle. I turned on the Cartoon Network to entertain him while I worked. He was happy. Johann didn't have a TV.

"Time to go," I said, when I was done. "We need to get your father's lunch."

"We don't have to go yet," he said, turning his big sad eyes away from the screen. "He can go for three days without food."

"Nice try, kid," I said.

I wondered how Tommy was coping. He had been so close to his dad that I couldn't imagine his suffering. I wondered if he'd been able to grasp what had happened or have any idea of how his life would change.

I lay down on the paving stones where Johann had fallen to share his last glimpse from the planet. Had he seen this same sky dotted with tufts of clouds and the swaying branches of black cherry trees? Did he know what was happening? Was he scared?

Skateboarders whizzed past, riding up the banks and doing flips on the way back down. Giggling children started drawing brightly colored chalk figures on the slabs beside me. The hazy laughter, boards popping, and the noise of rush hour traffic on Riverside Drive swelled my brain. Exhaust fumes made me gag. I rose and walked away from the chalk-covered slabs that had become his gravestone and my private memorial. Then, with still no sign of him, slouched back toward the subway.

I convinced the guy at a halal stand on Broadway to make me a veggie sandwich out of whatever non-animal products he had in his cart. He piled on overcooked onions and limp peppers and tomatoes and drowned the lot in some kind of sauce.

"Let me know if it's any good," he said. "I'll add it to the menu."

"I will," I promised, but I'd no intention of going back there again.

"Hey," he said, "my cousin is looking for a wife. He's good looking. Successful too. You want me to introduce you?"

I would have laughed had I any joy left.

"No thanks," I said.

"Ah," he said, seeing my engagement ring. "Big rock. You must be important."

"I hope so," I said.

Next morning, I rang Roisin's doorbell. I needed to find someone here who might not judge me and my strange story, and she was the only person I knew who still went to Mass. When she buzzed me in, an image of her in a wedding dress in the botanical gardens flashed in my mind.

"Are you and Des getting married?" I asked.

"No, why?"

"I just saw you in a wedding dress in the botanical gardens."

"We're going to a wedding there tomorrow," she said. "How did you know?"

"It's a long story."

The last time I saw Roisin she looked twenty months pregnant, waddling about in ninety-degree heat. I hadn't been on social media since Johann died, so I didn't see the photo albums of her son's red-face screaming into the world. I sent a gift from her Amazon registry. It was all I could do at the time. Roisin breastfed and changed diapers while I filled her in on the events of Virginia, the Spiritualist Church, the Edgar Cayce Center, and the notion of extraordinary encounters or signs from the hereafter.

"He's not showing you signs," she said. "He's burning bushes."

"You're not surprised?"

"Not really. He'd have to burn bushes to get your attention."

"No, I mean you're not surprised this happened at all?"

"No, I believe our ancestors can send us signs."

"They seem to have stopped now," I said. "I haven't seen any since I got back here. I've no idea why."

"You just saw me in a wedding dress in the botanical gardens."

"Yeah, but that's not a sign. You're not dead. And you're not getting married."

"I think you're psychic," she said.

"You're the second person to tell me that, but I'm not."

I wanted Rev. Cutler to be right. I wanted to believe I could receive extrasensory information, but I didn't want that word. It conjured up images of charlatans in headgear and cheap jewelry, charging $5.99 a minute to tell people what they wanted to hear.

"Maybe he's busy," she said.

Maybe she was right. Or maybe it was something else, something I was afraid to think.

"Here," she said handing me Sean. "See what you get off him."

"You want me to read your baby?"

"Yeah."

"No."

"Go on. Can you get anything from him?"

"*No.*"

"Ah, go on, try."

"I'm not psychic!"

"You are."

"Roisin ..."

"Never mind."

On the way home from Roisin's, I stopped by the park where Johann and I had idled away many lazy afternoons.

Can you hear me? I'm in McGolrick Park.

A bolt of static electricity crackled across my face. It was a strange sensation. Not like an insect flittering across my skin or a gust of wind. I felt my face, but there was nothing there. I closed my eyes and turned into the breeze just in case that had caused it, but all I got was a whiff of stale urine that made me gag. A crumpled old man had limped up the path and, ignoring all the empty benches, sat on mine.

"My dog is in the vets," he said, arranging his bags. "I went to Mario's meat shop to get him a treat." He pulled out a weird lump of bone that looked like something that had died in a Tod Browning sideshow. "He saw him *por bueno.*"

He smiled, and the skin around his dark brown eyes scrunched up. He must have been a handsome man in his youth before he ended up here with deep wrinkles, a leather tanned face, and a stench. He held his smile too long to pass it off for happy. His was a face of fear, fear that his dog would die. He needed a friend, not an asshole who wished him and his odor would leave.

"Will he be okay?" I asked.

"Hope so," he said. "He has a lump on his leg."

The image of a dog sprang to mind.

"Is he a black, short-haired dog?"

"Yes," he said, pulling out a tattered photo of an ugly dog that not many would bother to photograph.

"How did you know?" he asked.

"Lucky guess," I said.

"Are you psychic?" he asked.

"No," I said.

"Can you see the future?"

"No," I repeated.

"Do you think he'll be okay?"

He was desperate to believe I'd a magical power to tell him what he wanted to hear.

"I don't know, I'm sorry," I said, but his despair weighed on me.

"He's in good hands, right?" I said. "So, he has a fighting chance."

Hope scuttled across his tired, old eyes. How easy it would be to peddle false hope to the anxious and desperate. I felt bad for the old man. I wished I could comfort him, but I didn't know how. That dog didn't have long to go. I didn't need to be psychic to see that.

Back home, I kicked off my shoes and slumped onto the sofa, feeling fantastically futile. I could do nothing to help the living and could no longer see signs of the dead.

I ordered some food, opened my MacBook, and loaded the page I'd bookmarked for the Arthur Findlay College of mediumship. Its website claimed it was the world's foremost college for the advancement of Spiritualism and psychic sciences. It was affiliated with an online school run by the Spiritualist National Union that offered classes in meditation, healing, mediumship, and psychic development. Surely if anyone had answers, they would. I bookmarked a class scheduled for later that week and went to bed.

Truthfully, I was scared. I was scared that Rev. Cutler was wrong, and I didn't have some special faculty to receive extrasensory information, which was what she said I needed for our relationship to continue. But there was something else that scared me more. The professor said the bond of love made extraordinary encounters possible. I'd counted fifty-seven of those encounters in Virginia, but now I was seeing none. Was it possible that wherever Johann was, he was now happier without me, and, despite what the professor said, he didn't love me enough?

I knew I was dreaming. I was standing in front of a narrow skyscraper that crawled into the night sky like a beanstalk. The number 220 hung over the entrance in brass lettering. James appeared in front of me.

"Johann's back," he said pointing up to the building. "He's up there."

I peered through the glass to read "9A Johann Schmidt" on the buzzer panel. I was desperate to get up there, but the door was stuck. I heaved it open with all the strength in my being, squeezed through the crack, and pressed the button. Someone buzzed me in. The elevator wasn't working. I ran as fast as I could up the stairs, breathing hard, anxious to see him, fearing something awful would happen if I didn't get there quickly.

I was standing in front of 9A. The door was slightly ajar. I creaked it open. I already knew something was wrong. Inside, I found a dark, L-shaped apartment, minimalist, modern, very much his style. A wood burning fire set into a stone pillar in the center of the room crackled out warmth. A black leather sofa lay before it and beside it was a low-voltage lamp. Behind the pillar was a pristine Pullman kitchen, but there was no one here. I hadn't been able to get to him on time. I stood in the empty apartment and cried.

My head was throbbing when I woke, like two bottles of cheap wine throbbing. Cortisol jittered in my veins.

Morning light limped through the curtains. I dragged my feet to the floor, feeling like shit in sweaty slept-in clothes and yesterday's makeup caked onto my face. I brewed a pot of coffee, closed the blinds to block out the morning light, and opened the freezer door to cool my head. I could kill for a cigarette. I hadn't smoked in five years, but that didn't matter. All the work to get healthy in mind and body didn't matter. My nicotine craving was exacerbated by the faint smell of burning tobacco hanging in the air. I took my head out of the freezer and sniffed around the living room.

Is that you?

The smell was strongest nearest the middle window. Hope leapt in my heart, until I realized it was the window with the AC, the AC with open vents that was sucking everything in from outside.

I flipped open the blinds to see the peroxide updo, fake tan, and false nails of Nadia, the Polish neighbor dangling a cigarette in her bright red lips. She was in the space behind the building, directing her boyfriend Stanley to park his dually wheel pickup right up against my window.

"What the hell are you doing?" I asked.

"Didn't you hear?" she said. "Zybi sold this bit of land to be a parking lot, and we rented this space."

"You're blocking the window," I said. "All I can see is your dumb truck."

"Too bad."

"This is a fire exit window. You can't park there."

Stanley idled the truck while Nadia and I bickered, so the living room that was already filled with my shitty mood was also filled with carbon monoxide.

"Not my problem," she said.

"It's illegal to park there," I said. "Move your fucking truck."

She tottered off with her hand in the air and a smug: "I don't have time for this."

Rage surged in me. Rage I'd suppressed for weeks, maybe months. Rage waiting for a target. I wanted to grab her by the throat and shake her until her bleached teeth rattled, and her piercing voice broke, and her cheek implants melted off her face. I wanted that truck to drive over a cliff and explode in flames. There were a hundred ways I wanted her to suffer for her spite toward me, and each fantasy galvanized my hate. Her power trip was stealing the little light I had in my shrinking life. I was sick of being a victim to circumstances. I was sick of feeling powerless.

An image punched into my mind — vibrant green lines like leaves overlapping on a thick, lush plant. I was too angry to give it any thought. I clattered into the kitchen, threw dishes into the sink, and broke a few. I stormed into the bedroom and pulled a drawer out so hard, it flew out and crashed to the ground. Shades of green filled my mind again as I yanked clothes off their hangers and tossed them aside. Then I saw it, hanging limply on a hanger, my ivory sheath wedding dress that I'd found in a vintage store in the West Village the week after we got engaged. It was so pretty, I had to buy it, but this simple thing served no purpose now. It even seemed undeserving somehow. Or was it me who felt undeserving? Girls I grew up with fantasized about a big wedding in a meringue of a dress in a castle in the countryside somewhere, but I never did. I wanted to elope with my heart's desire and adventure around the globe. I slumped into an armchair looking at this unassuming dress that had asked for little and got even less, then I shoved it to back of the closet behind my winter coats so I'd never have to see it again, threw on some pants and a t-shirt, and stormed out the door and up the stairs to see Zybi, my landlord.

Zybi had no idea what I was saying; his English wasn't good enough to keep up with the abuse I hurled at him. He just handed me the address and number of the plot's new owner. I crossed the street and banged on his door and threatened him with a fire inspection. He had sense enough to know that one parking spot wasn't worth the fine.

"I'll tell her to move when they get back," he said.

"When's that?"

"End of the month."

"Tell her to move today."

"She left for the airport already."

"I don't care. Get that truck out of there."

An hour or so later, I heard Stanley start his engine.

"You fucking bitch," Nadia shouted at me through the window. She wasn't so smug now. "You made us miss our flight."

Tottering on four-inch stilettos, she dragged her enormous suitcase across the potholes and debris in this excuse for a parking lot.

"I think you lost a nail," I said and closed the blinds.

With Nadia gone, I was left with silence and an industrial dump outside my window. This had been a beautiful place to live when it was a garden apartment, but now the garden was gone. There was less space, more ugliness, and more anger. I collapsed into the mess my fury had created and cried.

"Stay positive," Rev. Cutler had said. "Maintain a high vibration and you'll be able to touch the spirit world."

She should try living in Brooklyn.

I was walking along West Street in another dark dreamscape. It was a moonless night. Warehouses were closed up and no one was moving about. One street lamp all the way down near Eagle Street lit up a small part of the block. I headed that way, walking through puddles that got bigger and deeper as I got closer. When I got to the street lamp at Eagle, I saw monarch butterflies all over the sidewalk — all dead — drowned in a puddle. One was feebly moving as if it were stuck in sludge. I gently pried it loose and watched it flutter away.

I woke with aching shoulders and a splitting headache. I chased down some Advil with black coffee and leaned against a window to watch the morning rush hour go by. The noise of traffic on McGuinness Boulevard rattled my brain. It must always have been like this, but I didn't remember it being this bad. Of course, now I had the added bonus of looking out onto a hideous parking lot of jalopies. I could pull the blinds and live in darkness. Anger rose in me again. I turned away. I didn't want to reignite yesterday's fury. Anger is exhausting. Hate is exhausting. Not only had I wished Nadia ill, I'd cannibalized my own feeble energy reserves and given myself a hangover.

I needed help. I needed answers. The online mediumship class I'd bookmarked was happening that afternoon. It was called a "lab" and was an opportunity for students to ask the teacher questions about their development, mediumship, and the spirit world. It seemed like a good place to find someone with more knowledge than me.

With couple of hours to kill before it started, I decided to drag myself out of the apartment and get some fresh air and decent coffee.

I was on my way to Grumpies when I bumped into Peggy heading for the subway. She was Johann's friend more than mine. I wasn't close to most of his friends, but I liked Peggy. She was one of that rare breed of people who experience many hardships in life but suffering makes them kinder not crustier. Other people had done less with better starts and easier paths than Peggy, but she never compared and rarely judged, not that I heard anyway. Life had made her a realist, but it hadn't made her bitter.

"Hey!" she said. "I heard you were back. How are you feeling?"

"Hi, I'm okay," I said. "How are you doing? How's school?"

Peggy was one of the first people I met when I moved back to the neighborhood. Roisin and I were in the gift shop off Franklin Street when Peggy recognized me as the new neighbor Johann had been talking about. At the time, she was drifting, drinking a bit too much, involved in bad relationships, but the last time I saw her, she'd enrolled in an undergrad program at a divinity school in the City. I couldn't understand why anyone would go to divinity school at the time. Now I did. It suited her. She had an acute social conscience. She listened as if every word mattered; she gave you the respect of her understanding without burying you in the hubris of unsolicited advice. What's more, unlike many people I'd encountered in my bereavement, I knew she wouldn't offer platitudes to assuage a fear that she might drown in my pain. You could drag yourself to her doorstep in shambles and come away feeling better. That was Peggy's gift.

"School's going well," she said. "But tell me how you're feeling?"

"I'm trying to settle back in," I said. "Build a new life, find a new purpose. Doing some existential questioning. You know how it goes."

"Yeah, I understand," she said. "I've been pretty shaken since Johann died. I can't imagine what it must be like for you. It must be hard to suddenly find yourself alone without him. He loved you very much."

"You think?"

"Of course. Why? Are you doubting his feelings?"

"I don't know," I said. "Maybe."

"Well, he was the most emotionally unexpressive man I've ever met."

"True," I said.

"Did he tell you how he felt or presume you knew?" she asked.

"Mostly presumed and occasionally expressed with the help of hard liquor."

She smiled. "Yeah, that's him."

"I felt loved," I said. "I never thought too much about the words."

"But you need to hear them now," she said.

"Yeah, I could use them now," I said. "I feel stupid doubting him. I mean, he asked me to marry him two months before he died."

"I heard," she said. "That was huge for him. He always swore he'd never marry again."

"I know. But now I'm questioning everything. He'd had so many flings. Des called them 'throwaway relationships,' but still ..."

"You wonder if you were special."

"Yeah, sometimes. I didn't before, but I do now. Isn't that stupid?"

"Listen, the only people who really know what's going on between a man and a woman are the man and the woman," Peggy said, "but I can tell you that from the day you moved into the neighborhood, it was obvious that you were very special to him. The way he talked about you was different. He was different. Hold onto that."

"I will, Peggy. Thank you."

The G-train rumbled underfoot.

"I need to run," she said. "I'm heading to the Midwest this week, but I can Skype if you want to talk more."

"Thanks," I said. "Safe travels."

"Be kind to yourself," she said with a broad toothy smile as she headed down the stairs. "Death has a way of making us feel insecure."

Maybe she was right that this was just insecurity, and I'd really nothing to worry about. Maybe I was confusing my grief for him with his feelings for me. I never doubted him before, definitely not after he got sober. Even before that, the bond we had was strong despite our ups and downs and squabbles and reconciliations. No, I wasn't insecure then, but now? Now, I didn't know what to believe.

I wandered the streets alone for a couple of hours and then headed home.

Twelve people logged into the virtual room. They had ordinary names like Pam, Annie, Jim, and a couple had foreign-sounding names like Solvang and Inga, but there were no "Mystic Mags," and presumably no turbans and crystal balls, which was encouraging.

"Karen, are you new?" asked Alicia, the teacher.

"Yes."

"Have you done any development?"

"No."

"But you have the faculty or at least an awareness of other senses?"

"Honestly, Alicia, I don't know."

"Well, don't worry. Everyone is on the spectrum to one degree or another."

I didn't know where I was on that spectrum, or if I were even on it anymore.

"Ok."

"Everyone has some ability, some more than others, but everyone can develop their natural ability to the best of their ability," Alicia said, turning to the class. "Okay, first, who can tell me the difference between psychism and mediumship and why it's important to know the difference?"

"Psychics use the five psychic senses to get information about the living and can sometimes get an idea of what may happen in the future based on choices facing someone now," Inga offered. "Mediums use the psychic faculties to receive information from people in the spirit world. So, all mediums are psychic but not all psychics are mediums!"

"Good," Alicia said. "Karen do you know what the psychic senses are?"

"No," I said.

"They're clairvoyance, which is seeing; clairaudience, which is hearing; clairsentience, which is feeling; claircognizance, which is knowing; and there are also clairgustance and clairolfactory, which means getting a taste or a smell. Okay?"

"Okay."

"Now, the spirit world uses the medium's psychic senses to communicate. This means the medium needs to develop their clairs to be able to receive the sounds and images and feelings from the person in spirit. Then the medium needs to piece all of this together to understand the spirit person's meaning. It's a highly intuitive process, and it works a little differently for each medium. If you're visual, you might see a lot of images. Musical people often hear more sounds. Very sensitive people tend to feel more. It really depends on you. You'll often hear mediums say 'so and so is telling me' but there's no running commentary happening. We're not hearing a voice rambling on in our heads. What's really going on is that we're combining all the different pieces of sensory information we receive to convey what the spirit person wants to tell their loved one here. This is the language of the spirit. It can be very subtle. Does that make sense?"

"Yes."

"Do you have any questions?"

"Yes," I said, explaining with as much clarity as I could muster, Johann's death, the signs I got in Virginia, and their absence in New York. "Why am I not seeing signs now?"

"Signs aren't mediumship," she said. "They don't use the mediumistic faculty. To really increase your ability to communicate with him, you need stop looking outward for them and start using your psychic faculties to look inward. Do you know what I mean?"

"No."

"Look inside, not outside. Start with meditation and finding harmony. You've been through a lot. You need time. It also sounds like you're worrying too much. Worry is a heavy emotion. It'll drag your vibration down. So will negativity, or anger, or sadness."

"Okay," I said. "I haven't been feeling great since I got back. I thought I'd feel closer to him here, but I've just felt empty."

"That might be part of the problem. Listen, hon, development tends to bring our issues up so we can deal with them. If you have any unresolved issues, like grief or denial or anger or depression, they'll all come up, and you'll have to work through them if you're going to be able to lift your vibration. Our physical vibration is very heavy, so you need to raise it to communicate with him and to allow him to communicate with you. If you're in the pits of grief and despair, you'll have a hell of a time. He'll have a hell of a time. So, you need to heal. He may be still part of your life, but his physical presence isn't, and you need to grieve that. You need to work through your sadness and anger and resentment, which are also part of the grieving process. Write down what you want to say that you didn't get to say. It might help you offload some of the weight you're carrying. There's no point in running around in the world looking for signs if you can't sense what's been offered to you internally. You have to be able to blend with him, but if you're ignoring what's inside that needs healing, that'll be very difficult."

"Okay," I said. "I understand."

I knew she was right. I could feel the weight of the baggage I'd been carrying since he died, and even more so now as I walked every day along the streets of our past. I was drowning in the past here. I may have been better served by dusting off my meditation cushion and looking inward as Alicia suggested than trolling the streets of New York in search of a sign, but truth be told, I'd been afraid to sit alone in the dark for fear of being consumed by grief or fear or something else that was scratching in my head that I couldn't name. I wanted to keep doing, keep moving, keep looking out there, keep doing anything except be alone in here.

Alicia was right. I had a lot of work to do.

"There must be a reason why things have unfolded this way," she said. "Trust him and trust the process."

I was being carried along by a noisy crowd in a massive theatre that was propped up by six massive columns in a disturbing dreamscape. The stage was more or less intact, with erratic light patterns cast by torn gels over floodlights on the floor downstage. Nick Cave was singing "Avalanche" somewhere, but I couldn't see where. The seats were long gone, as was most of the carpet. Stage right, Johann was shaking a cigarette out of a soft pack and laughing with a couple of men. I called him, but either I didn't actually speak or he didn't hear me. I called him again and again until my throat hurt and my voice grew shrill. I pushed through the crowd, but as I got close, a row of women can-canned their way in front of me in denim jackets, purple tulle, and wire rimmed glasses. Behind them, I saw Johann walk away, and I couldn't follow.

I lay in bed for some time the next morning. I looked at my cushion in the corner of the room, then crawled out of my bed and sat on it. I tried meditating to quiet my mind to make room for sounds in the silence. I'd been afraid of this space, afraid of looking too close at myself, afraid of seeing things I didn't want to see, worried I wouldn't find him here. I couldn't focus. I tried counting my breath but couldn't get past one. I felt heavy, like there was an 800-pound gorilla on my back. And I was antsy. There was definitely something in here I didn't want to see.

I got up and opened the blinds to let in some light. I made a pot of coffee and camped out in front of my MacBook. I googled "how to have a high vibration." There was nothing mystical about it. The tips said eat healthy, drink water, exercise, walk in nature, meditate, practice gratitude and random acts of kindness, and be conscious of your thoughts because what you think becomes your reality. This reminded me of Henry Ford: If you think you can or you think you can't, you're right. Or words to that effect. Everything suggested was, in short, the exact opposite of what I'd been doing. I couldn't knock the high vibration tips because just sitting reading the suggestions made me feel better and motivated me to get outside for some air.

On my way to the park, I passed Jose's flower shop. Its outdoor shelves were stacked with grasses and leafy plants that hadn't yet flowered: luscious, pretty, and peaceful. I went inside and came out twenty minutes later laden down with a ficus, a peace lily, devil's ivy, and a fern and took them home to stack on my windowsills.

My apartment was transformed. I made some tea and sat in an armchair admiring my new indoor garden that hid the ugliness outside and brought tranquility inside. Such a simple solution. As I moved the pots this way to hide the world outside, the bars on the windows that had cast vertical shadows along the floor became the curling shadows of sinuous leaves.

The leaves!

This was the image that had been forced into my head during my screaming match with Nadia.

It was the ficus! Were you telling me to hide the eyesore with plants?

I didn't know if this had been message from him or more nebulous images that just sprang to mind like Roisin's wedding dress or the old man's dog. What I did know was that I needed to do something to get myself out of this sinkhole into which I'd fallen.

I stood between a dumpster and scaffolding on West 30th and Seventh Avenue, peering through a glass doorway into a tatty looking lobby, fogging it up with my breath on the cold air. I was happy. My Google search on high-vibrations had returned a listing for an Edgar Cayce Center in New York City. It was holding a group Reiki share that Friday. Reiki had made me batty last time, but maybe it would help me get to a place where Johann could use my supposed mediumistic faculty to communicate with me internally. If that were the case, another Reiki meltdown was worth it.

A bumpy elevator spit me out onto a shabby looking floor of a century-old building. It was plastered in layers of lavender and lemon paint, which testified to the Caycean's effort to carve out a semblance of New Age mysticism for the spiritual seekers that wandered its hallowed halls. In the waiting area, twenty people hovered and whispered as if they were sitting under the Mahabodhi Tree in India, not crammed into a Chelsea office building shared with dentists and cheap clothing companies.

"Howdy." A peculiar guy flowed out of the elevator and into the conference room, like a tidal wave that sucked the twenty in behind him. He wore a bright blue T-shirt stretched over buff biceps and even buffer pecs and a black cap over three thick dreadlocks that reached down to the floor behind him. After the white tunic and hushed tones of Virginia, this guy was unexpected.

"Welcome, welcome, welcome," he said, popping the tops off colored markers and scribbling all over a whiteboard. He surveyed the group and settled on me. "Ah, we have a newbie. I'm Peter Goldbeck. I'm your local neighborhood light guy, and I'm here to share some light with you."

The twenty shuffled their chairs into a semi-circle around Peter. They were a normal enough looking group, your average cross section of New Yorkers. Except for Bertie. Bertie looked like a mad scientist lilting about in a lanky frame under a mop of wild, white hair. He alighted onto the chair beside me and offered an impalpable handshake. Bertie's weight on the world was feathery, intangible, like a mirage in faded jeans and a purple shirt. And he buzzed.

"We're gonna be working with some universal light force energy," Peter said. "The Japanese call it ki, the Chinese call it chi, the Indians call it prana, the Christians call it grace, and it's an awesome gift that comes from the Source, the Creator, the Divine, whatever you consider the Source to be. It's been here since the beginning of time, and it'll be here till the end of time." From the speed of that speech, he'd delivered it a thousand times. For the newbie (me) he explained that he was led into healing after being hit by lightning a couple of decades earlier and had done 40,000 healings in one way or another since then. No wonder he sparked. He swiveled the whiteboard around to show us a sun with a smiley face from which emanated a hundred rainbow-colored rays.

"This is the Source. These colors represent modalities: Reiki, reconnective healing, Shekinah Holy Spirit, cosmic regenesis, the violet flame, but they're all aspects of chi, and we're going to share some of that light now." He pressed a button on a tiny remote to play chimes and flutes and told us to take a deep breath and exhale slowly.

"Now, imagine there's a beautiful door above each of you," he said. "We're going to open the door wide as I call upon the Source, the Creator, the Divine, Father-Mother-Goddess to rain down life force energy, getting lighter, stronger, forming an awesome ball over each of you."

Following him was like trying to follow a horse-racing commentator on the radio; you'd no idea what was happening but you couldn't switch off for fear of missing the action at the finish line.

"It is my intent to bring that light in through the door and draw it down through your chakras. Allow the light to flow down to your light core, getting stronger and lighter, flowing down past your third eye, through your throat chakra, picking up momentum as it flows into your heart chakra ..."

My head started to tingle. Then I shivered, a shiver from deep in my spine that shook me in my chair. Bertie jumped beside me. I peeked. Peter was moving around the room waving his hands over people's heads.

"...flowing down into your navel, down to your root chakra, folding your vertical core center access, all around you, above and below you, getting still brighter, stronger."

I'd no idea what a vertical core center access was supposed to be.

"It's my intent with the spoken word that this will bless you, purify you, cleanse you, balance you, soothe you."

Bertie's shoulders were shifting up and down, and his head was bobbing back and forth.

"Now, we're gonna crank it up. If you're not a healer, you will be by the time we get done with this stuff here. Everyone raise your hands in the air, place one hand over your heart, and one hand over your solar plexus — this is the universal Reiki hand position. Now, listen to the sound of my voice."

Peter started speaking with the frenzy of a Pentecostal pastor presiding over a congregation falling down slain in the spirit.

"It is my intent calling upon the Source, calling upon the Creator, calling upon the Divine. It's my intent through the spoken word raining down universal life force energy, radiating all around me, above and below me, like an atomic bomb going off with wave after wave all around me, bringing down all frequencies of Reiki, all frequencies of all lineages: Usui Reiki, Tera-Mai Reiki, Lightarian Reiki, Imara Reiki, Shekinah Reiki, Jikiden Reiki, Karuna Reiki, all frequencies of Reiki, Shekinah Holy Spirit, cosmic regenesis, the violet flame, infinite energy rays; each wave stronger than the one before, moving into the cells in your fingertips, the cells in your hands, chromosomes, DNA, molecules, atoms, neutrons, protons, electrons, tachyon, subatomic particles; the spaces between are flooded with Divine light, now into your upper arms, your shoulders, your neck, your back, your chest, your hips, your thighs, from your nose to your toes, from the top of your head to the soles of your feet. It's now my intent through the spoken word to amplify the process, magnify the process, intensify the process by nine-hundred-thousand-billion-fold, times an exponential factor of nine-hundred-thousand-billion-trillion-fold, instantaneously, permanently, right now, and so it is."

Bertie was jerking back and forth so hard I could hear his chair bouncing off the floor.

A few minutes later, the room settled into silence. Then chimes. Then the silvery notes of the flute dancing around the room.

"People ask how they can increase their psychic abilities or their healing abilities," Peter continued. "You use your heart. You use your mind. You connect to source. Use the universal Reiki position to give yourself light. Say 'it's my intention to give myself universal life force energy, give myself divine energy, creative energy. I draw it into my chest. I let it radiate all around me, above and below me, getting stronger, brighter in every cell in my body.' Once you do that, you let the light flow every day. You don't deprive yourself of food or water or air. Why deprive yourself of light?"

He put his hands in prayer position, which told us we were cooked and could leave.

Bertie turned to me. "That was a good trip," he said.

I was halfway down that narrow, spiral staircase in the basement of the Girl Guides house again. Brigid Boyle, behind me, was afraid of the dark. "It's okay," I said. "There's nothing to fear." But she darted back upstairs. I knew I was lying. I knew there was something scary below, but I didn't want to run. This time, I wanted to face it. I stepped off the last stair and into the stone basement. The floor was a black and white checkerboard, but everything else was dark brown. The air was thick with dust, making breathing difficult. A narrow hallway led off the kitchen area and along it were hospital beds covered by dusty beige sheets. I passed five or six along the hallway before I stopped. I had a bad feeling about this. I lifted my foot to take a step when the creature rumbled loudly below, so loud that its ferocity shook the stonework, and its howl rattled my head. It was awake, this ancient, menacing creature, and it was pounding along the hallway toward me, hoof after hoof crashing onto the stone slabs.

I ran back up the stairs, racing as if my life depended on it.

A truck roaring along McGuinness woke me with a jolt. Another night of restless sleep and an early morning wake up to truck gears grinding and Zybi's obese wife stomping across the floorboards overhead. She must have packed on some extra pounds while I was away. I was tired and cranky. I wanted to bang on the ceiling with the broom handle.

Just for today I will not be angry.

I was seething.

I felt shaken, disoriented, as if the Reiki infusion was trying to cough up something I was trying to suppress. All I knew was that the light was too bright, the noises too loud, and the slight breeze coming through the vents of the AC felt like an assault on my nerve endings. This didn't feel good at all.

I picked up some coffee at the deli and walked to the waterfront, where I sat on the concrete barrier and closed my eyes. "It's my intention to give myself universal life force energy," I whispered. "I draw it into my chest. I let it radiate all around me, above and below me, getting stronger, brighter in every cell in my body."

I hoped I wouldn't spin out even more by topping up on universal life force energy, but I was trying to think positively. I was trying to raise my vibration, but it's hard when you're grieving, when you wake up in a panic and spend the day feeling sick, hovering on the outskirts of anxiety and abandonment. It's easy to be positive when you've plenty to be positive about, just like it's easy to be kind to kind people. But what happens when you feel unloved and unlovable? What happens when you don't feel good enough? I wasn't sensitive enough to reach beyond my physical form into something greater. I was small, inadequate, misery glued to the slab of a city street, unable to find a reason to be kind to myself. My friend Mac at the circus used to tell me to throw myself some bones: "Lighten the load," he'd say.

That word again.

I retreated into the Reiki principles: just for today, I will not worry; just for today, I will not be angry; just for today, I will be grateful. I idled away an hour or so listening to the sounds of planes ascending from JFK, the buzz of boats speeding by, the water lapping on the rocks, and the occasional duck quacking. Then I remembered another Reiki principle: just for today, I will be kind to every living thing.

Just for today, maybe, the living thing was me.

Next morning, I woke up from a blissfully dreamless sleep in desperate need of strong coffee. Grumpies had decent Wi-Fi, and at this hour, there would one person to a table with a laptop and a stoneware mug crusted with froth from a slowly consumed latte. Everyone would be surfing, trolling, and scribbling. No one would be talking. Rich roasted coffee and a quiet table seemed like a great way to start the day.

When I got to the café, I ordered coffee and slipped into a chair at a back table where I did a YouTube search on the term "afterlife communication." A video by an Australian guy calling himself Afterlife Phil popped up. The name sounded a bit odd, but he had a humble manner and a soft accent that was easy on the ears.

"Get their favorite coffee mug," he said, "and put it on the table in front of you. Just imagine that they're in the seat and talk to them."

That was easy. Johann and I spent hours in this place talking about stuff that seemed to matter and stuff that really didn't. I bought an Americano for the chair opposite. The idea of talking to a mug of coffee and an empty chair in public seemed deranged, but the locals were too absorbed in their own worlds to notice. I stuck my earbuds in my ears to listen to the YouTube video. Anyone watching would think I was on the phone.

"Say the things you didn't have a chance to say," Afterlife Phil said. "Talk about things that have happened in your life. Reminisce about old times, happy times. Whatever it is just talk to them as if they're there and you're having a real conversation."

Although I felt stupid playing make-believe with a latte, I could feel something trying to rise up out of my throat to be heard.

"Talk," Phil had said.

But I couldn't. Something was there, something that didn't want to be heard.

"Talk to them as if they're there and you're having a real conversation," Phil had said.

Rising. Uncomfortable.

"Speak," Phil had said.

A bitter, ugly feeling.

"Say it."

The weight of the beast pounding on the basement floor.

"Speak."

The panic of the monster dragging me down. The weight of something that wanted to be said. The something I'd unleashed on Nadia, on anyone, anywhere except where it belonged. The something that had been lurking in the dark all along.

"Say it."

It rose.

"I hate you."

I'd said it.

"I hate you."

Tears welled up in my eyes.

"I hate you for dying. I hate you for giving us no time. I hate you for assuming I knew you loved me because now I need to hear the words. I hate you for showing me you survived and leaving me again."

I turned away from his empty chair. My stomach heaved. I needed to vomit the stench of my guilt. I went to the bathroom, leaned on the sink, and stared into the mirror hanging under a harsh overhead light. I looked haggard. How could I have given voice to those things? I couldn't take them back now.

I splashed cold water on my face and wiped away the smudged mascara with paper towels that were like sandpaper grating across my eyes. No, I couldn't take them back because they were the truth.

97

I wasn't only angry that he died. I was angry with him *for* dying. But those words weren't the whole truth. I missed him. I missed him in every moment, in every word in every conversation, in every perfunctory exchange that feigned functionality when life was a churning stomach and a headache and an endless horror.

"*Liebling*, if you can hear me, I love you. I'm lost without you. I don't know how to find you. I don't know what to do."

I felt the 800-pound gorilla climb off my back.

Back at my table, I found five loud teenagers had moved into the back room. I put my earbuds in and clicked play on my MacBook and turned up the volume to drown them out.

"I want you to pause as you talk to them," Afterlife Phil went on. "What you'll find is you'll start to imagine them talking back to you. It could be imagined, it doesn't matter. Just do it anyway. Ask them to tell you something you need to know."

I paused the video. The teenagers went to the counter in the front to order. In the quiet, I composed myself by focusing on my breath, relaxing into my own space as Peter had done in his circle, breathing into the space around me, letting myself expand into it.

I heard something, but not like a sound — at least not just a sound — more like the feeling of a thought being whispered somewhere beyond me.

... here ...

The noisy teenagers returned. I removed my earbuds and closed my laptop. Did I imagine the word? I didn't think so, but it was too loud now to try again.

Zybi's fixit guy was leaving with his sack of tools when I got home. Inside, my apartment was toasty. The fixit man must have set the thermostat to seventy-five. Zybi would have an anxiety attack and would set it back to sixty by nightfall. For now, it was fabulous.

I am grateful.

I settled down to try Phil's exercise again. This time I didn't bother with the coffee or the chair. I sat on my cushion and focused on the light and on lightness as Peter had suggested. I held my hands over my heart and solar plexus and focused on positive thoughts to raise my vibration. I was nervous. I was afraid that I hadn't heard anything at Grumpies. I was afraid that he wouldn't come. Fear, the heaviest vibration. That wouldn't help.

Just for today, I will not worry.

As Peter had done, I imagined a light under my hands that spread from my heart up to and through my head, down to and through my feet, and then out around me like a bubble. Some recess of my mind said this was corny, but it felt really good in here, the calmest I'd felt in ages. I felt part of something more in this space. I didn't know what. All I knew was that this was the best I'd felt in weeks, maybe ever, and I didn't want to leave. When my mind wandered, I brought my attention back to the light, and before long, I felt myself getting lighter and lighter.

"Ask them to tell you something you need to know," Afterlife Phil had said.

"If you are here Johann, tell me something I need to know."

Something yellow flashed through my mind. It looked like a folded yellow blanket. Yes, it was a folded yellow blanket. That was absurdly meaningless, hardly something I needed to know.

Frustration with my inability to understand deflated my bubble. So much for Alicia's and Rev. Culter's theories about my supposed mediumistic ability and my wonderful spiritual path. I felt about as sensitive as a boiled potato and just as clueless.

I gave up, shuffled into the living room, and absentmindedly scrolled through the program guide on TV until I came across *The Lovely Bones* on pay-per-view. That would do. I'd read the book. It was narrated by a murdered fourteen-year-old who watches her family fracture after her death, the murderer escape suspicion, and her first love take up with a weird student who happened to be a medium. It was a chilling opening chapter that later dissipated into a view of the hereafter that has lingered since Patroclus wandered the earth, unable to enter Hades until Achilles honored his remains and freed his spirit. Here again was the tale of spirits lingering until they took care of their unfinished business. Admittedly, it made for a good story. I mean what would have become of *Ghost* had Patrick Swayze not had a murderer to catch. But it was a bedtime story, this unfinished business. Bad stuff happens. Bad people get away with bad things all the time. If a dead person could orchestrate the meting out of justice, wouldn't all murderers get their comeuppance? I was tired of the myths and fairytales that mitigated our fear of death with neatly tied bows and mollified our need for justice or reward by promising it in afterlife. We could doll death up as much as we liked, but it was random, unfair, and it certainly wasn't neat.

My mood had definitely tanked.

I rustled around the kitchen to comfort eat away my failure to make any sort of meaningful contact and flopped back down in front of the TV. Toward the end of the movie, there was a scene where the murdered girl follows her former boyfriend and the medium whom he's now dating on a picnic. Something caught my attention. I stuffed my chocolate croissant in my mouth, grabbed the remote, rewound, and froze the frame. There it was, the something I needed to know, the message that told me that the static electricity in the park, the vibrant green plants in the midst of my argument, the word "here" whispered at Grumpies were him trying to get my attention. He was doing as Rev. Cutler and Alicia had said. By not showing me signs out in the world he had forced me to focus inward and find true connection inside, where we could be one, where he could communicate with me directly. He had been guiding me to heal, to think differently, to see the world with fresh eyes, to own what Rev. Cutler said I needed to own: I wasn't a boiled potato. I had that inherent human quality that would allow our relationship to continue and a new path to unfold.

He did all of this with one simple but powerful message. He had pointed to the medium. She was sitting under a tree on a folded yellow blanket.

Speaking

The great and sad mistake of many people ...
is to imagine that those whom death has taken, leave us.
They do not ... They are ... living near us, transfigured ...
into light, into power, into love.

Karl Rahner SJ

Mrs. Zybi thundered across the ceiling into her kitchen and pummeled tenderness into her husband's Sunday breakfast steak. My bedside table rattled as the building shook under her flat feet. Moonlight was still trickling through the curtains. I willed her to go back to sleep, but the vacuum came out, which meant everyone was up for the day.

Just for today, I will be grateful.

A long, hot shower would have been delicious, but given Zybi's reluctance to heat it to the temperature New York tenant law demanded, I had to settle for a tepid one.

I realized, as I let the water run, that I felt very different today, lighter, optimistic even. Johann had obviously heard what I'd said at Grumpies, but he didn't judge me. He must have understood that I needed to say the words to be rid of the anger and guilt that was festering in my grief. Then he helped me by wrapping layers of reassuring information into the yellow blanket so I could stop doubting and move forward.

I dropped my towel and stepped into the gush of lukewarm water.

By being absent outwardly, he'd forced me to look inward to the fear hiding in my own shadows as well as to the place where extrasensory whispers resonate. I was beginning to see how it was all connected: my awakening to his continued existence, our ongoing relationship, my thoughts, and my healing.

Are you here?

He always liked sharing showers.

A tingle shot up my spine. Quivering and pulsating through my body. Orgasmic almost. I held onto the sensation for as long as I could, astonished by but reveling in the sensation. Once it faded, I couldn't bring it back.

I wondered if this sensation had been possible because I'd surrendered to the altered state into which Afterlife Phil had led me. It wasn't a meditative state, at least not in the passive sense I was used to; it was active; it had intention. I didn't still my mind in order to experience the inherent emptiness of all things as I did, or tried to do, with zazen. This was more like an expansion — of what, I didn't yet know. I felt bigger, as if my physical body was more subtle than I'd realized and could expand and distort up and out beyond the limits of its physical space. When I felt Johann in that space, just for the tiniest fraction of a moment, it was glorious. I felt a oneness there, a sense of belonging that made life seem larger and more purposeful. For the moment it lasted, I felt loved completely, without shadows or shame or conditions.

What is this space?

Words like "soul" and "spirit" flitted around like the nebulous labels used through the ages to define non-material concepts. I was limited by language. Language evolved to help us communicate experiences *within* our frame of reference not *without*. What language can be used to explain something no one has ever seen, known, or experienced and therefore was never in need of a word? Trying to describe a world outside language seemed like trying to explain nuclear physics to a three-year-old. I was experiencing a state of belonging that I've never known before—the state of existence that poets and philosophers through the ages approximated with metaphors and similes. His life, how he felt, how I felt with him was ethereal, fundamental, something that came with a knowing that couldn't be explained or approximated or expressed verbally. I was, for the first time, beginning to grasp what Master Hanh described as interbeing—the oneness or connection of all things, something that has to be experienced to be understood.

Speaking

I looked at Johann's photo while I laced up my boots.

I have a funny feeling that if I want to learn to go deeper into this space and hold it for longer, I'll have to drag all *my shadows into the light.*

The Nike swoosh popped into my head.

Just do it? Seriously? Just like that?

It sounded like a lot of hard and even painful work, and I didn't know where to start or what to do.

I grabbed my keys and went for breakfast on the East River at dawn. This was definitely not a memory we shared. We were never up that early on a Sunday morning. The only place open for coffee was the corner deli that doled it out like bitter swill in "we are happy to serve you" cups. At the river's edge, the sky turned from indigo to purple, and the light of the rising sun reflected off glass skyscrapers in the former slaughterhouse area on Manhattan's East Side. The longer I looked at the skyline the more there emerged the sleek black walls of billionaire developer Sheldon Solow's architecture — mysterious buildings that snuck up on you, not like Trump's towers that heralded their arrival with his name emblazoned in gold. Money and power. That world was further from me now than it had ever been.

An hour or so later, I left the riverfront and took the long way home through McCarren Park and along Humboldt Street past St. Stanislaus Kostka Church, a gothic giant with twin spires hulking over the south end of the neighborhood. It had Masses on the hour on Sundays, alternating between English and Polish for the thousands of Catholics in the neighborhood. A Mass in English was underway. I slipped past a statue of Pope John Paul II and into a pew at the back. I wasn't there looking for God, I was just floating through my morning, following the brush strokes in the painting of my day.

"Knowledge inflates with pride, but love builds up," a parishioner read from the altar. I picked up a creased missalette. She was reading from 1 Corinthians. "If anyone supposes he knows something, he does not yet know as he ought to know. But if one loves God, one is known by him."

Considering the extent of my newfound ignorance, I found St. Paul reassuring. It reminded me of Socrates's saying the most reprehensible ignorance is to think that we know what we do not know.

I'm in the clear today, Liebling. I whispered to him in my mind. *I know nothing.*

I felt him smile. It felt like my entire being, from the inside out, was smiling.

While the parishioners stood up, sat down, knelt, and said their refrains, I noticed the religious mosaics in rich colors and gold leaf that were set into large gothic archways. Jean Paul II had served Mass there when he came to New York, which presumably was the reason for his statue. I saw him twice, once in the Phoenix Park in Dublin as a child and again at fourteen when my grandmother took my cousin and me to Rome. I'd say I shook his hand, except he only brushed limp fingers across the outstretched arms of the faithful as he breezed past in his Popemobile. That was before someone shot him, and the Popemobile was redesigned to keep him safe inside bulletproof glass.

These pews must have sat a thousand people twenty times a week, and this was only one of hundreds of churches, synagogues, and mosques in the city where people flocked for spiritual care. I'd assumed the modern world was more secular, especially in a liberal bastion like New York, but looking at these numbers, it was clear the materialistic paradigm wasn't satisfying a human yearning for something more. As a skeptic, I'd believed the observant to be delusional, and while I still wasn't enamored by organized religion, I saw how it served: communities of people were having a personal experience with God and with the godliness in each other and themselves.

"And fear not them which kill the body," the priest read during the Gospel, "but are not able to kill the soul: but rather fear him which is able to destroy both soul and body in hell."

This is the Mass I remember. Sooner or later, we are all threatened with hell.

Static crackled across my face.

You remember it too.

As communion started, a soprano in the choir loft began singing "Come Down, O Love Divine." Her voice was so pure that I closed my eyes and forgot about the pride and death and hell of the readings and was back to those airy mornings in Virginia when the tenor sang the "Ave Maria," giving me the only peace I knew back then. This soprano's voice resonated even more deeply now, as if, instead of hearing only the melody, I heard the notes from inside like delicate chimes. Such was the tranquility I experienced in the church that day.

After crawling into bed that night, I placed my hand over my heart and focused on the light, breathing into it as I'd done before, allowing it to expand around me, and resting into the calmness and sense of belonging that came with surrendering to that place.

This time, something different happened. I started to lose body awareness, at least, I began to feel my body stretching and contorting up and out beyond its physical boundaries. It must have been the energy around my body because I hadn't moved. The more fluid and expanded I felt, the more I could sense him around me.

Liebling, are you here?

Ith-voll-ta-dear ... came his faint and fragment reply.

I tried to hold the altered state to hear more clearly, but I couldn't. I hoped I'd learn to hold this space better. I desperately wanted to be there fully. That place with him was the closest I'd ever come to knowing pure bliss.

Next morning, upon waking, I felt the static of his presence close to me again. It was like being caressed by tiny, soothing tingles.

Shone-ima-zag ...

The end of the phrase seemed to drop out, like a bad phone connection.

I'm sorry, Liebling. I'm not able to understand.

No more sounds came. I was disappointed in myself. He was trying. It couldn't have been easy for him either. He was probably learning to communicate just like me, and I was letting him down. I needed to be able to hear better but didn't know how. I was hungry for knowledge. There was so much I didn't know.

I picked up a book I'd found called *The Teachings of Silver Birch*, stopped by the Greenpoint Coffeehouse for an Americano, and then wandered down to the East River to read.

Silver Birch, who was depicted as a Native American, was a spirit guide who began speaking through a British journalist turned trance medium called Maurice Barbanell in the 1930s. Over the course of many group sessions, the guide offered considerable information through Barbanell about the nature and purpose of life and our relationship to those in the afterlife. Despite his archaic locution and his tendency to speak to the audience like they were children, his teachings made for some easy and interesting riverside reading.

My interest was piqued when I came up on a chapter called "Problems of Communication." He talked about the difficulty involved in trying to impress thoughts on an individual's mind. "I am limited, not only by my medium's vocabulary, but by the state of his soul evolution, because that limits the amount of myself that I can express," the guide said. People's subconscious mind was apparently so programmed with associations and perceptions that trying to get past this interference to clearly communicate a single word to that individual very often triggered a heap of associations with that word that the person had formed over the years. This sent his mind off on a tangent only to arrive at an interpretation that was not the spirit's intended meaning. It took Silver Birch years to learn how to work with Barbanell's mind to get his message across, years, he said, to get through the references that were already there before the guide arrived. Once, when asked by an audience member to elaborate on this, the Silver Birch replied, "When you ask these questions it is like trying to explain to one who has been blind from birth what the color of the sky looks like when the sun is shining. You have no standard of comparison."

Silver Birch had perfectly described my struggle to verbalize my experiences.

The wind picked up on the waterfront, so I gathered up my books and headed for home. I paid little attention to anything except my own ruminations. A car horn beeped and a driver yelled Polish obscenities at me when I stepped out in front of him on the corner of Kent.

I wandered down Franklin Street wondering what the sound Johann had been making could mean. *Ith-voll-ta-dear... Shone-ima-zag...* It sounded like gibberish. Or maybe, as Silver Birch said, I wasn't getting it because I was trying to interpret using a frame of reference that belonged to this world, not the next. I was growing frustrated with the limits of my knowledge.

Monique was opening her gift shop near the corner of Franklin and Greenpoint Avenue. I wandered in and looked at all her pretty things: handmade jewelry, crystals, oils and oil burners, little boxes made of turquoise and shell, and notebooks that were too pretty to scribble on. Even this early, without the incense burning, it smelled delightful. She had a shelf filled with decks of oracle cards that I hadn't seen before. The idea, the box said, was to ask for guidance and pick a card, which should tell the seeker something helpful or something they needed to know. I spread out a sample deck and ran my hand across them.

Okay, Liebling, if you can see me, tell me something I need to know.

I picked a card and turned it over. It was a picture of an angel walking up a staircase holding a lantern. The angel's name was written at the bottom of the card.

It's your name! That's unbelievable!

Under his name, the message read: "Ascend. I am leading the way through your intuition and dreams."

Did you do that? How did you do that?

Static electricity bolted across my face and danced lightly around my eyes.

Speaking

Obviously, he hadn't shuffled the deck, so he must have been able to influence my hand to pick that card. Still, all the cards were face down, so I couldn't quite figure this out.

How did you know what card I'd pick?

Static flitted across my face like feathery tickles.

Are you like a puppet master controlling my behavior?

I could feel him laughing. At least, laughter bubbled up in me, and I knew it wasn't mine. I also knew — and I didn't know how — that he was telling me that he couldn't make me do anything, but he would find a way to help when I asked.

Except for the angel cards on display, Monique had no more in stock. That was fine. I didn't need them. I already got my message. I bought a handmade, scented candle and headed for home. I wove through people bustling along Manhattan Avenue, running to the subway, queuing in Rite Aid, pushing strollers, standing on corners having a catch up, beeping car horns, and getting frustrated in traffic jams. I slipped past them all.

We were in our own private world. We had a secret life and shared secret messages. All of these people could see me but not know he was with me. Happiness trickled through my nerve ends. The intimacy of our new relationship was thrilling, electric. My day, far from empty, was filled with surprises — his surprise appearances, chiming in on the most seemingly mundane tasks like pulling a card in a store and wrapping into it some clever message.

This was Johann doing what he always did, being emotionally unexpressive but making me feel loved by his actions. Why had I worried so much about him not saying the words "I love you"? I felt stupid now, needy, and even a little neurotic. He was with me. He was looking out for me. His actions made me feel loved the way they always did. Of course he didn't need to say the words.

Later that week, for reasons I neither comprehended nor appreciated, I woke up with him filling my mind with the image of a spider. Sharing complex messages in images seemed to be his preferred method of communication. He was an artist, and art was his natural habitat, so this made sense, and given I hadn't a musical ear and didn't have the best extrasensory hearing ability, it must have been easier for him to show me messages than speak them.

Why are you showing me a spider? You know I hate spiders.

I got no more details, so I got up, brewed an Americano and checked my messages. There was a voicemail from my insurance company to say that month's direct debit payment was declined. I called them to pay by credit card over the phone. While I was holding, I noticed that my driver's license had expired, which invalidated my insurance coverage and meant I couldn't legally drive. It hadn't been a problem until now because I hadn't really driven since I got back to New York, except to move the car from one side of the street to the other on street cleaning days. I went to the DMV website to renew my license online but learned it could take a couple of weeks to arrive. I needed to go into the office, but rattling along on the G all the way to the government offices in downtown Brooklyn was more than I could face. The G train kept to its own timetable. If I left now, mid-morning, I'd arrive so late, I'd be last in a queue of hundreds, but I could be there in fifteen minutes and get ahead of the throng if I drove. I deliberated. Surely, it would be okay if I drove carefully.

I got into the driver's seat and was putting my key into the ignition when a huge black spider skittered down a cobweb in front of my face and disappeared under the seat.

"Oh shit!"

I leapt out of the car, and stood there staring at the open door. Eventually, I leaned in and saw the creature hiding under the passenger seat. I reached in with a Mastercard and tried to scoot it out, but it ran every direction except toward the door and then scuttled across my hand. I shook it off like mad, got my useless driver's license, trapped it between the two cards, and threw it onto the sidewalk.

I felt Johann's subtle presence wrap around me.

You're here! You saw that.

Then the penny dropped.

Oh, I get it. You don't just show me things ahead of time, you're telling me that you're with me when you show me the images in the morning, and you're also with me when I see them later.

It made sense. He couldn't show me things after the fact because I would think I was remembering something I'd seen earlier. If the image of a spider came to mind tonight, I'd think it was recall. He couldn't show me images at the moment I saw them because his sensory input was so subtle, it'd be overpowered by the chaos of Brooklyn. Besides, I couldn't float around in the proverbial ether all day being receptive to messages — I'd end up so strung out from hypersensitivity that I'd probably end up having a breakdown or walking under a bus. Instead, he'd found way to say, *I'm with you now in the quiet, when I can connect with you easily, and I'm telling you ahead of time that I'll be with you during the day.* It reminded me of the promise he made watching *The Lives of Others:* "I'm with you now no matter what!"

Static crackled across my face. I'd figured it out. I was learning, and he was happy. At least somewhere inside me I felt his happiness.

Whether the spider was all he saw and he thought it funny, or whether he saw something worse happening with me driving illegally down the road, I didn't know, but I slammed the door and went home, prepared to spend the following morning rattling on the G to the DMV.

I arrived at the DMV just before ten, plucked number 154 from the ticket machine, and settled into a hard pew for a couple of hours.

The spider, I decided, like the yellow blanket, raised an existential conundrum. He showed me the image before I saw it, which meant he had foresight, so either he could move through time or he was outside time, which intellectually made sense; time after all is a property of the physical universe.

If you can see what has not yet happened, does that mean everything I do is predetermined? If that's the case, what of choice or self-determination? If everything I am going to do has already been done, why do I bother grappling with decisions at all?

I had the strangest sensation that a wealth of information was dancing around the edges of my mind. I felt the energy of my body shifting somehow, distorting, expanding. It was subtle, but I couldn't grasp the information I was itching to reach. It were as if I were seeing a musical note or hearing a mathematical equation or smelling a color all at the same time. He was trying to answer, but I was asking a complex multi-dimensional question, and his effort to answer wasn't comprehensible to my three-dimensional being.

In an effort to be helpful, my mind raced through its stores of information about time and predetermination. It alighted on Thomas á Kempis, a medieval German priest I'd read in undergrad philosophy who described the "now moment" into which past, present, and future collapsed. He called it the complete, simultaneous, and perfect possession of eternal life; one moment that contains eternity and steps out of time entirely. Even with my new world view, Kempis was as incomprehensible to me now as he was then. If I'm in this moment, how can I arrive in the next moment if there is none? I knew my thinking was wrong, but what was right? I'd no idea. Concepts of time or its absence and predetermination versus self-determination were far more than my humble neural pathway could handle. I felt unevolved and unenlightened. I was in Plato's cave watching dancing shadows on the wall.

"I'm with you now no matter what," Christa's line from *The Lives of Others* sounded in my head again.

Wait! Could those sounds I'm hearing be German?

Maybe they weren't gibberish at all.

I texted Karl, a Berliner I knew.

"Can you translate something for me if I say it phonetically?"

"In a meeting but if you call me for one minute, yes."

I dialed. "Hi Karl, sorry to interrupt. It sounds like *ith-voll-ta-dear* and another one is *shone-ima-zag-in*."

"Is it possible to be *Ich wollte dir schon immer sagen*?"

"Yes, that's it! What does it mean?"

"It means 'I always wanted to tell you.'"

"I always wanted to tell you what?"

"Nothing else. I need to go back. See you later."

"Okay, bye."

You always wanted to tell me what?

Irises.

I woke up to find Johann filling my mind with irises. Irises held no particular meaning for me, so I didn't know what they signified, but I picked up purple and yellow pencils to sketch them in my notebook. I felt as I outlined his images, filled them with color, and added details, that I was savoring his longest kiss or inhaling his delicious smell or listening to the rhythm of his German accent dancing along his English words.

The experience would probably feel more intimate in the solitude of the riverfront. That, I decided, would be my new way to start each day with him.

A mediumship class at the online school was scheduled for that afternoon. It was a closed group, it said, which meant only members practiced, but anyone was welcome to listen and learn.

Later, after I logged in and was waiting for it to start, I searched for more books to read. There was a huge body of work in the area of mediumship, Spiritualism, parapsychology, and consciousness theory. There were a lot of academics and scientists working in the gap between spirituality and science or at least exploring a more holistic understanding of reality. Some books were by older writers, such as Rudolf Steiner and Anthony Borgia. Some were delivered in trance states, which I didn't love because it was impossible to verify how much of that information came from the imagination of the receiver. I made an exception for *The Blue Island,* which was supposedly transmitted through a medium from W. T. Stead, one of my favorite Victorian journalists. There were books by doctors, such as Eben Alexander and Raymond Moody on near-death experiences and Ian Stevenson on reincarnation. There was Robert Lanza on consciousness and Robert Monroe on out of body experiences. My reading list was getting very long.

"Can everyone hear me okay?" asked Dora, the teacher.

A dozen or so people said yes.

"Great. I'm delighted to see so many people logging in to support our six advanced mediumship students," Dora said. "Today, we're working with evidential mediumship, which means sharing evidence about the spirit communicator so the mediums can prove who they're connecting with before giving messages. But I also want you to be aware of the healing power of mediumship. Just as we heal and grow here, they are healing and growing in the spirit world, and we should be able to see evidence of this growth. Now, I know the message from the spirit world can be very simple, but for those of you who have loved ones who communicate a lot, your mother, for example, is not going to come with the same message every time. She may want to help you with something going on in your life or say something she needs to say so that she can heal or grow herself. There is always a lot more information there than you're aware of, so reach for it, and make this a healing practice. Everyone understand?"

The six students said yes.

"Everyone in the audience, if the medium comes to you or you recognize the spirit communicator, just say yes, no, or I don't know. These will be short contacts, and I don't want you feeding the medium any information."

A woman named Lizzy started working the way I'd see the mediums do it on YouTube: "I have an old woman here with white hair. She feels like a mother. She died of a heart attack. Who can understand that information?" A lot of people could.

"Ask her for something specific," Dora said.

Lizzy was quiet.

"Don't think about it Lizzy," she said. "You'll end up in your head and the power will drop."

While Lizzy was silent, I searched for "power and mediumship" and found an article by a tutor at the Arthur Findlay College called Glyn Edwards on a practice called "sitting in the power." His description sounded like my own effort to hold the white space of the altered state where I tried to blend with Johann. Apparently, I was expanding my energy field or power, as Glyn Edwards called it, and that made me sensitive to other sources of energy. What I wasn't doing, but should be doing, was expanding out into the universe and asking the infinite consciousness to blend with me. This blending enhanced the sensitivity of the mediumistic faculty, he said, and had the added benefit of facilitating visions and bringing a sense of peace.

"She is showing me four boys," Lizzy said. "And she wants to speak to one of them who's in this room."

A guy called Jas claimed to know the woman, so Lizzy asked to work with him to give him his mother's message.

"There have been some problems with one of your brothers," she said, "and your mother is aware of the effort you've made, but there's nothing else you can do. It's time for you to take care of yourself now. You understand?"

"Yes, I do," Jas said. "That's good to hear, thank you."

"Wonderful Lizzy. Nice healing message for Jas and his mother. Okay, next. Iris," Dora said.

Iris turned on her microphone. "Can you hear me?" she asked. She had a guttural accent, German definitely.

"Yes, we can hear you fine," Dora said.

"I have a man here with me who's about forty. A heart attack took him to the spirit world." She paused. "He had blonde hair, but it was the darker type."

Whoa! Is this you?

"The connection to the recipient here is a romantic connection." She paused again. "He is showing me the *Sieggessäule* in Berlin. That is a monument with an angel on the top, so he might be from Berlin. Or maybe I am imaging this because I am from Berlin."

Liebling, that's the monument from Wings of Desire.

"Does anyone know this man?"

"Yes, I do," I said.

"Thank you," she said.

"He was not very emotional — no wait, that's wrong." She paused. "He didn't speak about his emotions. Do you understand?"

"Yes."

"He's giving me the sense that he went quickly to spirit and never said many things he wanted to say."

"Yes."

"He is very sorry for this. I am hearing some words, one moment." Pause.

"He always wanted to tell you ..."

Pause.

You always wanted to tell me what?

"He is showing me a very big pink heart. Pink is the symbol I see for undying love, so he is using it to tell me that he always wanted to say, 'I love you forever.' Do you understand?"

"Yes, I do," I said. "I do. Thank you, Iris."

"Well done, Iris," Dora said and called the next person in to work, but I'd stopped listening.

Iris! The irises! You planned this. All this time, you knew I needed to hear the words, and you were trying to say 'I love you forever.'

That night, I was too happy to sleep. I lay there, one, two, three o'clock, as the noise of traffic on McGuinness Boulevard tapered off and the neighborhood fell into an hour or two of silence. I traced and retraced the outline of his message, first resting in the joy I found there.

What an effort you made for me, Liebling. Thank you. You've made me unbelievably happy.

As the hours passed, I began to wonder why he'd made such an effort to give me a message in German when I don't speak German.

Why ...?

His answer interrupted my thought. I couldn't tell if I'd heard it or felt it or saw it. I just knew it. I knew that if I'd heard the words "I love you" in English flitting across my mind, I may have mistaken it for my own thought, so subtle and fragmentary are these whispers, but in German, it had to be from him. He made sure to give me this message in such a way that it eliminated any doubt.

What patience you're learning on the higher side.

I laughed. Patience was never his strong point. It must have been taking some effort on his part to baby me along in the workings of this new relationship.

How do you feel now?

He flashed an image of himself sleeping into my mind.

You're exhausted? I bet you are.

Not only had he gone to so much trouble to overcome the challenge of interlife communication at all, he must have struggled with whatever caused his fear of vulnerability in order to express himself with such persistence and honesty. This must be what Dora had meant by those in spirit continuing to heal and grow. It must have taken a great deal of healing and growing and commitment on his part to send these expressions of love at all. The more I thought about the effort that went into his communication, the more I realized it was, without exception, the most perfect expression of love I'd ever heard.

Gold.

Glittering.

My half-awake brain was trying to make sense of the image that he put in my mind. It was so close, I could see the texture in the gold, but it was too close for me to see the whole image, which was bigger than my field of vision. A moment later, it shrank, and I could see it was a gold heart. It was as if he had to account for spatial logistics in some way. Communicating this way must be a learning process for him too. I rolled over not wanting to open my eyes, trying to hold onto the image, not wanting it to go away.

I love you too.

It was the early afternoon when I woke again. I felt like I'd slept off decades of weariness. A jackhammer was destroying McGuinness Boulevard — probably had been all morning, but I'd slept through it. I woke up starving. I made some toast and did a quick email check. There was one from an editor asking if I was still interested in a stringer assignment in Afghanistan. I'd asked him for the beat almost a year earlier, not long after I got back from Iraq, but at the time he'd a staffer covering that beat from Pakistan. I was miserable then. But not now. I had no interest in war. I'd no particular interest in politics either. Covering politics had become like Groundhog Day: different faces, same stories, same power playing and deal making, people presenting ideas and being beaten into the same old results. There was always a greater power behind the curtain. I'd have to go back to work sooner or later, preferably later, but for now, I'd enough left from the advance on my first book to take the time to explore what had suddenly become a far more interesting world.

I had a gloriously lazy day. I read. I replayed Iris's message in my head. I relaxed into Johann's delicious presence. When I ran out of energy to hold that space with him, I ate. I replayed Iris's message. I read more. In the afternoon, I got back into bed with my iPad and read from *The Blue Island*, which is an account of the afterlife transmitted by W. T. Stead after his death on the Titanic to his daughter Estelle Stead via a medium who apparently wrote in a trance.

Stead spoke briefly about the night of the Titanic, how the drowned souls were taken upwards to be met by loved ones who had passed over years before. They were brought to the first sphere of the afterlife, the transition place, which he called the Blue Island, not because it was blue but because of the amount of blue in the various buildings and scenery of the landscape. Yes, there were buildings. In fact, the description of this transition plane sounded both familiar and exotic. It was designed to help people whose consciousness had left their physical form to acclimatize. "Death is only the doorway from one room to another, and both rooms are very similarly furnished and arranged," he wrote. People there communicated mind to mind without the need of vocal expression. The mind was all powerful, and happiness or angst was determined by each spirit person's demands. "The vast majority by force of habit, the desire for business gain, or social gain, or any kind of gain," he wrote, arrived with "poor undeveloped egos, preparing their own discomfort and suffering — not a hell fire but a mental torture."

From this account, the choices we made in the physical sphere and not the vagaries of an all-powerful creator determined our state in the next. Progress was possible but up to the individual. To this end, he reported, everything offered was designed to help the spirit advance toward knowledge and enlightenment. Limitless opportunities for learning were presented.

"In this land we are much more sensitive than whilst on earth," Stead explained, "and when thoughts are directed to us by people on your side, we have a direct call from those currents of thought thus generated, and we are practically always able to come in close contact with the person who is thinking of us. ... Anyone who sits for a moment and allows his mind to dwell on some dear one who has 'died' will actually draw the spirit of that person to himself. He may be conscious or unconscious of the presence, but the presence is there." It was also possible, Stead reported, for those in the next sphere to be in constant contact with those with whom they had an intimate bond, a friend or family member still on the earth. They could even follow the loved one's thoughts to help and influence them.

In short, according to Stead, there was always someone listening to our whispers.

I knew now that Johann could see what I was doing ahead of time *and* while I was doing it in the present. I knew that he could hear my thoughts when I spoke to him in my mind. Now, however, Stead was saying he could hear *all* my thoughts even when I wasn't aware of his presence because we were part of the same wave of universal consciousness where all thoughts are shared.

I felt a prickle of discomfort. If he could hear every piece of nonsense that ran through my mind, then I'd no privacy, no boundaries. I reddened. If he could hear all my thoughts, he hadn't just heard me hurling insults at Zybi and heaping spite on Nadia, he could hear the entire monologue of my monkey mind: the desires, hopes, anger, sadness, fears, freak-outs, criticisms, self-criticisms, resentments, irritations, petty jealousies, petulance, self-pity and self-indulgence that come and go like flickers across the consciousness; the shadow places that other people never see; the shadow places I didn't want to look; the candid thoughts untempered by tact and reserve; the machinations spinning in the background of life and self-edited so I could speak social truths and not the rantings of a disordered mind. *You look like shit, your story sucks, you're not all that, oh, please, shut up*! Let's face it, sometimes the kindest thing I could do was keep my thoughts to myself. Then there was the solitary chatter that defined my silent relationship with myself — *I can do it, I can't do it, I feel good, I look like shit* — and the remnants of my childhood — *Mary is smarter than you, Sheila is prettier, Richard does everything better.* The dings I took and the shame I ended up owning became the secrets behind which I hid from judgment or rejection or humiliation. Then there's the normal stuff of society: the products we must buy to be like those who are more beautiful, the grades we much reach to be like those who are smarter, the salaries we must earn to be like those who are more successful. These remind us from birth to death that we are not enough. What kind of society would it be if we could accept ourselves as we are? Not this one, that was certain.

In physical form, Johann couldn't see all my shadows, but now, he could see everything — the nasty little id impulses, the tears behind every outburst. He saw me stripped, revealed, vulnerable, and defenseless — everything laid bare — no gimmicks, no manipulations, no secrets. In the 12-step program, they say that we are only as sick as our secrets, and those are never as toxic as when they're whistling around in the dark. Well, there were no secrets now.

Master Hanh said that to love more completely you "have to have trust, respect, and confidence in yourself. Trust that you have a good and compassionate nature," he said. "When we learn to love and understand ourselves and have true compassion for ourselves, then we can truly love and understand another person." Until then, he went on, there could be no true intimacy or interbeing with another.

Interbeing. That lovely word again. But now the magnitude of what it demanded brought me intense amount of agitation.

I turned toward the only thing I knew to do — sit on my meditation cushion. I dusted it off and sat with the doubt, the uneasiness that was clouding the love I had been shown, the shrinking of personhood that can prompt anger, jealousy, blame, and self-denigration. For hours a day for almost two weeks, I practiced recognizing *shenpa*, a practice I learned from Buddhist nun Pema Chodron of noticing a hook or attachment and sitting with whatever discomfort arose around it. It's a simple and excruciating practice of body, heart, and mind. For days, I sat with uncomfortable feelings that I had long repressed. I squirmed. I resisted the urge to escape shame or shift blame to someone else. It's desperately hard work, the work of self-acceptance. It was a brutal two weeks of my legs cramping and my head aching, of walking into the world without my skin, facing the City head on — defenseless in too many ways — not meeting obnoxiousness, or rudeness, or injustice with more of the same, just watching responses arise in me and doing my best to let them go.

One morning, I was reading the writings of Buddhist teacher Jack Kornfield: "Part of the art of quieting yourself is also to honor the tears that you carry." I burst into tears and cried all day. Every day for another week, I did this agonizing practice. When I wasn't on my cushion, I read or took long walks. I unrolled my yoga mat and revived my home practice. I was a loner.

Except on Sunday. On Sunday morning, I struggled to St. Stan's desperate to sit in the peace of the aria. I was feeling raw and overly sensitive, but the atmosphere created by the elegance of the soprano in the choir loft was soothing. Vibrations rippled down my spine like tiny healing tingles. Scientists say we are moved by music because it affects our limbic system, and this is why we have emotional experiences when listening to music, but this woman's voice testified that the ancient Greeks were right: music was the sound of the spheres that imparted grace as it found its way into the inward places of the soul. Grace. Even the word was peaceful.

Unfortunately, the harmony was broken by the discord of the Polish priest's sermon. He began to rant about an Evangelical Christian who had stopped him in the street that week, offered him a flyer, and tried to educate him on the good book and the good news of our Savior, the Lord Jesus Christ.

"Who is he to tell me?" he bellowed. "He hasn't been to seminary. I have been to seminary. He can't tell me about Jesus. I tell him about Jesus."

That was it. The atmosphere ruined. My little trips to Stan's for a moment of universal harmony ruined. He was angry, and now I was angry but struggling to talk myself into a better place. *Breathe,* I told myself. Maybe it brought up memories of repressive nuns in school and oppressive priests on Sundays. Jesus was the triumph of love over death, but we were still being lashed and scourged for our unworthiness. If there was anything I couldn't handle, it was a priest, or any clergy member, telling people how to think. *Be here now,* I told myself. I waited until the end, hoping that he would wake up and make it possible for me to stay, but he didn't. *Let it go,* I told myself. He just battered us with his ego until it was time for the profession of faith. I slipped out of the pew while the parishioners mumbled, "I believe in one God, the Father Almighty, Maker of heaven and earth, of all things seen and unseen ..." and closed the door behind me.

I knew he wasn't the voice of all priests. I'd known one or two great priests in my childhood, and where would I be without Father Peter in Virginia? But it didn't matter. Returning to the familiarity of the church was no longer comforting. I couldn't go back, which meant I'd no longer hear the choral singing, which had brought me such peace.

More shenpa; more hooks, more reactivity, more old resentments. My practice had followed me off my cushion and into the world and was forcing me to face my reactivity everywhere.

I stopped into the supermarket on the corner of Driggs to get a bottle of water. The word "supermarket" was generous. It was more like a warehouse with tall narrow aisles stacked with dust and high-fructose corn syrup. There was an argument brewing at the cash register among a couple of customers. I slipped past and grabbed a small bottle of Poland Spring. As the argument got louder and the aisles more claustrophobic, the remnants of my good mood shriveled.

I got in line to pay. A Muslim cashier was trying to communicate in broken English with a Latino woman counting out quarters and dimes who spoke no English. The obnoxious man who'd been arguing was pacing in front of the counter and up and down the aisles.

"What the fuck, lady," he shouted. "Pay for your fucking shit and get out of here. Go back to fucking Mexico you fucking beaner, and you fucking raghead terrorist go back to whatever godforsaken Arab shithole you came from."

The woman dropped her change all over the floor and muttered anxiously in Spanish. I helped her pick it up and incurred the wrath of the rageaholic. Up close, he didn't just sound obnoxious, he smelled obnoxious. It wasn't alcohol, it was piss and puke and body odor. I gagged. He waved his arms around, pointing at "raghead" and "beany" and me and the nervous old man clutching a box of cereal in line behind me. The woman put all her coins on the counter and ran out. I stepped up to pay. The rageaholic muttered in line behind me. I handed the cashier a twenty for a dollar bottle of water. He had to get under the counter for change. That was it.

"Fuck you, you useless fucker," the rageaholic yelled.

My heart started pounding with his rage. A thought was forcing itself into my head. I could feel the pressure of it. Angry. Determined. My stomach lurched as something spiteful gained traction in my mind.

I hope you get hit by a car!

It was sharp and toxic, crisp as if I'd heard someone else say it. Shame washed over that ugly voice in my head. I grabbed my water and my nineteen dollars and made for the door. The rageaholic blocked my path and leaned into me. His stench made me gag.

"I hope you get hit by a car," he said, spraying my face with spit.

I rushed out the door and fled to McGolrick Park. Trembling, I poured the water on napkins to wash his spit off my face and his rage out of my being.

It wasn't my thought. It was his thought! It wasn't mine.

I'd been working so hard to release the anger I'd carried since Johann passed, probably the anger I'd been carrying all my life. I was terrified to think that much remained. But it hadn't. Thank goodness, that ugliness wasn't mine.

I had always been sensitive, but never like this. As a child my mother criticized me for it, so I took it on as a shameful thing and became withdrawn. Now, I'd become overly susceptible to other people's emotions again. I was angry with the priest, fearful with the Spanish lady, and murderous with the rageaholic. All around me ugliness in all its forms was being dragged into the light. Was this the result of the shenpa practice I was doing? The more I tried to bring light to my own darkness, the darker the world seem to be.

I went home and crawled into bed. I didn't sit on my cushion.
I'm baked, Liebling. I'm sorry. I need to stop.

That Friday, as I woke, Johann put the number 496 in black letters on a yellow and red background in my mind. I didn't know what he meant, but I drew it in my notebook. It would probably make sense later, the way these images usually did.

I needed to get out. I needed a change of scenery. I hadn't been out since the incident in the deli a few days earlier. I missed St. Stan's or at least I missed the peace that had once washed over me on the waves of the aria there.

I decided to go for a drive.

For months, my old Mustang had been battered by wind and rain. It was covered in the remnants of winter city sediment, but it started right up. I squeezed out of my parking space and drove into the old-fashioned carwash down the block. I hadn't been in one of these since I was a kid. My cousins and I would cram into the back seat of my uncle's car and watch jets cover the windows in suds while the plastic strips battered the dirt off the exterior. We'd giggle and squeal because we were safe inside from the mayhem beyond. I felt much the same today, cocooned. The rhythm and swish were easing the headache I'd had since the rageaholic day. Maybe I'd benefit from a drive down to the Botanical gardens and a day among the trees, but I was tired. Was I up for hustling through the traffic?

Are you here?

Static danced across my eyes like his gentle kisses.

Thank you, Liebling.

My car rolled off the tracks and was dumped onto McGuinness Boulevard. I'd driven halfway down the block when an ambulance siren squealed behind me. I pulled over behind a yellow cab, both of us nestled by a hydrant trying to get out of the way. My ears were splitting from the squawking siren and honking horn and the EMT yelling "pull over to the side" on a megaphone. The traffic light was red, but one car beside me made no effort to creep into the intersection or get out of the way. In my rearview mirror, I fixated on the flashing lights and the letters FDNY on the ambulance.

"Get out of the way!" I shouted at the driver of the car sitting in the middle of the lane. "They're trying to keep someone alive."

It was that day again. His ambulance was screeching down Riverside Drive, cars were in the way, EMTs were trying to keep him alive. He was dying. *He was dying.*

Blood drained from my head. I felt frightened, disorientated, lightheaded, like I was leaving my body. I burst into tears, overwhelmed by the confusing sensations my body couldn't contain while it relived a time that couldn't be stopped.

Is this death?

I needed him to touch me or speak to me or show me he was okay, but I was too distressed and the traffic too loud to hear or sense anything.

The ambulance screamed past. The cab in front indicated to pull out. That's when I saw it. On the yellow paint over his red brake light was his cab number: 496.

You're here! You're seeing what I'm seeing. Are you okay? Please tell me you're okay.

As I wiped the tears off my cheeks, I felt the richness of his presence surrounding me, soothing the hollows of my distress. He'd anticipated how distraught I'd be in the moment I experienced his death and showed up for me. But more importantly, he seemed to be facing the moment of his own death without any distress. He was calm, happy, as if that day were just another day, as if he had just slipped out of one overcoat and slipped on another and kept moving along life's continuum, loving the same people, growing, healing, learning, and being an even more beautiful version of himself.

In that moment, he took away my fear of death.

I desperately wanted to kiss him, bury my face in the crook of his neck and stay there forever. As I buried myself in this memory of him, the air around me grew softer and warmer. He was drawing close to me, surrounding me. Static caressed my face. Yes, this was him. Tingles ran up my spine. It was tantalizing, orgasmic — this melting into his presence and the bliss it promised, relaxing on a deep exhalation, releasing into my subtle body to intensify the sensations and …

HONK!

A guy in an SUV who was looking for a parking spot shouted out his window, "You leaving?"

I pulled out, and went home. I was exhausted and hungry. I ate lightly, drank some tea, ran a bath, watched *Wings of Desire* again, and went to bed wrapped up in the comfort of his embrace.

I wanted to be free of the weight I was carrying to reexperience the bliss of interbeing that I'd only barely touched in that moment in the car, so I spent the second week of this practice allowing uncomfortable feelings to arise until I could observe them without judgment and let them go. It's easier to be angry than look at our scary places, easier to find distractions than look at our own underbelly. But I had to navigate through these dark, scary places. The sooner I did, I knew, the sooner I'd be free to really be.

The priest had threatened my right to independent thought, I realized. He had stolen my peace and my pleasure. This wasn't new. It was old. Very old. Triggers stemming from the authority of nuns and priests in my childhood who told us what to think. Over many days, I watched my reaction to the Polish priest arise and eventually came to let it go. The rageaholic had stolen human decency and dignity and destroyed my tranquility. I could see now that I was letting people steal my peace. I was absorbing their issues. I needed to learn to hold my space and peace for myself, in myself, no matter who was ranting or raging. I needed to sit, be calm, and allow it to be, and let it go without judgment.

One morning, I climbed off my cushion after an early morning sit, which was the only ritual I had to replace St. Stan's. I shuffled into the kitchen and had just made tea when an enormous comma with two dots on the outer side of the curve popped into my mind.

What on earth is that?

He showed me nothing more.

Another assignment, something new to investigate.

I fired up my MacBook to try to decipher his message. I drew it in my notebook, photographed it, and dropped it into Google's image search. Google returned an F clef, the sign at the beginning of a musical staff that determined the pitch of the notes that followed.

I don't know what to do with that.

I could feel him by me, quiet, waiting for me to follow the story.

I refilled my mug, leaned against the sink to think, then sat back on my stool and searched for the clef. I read that it was an old and rarely used clef, mostly found in vocal music scores and last associated with Leipzig composer Heinrich Schütz. The German connection had relevance. Heinrich Schütz turned out to be an early seventeenth-century composer and one of the most important to emerge from Germany before Bach. He was best known for his sacred music, ranging from solo voice with instrumental accompaniment to a cappella choral music. Amazon music had a clip of his called *Selig sind die Toten*, which Google translated as "Blessed are the Dead."

Speaking

I downloaded the MP3 of *Selig sind die Toten* on Amazon Music for eighty-nine cents and clicked play. For the next four minutes and twenty seconds, the most beautiful choral singing I'd ever heard poured from my speakers — rich, delicate, and haunting.

Liebling, angel, you've given me back the music!

The next morning after a deliciously long uninterrupted sleep, I woke to hear Johann singing something in my mind.

... ... I am, I am, ... I am.

It sounded familiar, but I couldn't place it.

What is it? Something, something, I am, I am. Something, something, I am.

I rolled over and replayed the fragment in my head.

This will drive me crazy.

I showered and went out to Forest Natural for coffee and breakfast. The day was lightly overcast, and the tiny water droplets in the cool air felt fresh on the breath. The forecast said fifty percent chance of rain. I remembered Johann telling Tommy that meant it would rain on every other block. "No way," the child protested, and we laughed.

I was sitting at an outside table churning the beat over in my head like an itch I couldn't scratch when Roisin passed by with her stroller.

"Are you in pain?" she asked.

I laughed. "No, I've a song stuck in my head. Where are you going?"

"I'm taking Sean to the pediatrician," she said. "Do you want to come over for dinner this week?"

"Sure. When?"

"Saturday, maybe. I'll text you." She pushed her stroller on. "What's the song?"

"I don't know. It goes 'something, something, I am, I am, something, something, I am.'"

"I'm Henry the Eighth, I am, I am," she said. "It's from *Ghost*. Remember, Patrick Swayze sings it to keep Whoopi Goldberg awake."

"Oh right! Yeah, that's right."

"Okay, I'm off. See you later."

Henry the Eighth was stuck in my head.

I tried searching for the song on my old phone, but that thing was on its last legs. I didn't want to replace it because all of Johann's texts were in it, but it was a dinosaur. T-Mobile on Manhattan Avenue was selling the new iPhone, so I went in and got one and sat in McCarren

Park to set it up. It was a huge improvement, but the comfort of having his texts in my pocket was gone. Another little piece of our past gone. It shouldn't have mattered, but it did.

I opened the browser on the iPhone and searched YouTube for Patrick Swayze and Henry the Eighth and clicked play. That was the song all right. I looked closely at Swayze. There was a resemblance; a similar build and hair color. When the clip ended, I opened the phone's browser and searched for Johann's name. I'd done this a lot since he died, as if I could find him somewhere in Google. Nothing new had ever shown up. Until today. Google returned an Ancestry.com listing of his death record. The blood drained from my face. That very moment made his death official. One little listing put a period at the end of his life: born, died, and relegated to the ancestral tree, just like that. With my stomach lurching, I clicked the link. It loaded a sign-up page for Ancestry.com membership. To the right, it showed a sample of the type of record I could access were I a member. I zoomed in. The sample was the death record of Patrick Swayze.

I burst out laughing.

People looked at me. I didn't care. They had no idea that he'd just shaken me out of the past and out of my pessimism.

Thank you, Liebling. I love you forever.

Static flickered across my face and caressed my eyes like little kisses.

Over the next week or two, bit by bit, person by person, circumstance by circumstance, I learned to let things go — not to get caught in either the shadows of my own psyche or the darkness of others. It was desperately hard work that required constant vigilance, until finally, one night, I came to the realization that the only real way out of the darkness was through self-compassion and forgiveness for all my wrongdoings, real, imposed, and misperceived. It was shame, self-blame, self-criticism that kept me hooked in negative places. Yet, he saw all of me and didn't judge or criticize. He seemed to understand that I was just like everyone else, struggling and suffering and doing my best. He knew that I didn't want to be angry or jealous or spiteful or hopeless. He knew I wanted to be happy, and he was doing his best to contribute to my happiness. I wanted to be bright and open so that I could meet him in that state of interbeing of which Master Hanh spoke, the place where we could leave ego aside and be one. I wanted to learn to meet him at the depth and breadth of love that he could reach.

Speaking

I sounded like a Sixties bumper sticker — God is love, the universe is love, you are love — but I had to admit that those hippies were right. Love is why every day millions of people shared clips of animals being rescued and stories of the triumph of the human spirit against the odds. It's why we feel good when we perform random acts of kindness or see others do the same.

We rise by lifting others, I realized, but to do this, we must first be kind to ourselves.

For the first time in my life, I was beginning to truly understand the essence of love.

Later that week, I cleared some space to be quiet and focused. I cleaned and tidied the apartment, took out the garbage, showered, and dressed in comfy clothes. I closed the blinds to shade my space, put on some music to neutralize the traffic noise, and lit the scented candle I'd bought from Monique. It took some time, but the energy of the apartment calmed down. I clicked play on a digital download I found of an old Glyn Edwards recording on what he called "sitting in the power." How great it would be, I thought, to do this well. It would make communicating with Johann so much easier.

Whether it was his old-school, upper crust British accent or the seventies organ music with the occasional simulated sound of waves or his frequent reference to "this side of the tape" and "the other side of the tape," listening to Glyn Edwards was like stepping out of time. He talked about spirit communication being natural not supernatural and how it was important to approach it in an intelligent and rational way. I loved his unpretentiousness. I expected him to talk about expanding the power to enhance the mediumistic faculty for spirit contact, but he focused on mediumship not as an end in itself but as a vehicle for healing and personal development. His philosophy seemed to be consistent in many ways with the Buddha dharma on non-reactivity and non-attachment.

Glyn's version of sitting in the power started off much like any form of meditation: sitting straight, getting comfortable, focusing on the breath, letting thoughts go as they arise, not trying to control them, but not letting them control me. Once settled in the silence, he offered three sentences to be repeated like mantras and allowed to sink into the subconscious without questioning: I am spirit. Repeat five times. God's presence and power is within me. Repeat five times. I am one with the spirit world. Repeat five times.

"Expansion moves you out of the room you're resting in. It allows you blend with nature, the birds, the grass, trees, sky, sun, rain. Listen into the distance, into the whispers of life, the cries of humanity, and the demands of men," he said. "Expand out and relate to the power that is. Recognize that power is flowing back and blending with you. Expand more to feel the power of God in nature. Recognize this is flowing back to you. Expand into the universe. Recognize the vastness and the limitlessness of space, and feel that flowing back to you. Everything will come to you in this stillness."

I hadn't tried to expand the light around me this much before, but I followed along. With each breath, it grew bigger until I felt myself pouring into the room, and then the block, and then the sky, and then into a vast white space.

Something shifted. My center of gravity changed. I wasn't physically moving, but it felt as if my upper body was shifting to the right and then to the left. My hands seemed to float upwards. This was the subtle body I'd briefly experienced before, and it was expanding beyond my physical limits. It was a liberating, exhilarating.

Johann emerged from the light and stood in front of me in the royal blue shirt and jeans he wore in a photo taken on West Street. Not only could I see him more clearly than ever, I could feel him more strongly, as if he were out there and within me at the same time, as if he were separate and the same. He handed me a small, black and white, heart-shaped box tied with a ribbon. It had tiny red hearts and lines of handwriting that read: "I love you from the bottom of my heart. I love you more than you know."

Liebling, that is beautiful.

His presence felt gentle and joyful. He smiled and took my hand, his touch an electrifying sensation, as if every neuron in my hand was excited. He drew so close that his essence began to touch mine, sending energy tingling along my spine, energizing me, leaving me with the lightest most wonderful sense of belonging to something greater than me, something greater than both of us together. The experience lasted for just a second before I ran out of energy, and the white space around me collapsed.

Liebling, that was extraordinary.

I fell asleep that night absorbed in the bliss of his presence. It was a remarkable experience, that blending. There was a knowing beyond the body into the essence of him. He wasn't beside me as he had been in life; now, it felt as if we were occupying the same space. His essence was pouring into mine. I felt complete, connected, and loved beyond measure.

Ram Dass once said, "... just love until you and the beloved become one." This was how his presence felt in those fleeting moments: beyond the most intimate moment we'd ever had.

Liebling, I've never felt happier in my life.

Purpose

*What brings order in the world is to love and
let love do what it will.*

Jiddu Krishnamurti

"In town for weekend. Let's meet!"
My phone beeped with an early morning text from my friend
Justin. I hadn't seen him for a few years, not since he moved to LA to
break into television. I was still feeling sensitive and not particularly sociable
after my intense inner journeying over the previous few weeks. I was sitting
in the power each evening and added a yoga practice, which kept me bit
more grounded than I had been floating about in the ether. Still, death can
make people uncomfortable, and the idea of having a catch-up conversation
that would have to include Johann's death, without talking about what had
been happening, sounded like a torturous amount of awkwardness and
dishonesty. I didn't imagine Justin would be open to what I had learned.
It's a tough story to sell when you're known as a hard-nosed skeptic. "That
poor woman," I expected people to say, "she had such promise, but her
fiancé died and she lost her marbles. She thinks he's sending her messages
from the heavens." I was annoyed with myself. I was creating new secrets
and shadows from ego and self-consciousness. Johann was making every
effort to show me that I was loved and not alone, and my response was to
cave in the face of social pressure like a primate afraid of being devoured
by a predator should I be ostracized from the tribe. Roisin was a believer,
so telling her didn't count, but had I the courage to risk being labeled a

crackpot by people who had neither my knowledge nor experience to make a cognizant assessment? Crazy was feeling diminished by other people's uninformed opinions, so in that sense, yes, I was crazy.

Justin and I lay propped up on our elbows in Sheep's Meadow in Central Park, making the most of the early spring day, talking for hours about his boyfriend Donny, his job, my job (or lack of one), life in New York, life in Los Angeles, dancing around what Justin thought was the elephant in the room — Johann's death — and me dancing around the real elephant in the room — that we don't die, at least not in the way we traditionally define death. We rambled up to the Alice in Wonderland statue, with me hedging around the subject, trying to gauge his response if I told my tale. He was leaning against the White Rabbit, and I was sitting on the Mad Hatter's mushroom when I outted myself.

"Here's the thing Justin, when Johann died, things started creaking and moving around. Creatures were showing up and electronics were turning on by themselves, so I went to a priest and a grief counsellor, and then to the hospital of a nineteenth-century psychic, and then to a Spiritualist minister, and then read everything I could find, and learned that, well, we don't actually die. It turns out the body dies, but what is us — our consciousness — that exists independently of the brain."

There was a long pause, plenty of time to project my paranoia into his expression.

"And if that's not enough," I added hesitantly, "now I'm picking up living people's thoughts and moods, and he's showing me hearts every morning except for the other morning when he sent me on a search for an obscure seventeenth-century German composer."

I searched his expression for a response.

"Interesting," he said.

We burst out laughing.

"I'm serious," I said.

"I believe you. I totally believe spirits are around."

"You're the second friend who said that," I said.

"Why did he send you looking for a German composer?" he asked.

Of all the questions he could have asked, that was not the one I expected. I told him about the tenor in Virginia and the soprano in Brooklyn, how much comfort they gave me and how the parish priest ruined it. I walked him through the steps of my search for the F clef and how it led me to the German choral singing, which I now had in a playlist along with Henry the Eighth.

"He really gets you, doesn't he?" Justin said.

"How so?"

"The journalist bit, right? He's giving you clues because he knows you'll follow the trail to get the story."

"Right. I hadn't thought of it like that."

Brains ticking.

"Amazing," Justin said. "Your relationship dynamic is the same."

"Yes," I said.

"That's amazing."

"Free at noon," read the text from Justin the next morning. "Meet at Met? I'm UES."

Justin was sitting on the steps of the Met when I arrived.

"You want to sit in the park?" I asked him. "It's warm for spring."

"Yeah, sure."

We had only just sat on a bench in the park when the image of a woman flashed into my head and disappeared. I didn't know who she was. This wasn't from Johann. It felt different. And it wasn't just an image, there was feeling with it, mixed feelings, as if she'd layered information into one picture and then disappeared, leaving me to unravel her story while Justin chattered away.

"You think if Donny died, would he come back to haunt me?" Justin asked.

"Johann doesn't haunt me."

"You know what I mean."

"I do," I said before continuing apprehensively. "Hey, do you know a middle-aged woman, about sixty, with medium-length, white, curly hair. She's thin and she wears a blue dress with white flowers?"

"No. Why?"

"I don't know. I don't know her. I thought you might. She feels complicated. Serious and relaxed at the same time, like she's determined to let me know she feels peaceful, which sounds contradictory, but it's hard to describe."

"Oh, you mean a *dead* woman?"

"Well, yeah."

He chewed on this for a while. "My friend's mother was fifty-eight. She had bleached blonde hair that was almost white. It was totally straight, but she hated it, so she was always curling it. She was thin, yeah. But I don't know about a blue dress with white flowers. She died of suicide last year, so sad, yeah, that'd make sense."

I felt a sense of relief flood through me. I knew those were her feelings.

Something darted past him, headed for me, and hovered a couple of feet from my head.

"My goodness," I said. "It's a hummingbird. It's a tiny, brown and red hummingbird."

It shot off.

"Did you see that?" I asked. "I've never seen a hummingbird up close before."

"Yeah, me neither," he said. "That was cool."

"They move really fast."

We looked for it, but it was long gone.

"You know, I do think that woman is my friend Anabel's mother," he said. "I'll call Anabel and check."

"You're going to tell her some person you had lunch with saw her dead mother in the park?" I said. "It's a bit insensitive, no?"

"I'll handle it," he said. "I'll call you and let you know how it goes."

Home alone that evening, I had only made some tea and curled up on the sofa to read when my phone rang.

"Hi, I spoke to Anabel," Justin said.

"Please say you didn't upset her."

"No, I didn't, but you won't believe this," he said. "I told you it's a year since her mother died, right? The doctors had tried different medications, but nothing was working, so she stopped taking everything without telling anyone and ended up overdosing. Anabel and her father have been in a bad way for the last year. I think they feel really guilty for not helping her, you know? Anyway, when I called her, she was at her father's house clearing out her mother's wardrobe, and at the same time that we were in the park she had taken out her mother's favorite dress and tried it on. Guess what?"

"What?"

"It's blue with white flowers."

"Are you serious?"

"She started crying," he said.

"Oh no!"

"Wait, there's more. Her father came into the room when we were on the phone, and she filled him in. Then he took the phone and told me that his wife loved hummingbirds. She had feeders all over the garden."

"No way!"

"Yeah. Amazing. So, I told them you said she was peaceful and that she was determined to get through to you to tell you this," he said. "So, they're totally relieved. You took a huge weight of their shoulders."

"Wow," I said. "I don't know what to say."

What an orchestration! Since her husband and daughter wouldn't have gone to a medium of their own volition and Justin didn't have any other mediumistic friends, Anabel's mother had not only waited a year for an opportunity to get a message to them, she had to wait until a friend of her daughter met up with a friend of his whose ability to hear or see her had only recently been reawakened. Had Justin and I met a year ago, it couldn't have happened. Had we not met that afternoon, Anabel wouldn't have been trying on her favorite dress at the same time. Had we been indoors and not in the park, we wouldn't have seen the hummingbird. The preparation that went into stacking up all of those elements to make this message happen in that way was astounding.

"That's a great gift you have." Justin said. "You should do something with it. You could help a lot of people."

I was delighted to have been able to help. I was also delighted that Justin hadn't known the information I gave him. Glyn Edwards said that all our memories are stored in our aura and that a psychic can pluck those out and offer them up as information from the spirit world without being in contact with the person in spirit form at all. But I couldn't have gotten this information from Justin because he didn't have it to give. It had to have come from Anabel's mother. That little fact eliminated any modicum of doubt I may have had that the continuation of consciousness was real, and it boosted my confidence in an innate ability to communicate mind-to-mind immensely. Not only had I helped Anabel's mother, she had helped me. I reflected on the day's events late into the night, immensely gratified to have been able to help.

What do you think, Liebling?

Johann popped the image of a little doll wearing a pointy hat into my mind

A witch? I laughed. *You're funny.*

Peter's Reiki healing share was packed into the large room at the Edgar Cayce Center in Chelsea. Bertie was sitting up front, getting a buzz going, while Peter ushered the latecomers into the room. I had been looking forward to this.

"Welcome, welcome, welcome, find a seat. Any seat," he said.

A woman asked the people on either side of an empty chair if it were free.

"That's Uncle Aloysius's seat," Peter said. "Take it. He won't mind."

They laughed. The spirit of Uncle Aloysius taking empty seats in his nephew's healing events was Peter's little joke. I smiled at Bertie and sat at the end of a long row next to the only empty chair in the room. Peter started his routine of relaxing from your nose to your toes and inviting the healing energies to flow. I settled into the peaceful space that the Reiki healing creates. On each breath, I took in healing from the universe for me, and on each exhalation, I sent it across the world to wherever it was needed. After about fifteen minutes of this, my attention was drawn to the chair beside me. Energy was building. Someone was there. It wasn't Johann. It didn't feel like him.

Uncle Aloysius?

A large bunch of daffodils were shoved into my mind, followed by the image of a tiny woman in a long pink dress, and what looked like a Victorian maid's day cap. Definitely not Uncle Aloysius. She sat in a BarcaLounger and flipped up the footrest to show that her tiny feet barely reached it. I felt her laugh. She was funny in a Yoda sort of way. I could tell she took adversity in her stride, and I sensed she'd known plenty of adversity. Next, she showed me a large animal, a dog maybe, a really big dog. Then as fast as she arrived, she, her chair, and her dog were gone.

Peter was in full flow, and I did my best to settle in to a half-hour sizzle in his violet flame and Reiki frequencies, but I was curious about this woman. She felt quirky and vibrant. I wanted to know who she was, but I got nothing more from her. Afterwards, Peter went around the room asking people what they experienced. Most shared sensations like heat, tingles, shivers, and cold.

"Anyone have anything else?" he asked.

I deliberated. I was a stranger in a large, cliquish group that had clearly been meeting for a long time. My experience made me feel like even more of an outsider. They were giving and receiving healing, but me, the odd one at the end, brought a dead person. Maybe I could just stay quiet or at the very least admit to tingles or shivers like everyone else. No, I couldn't do that. That woman came to me to give her a voice. That was more important than my own fear of looking foolish.

"Okay, then," he said, moving on.

I raised my hand.

134

"Yes?" he said.

"I had someone's grandmother."

All the heads in the long row turned to look at me, some with interest and some, it seemed, in bemusement.

"Excellent," he said. "Whose grandmother was it?"

I explained what I'd seen and the feelings I'd sensed.

"Is this anyone's grandmother?" he asked the room.

No one answered. One by one, I watched their anticipation of some sort of supernatural event fade and all of them turn away, interest lost.

"Maybe she just needed some healing, so she came to our Reiki share," Peter said.

The group accepted this as a plausible explanation. Peter had allowed me to save face. They probably didn't think I was a crackpot, but that's how I felt. If that woman were really communicating with me, why would she want me to speak for her in a room where she wasn't known? Maybe she didn't come at all. Maybe I made her up.

We were given a ten-minute break. I was snacking on a bag of pretzels in the kitchen, feeling small and stupid, when an Asian woman in her late twenties sidled up to me.

"Hi, I'm Meera," she said, reaching out her hand.

"Karen," I said, wiping pretzel salt on my pants.

"I think that was Nonny, my grandmother," she said. "She was tiny, and she had a great sense of humor. She had white hair that she combed back into a tight bun, so I could see how it would look like a cap. And she had a pink dress that she loved. She wore it all the time. I hardly remember her not wearing it."

Meera smiled.

I wanted to hug her on the spot. "I am really glad you know her," I said.

Peter was talking with someone nearby, half listening to them, half listening in.

"I was thinking about her this morning," Meera said. "My boyfriend broke up with me last night, and I was sitting in the garden looking at the daffodils and thinking about her. I missed her so much."

"Ah, she was there with you," I said. "That's why she brought you daffodils."

"That's beautiful." Meera said. "Thank you so much."

She took a handful of cards out of her bag. "Here," she said, signing one. "Let me do something for you. I'm a cop, and this is a Police Benevolent Association card. If you ever get into trouble with the cops or get a ticket, show them this, and they should help you out."

"Great," I said. "Thank you."

She was squeezing past Peter to get to the bathroom when I remembered a detail.

"What about the huge dog? Did you understand that?"

"Oh no, it wasn't a dog," she said. "It was a donkey. Oh my God, she loved that donkey."

She was still chuckling when she closed the bathroom door.

"That's some lightwork you're doing," Peter said. "Do you work as a medium?"

"Not at all," I said.

"Well, you should," Peter said. "There are lots of folks out there trying to reach their kids or their partners or whoever. Lots of folks and lots of fakes, but you're the real deal. You should do the lightwork."

"You're the second person who told me that," I said.

"Then take that as a sign from the Divine," he said.

At home in bed, I curled up in the comfort of Johann's presence.

That was unexpected, Liebling. I'm delighted we were able to help Meera and Nonny.

I fell to sleep with his tantalizing energy tingling along my spine, but at 3:00 a.m., I woke abruptly in an entirely different mood. Peter's and Justin's words lay heavy in my mind: Do this for strangers out there in the world for all to see and all to see and judge? No, I wasn't comfortable with that. For months, my entire focus had been on learning this language to maintain a continuing bond with Johann. I'd attended classes, not to develop the ability to work with others, but to find answers to questions about us and how to be in this relationship. I was a journalist not a medium. I'd identified as a materialist and an atheist my whole adult life. I'd gravitated toward Zen because it was non-theistic and because mediation practice would help me manage my own life. I'd neither the courage nor interest to advocate publicly that there was an afterlife and not only was it possible to communicate with it, I, the erstwhile cynic, could mediate that conversation. Who would believe me? I wouldn't have believed it had he not sat on my bed, squeezed my shoulder, and turned on my electronics. How could I expect those who hadn't my experiences to believe? I knew what I'd be up against. I'd be ridiculed by people like the old me. Added to that, I'd be stepping into the sensitivity of others' grief, and representing their deceased loved ones. What if I got it wrong? What if I upset or harmed someone? No, this wasn't for me. If someone like Nonny or Anabel's mother came along and I could help, well and good, but that was it. I knew I was caving to the pressure of other people's opinions, but I didn't care. I couldn't be the person Peter or Justin wanted me to be. It was too far from the image I'd constructed around who I believed myself to be.

I know you're here. I know you have something to say.
Grow.
Okay, I'm small. I know. I don't care.

I tried to kid myself that there was self-compassion and self-protection in a choice to hide out together in this space between worlds and let no one else in, but when I was still tossing and turning at 5:00 a.m., I knew there wasn't.

Then he whispered.
Offering.
Offering? Did you say "offering"? What do you mean "offering"?
He said no more.

After another hour or so, I fell into a heavy sleep and woke into a lucid dream.

It was dark, and I was gliding along on the back of a large, purple butterfly whose wings moved almost imperceptibly toward the dawn breaking over the horizon. I could hear the faint hum and swish of the wings in flight, and I could feel the comfort of Johann's presence beside me: the tingles of his energy along my spine, soothing my mind, and guiding me forward.

I turned to see his vibrant face.
Liebling, I know I have to do better.
You do.
I should really get over myself and help other people.
Silence.
Was Nancy right when she said our dharma was to walk together between worlds?
Yes.
And that maintaining our bond and mediating for others are fused?
Yes.
And that's the offering?
Yes.

I leaned into his chest, becoming one with him, feeling his arms wrapped around me, feeling that I belonged.

The butterfly glided toward the breaking dawn, and my field of vision was soon flooded with bright morning sunlight.

Okay, Liebling. I'm in. I'll do my best. I promise.

Reason

Each soul that moves out of darkness into the light,
out of ignorance into knowledge, out of superstition into truth,
is helping to advance the world.

Silver Birch

I felt lighter. Johann and I had a new purpose together. I'd offloaded the 800-pound gorilla. I'd faced the monster of secrets, and fear, and shame in that putrid basement. Life was finally looking bright, and I was happy again.

I'd no idea how much more darkness was yet to come.

My existential perspective was broadening, but my social life was shrinking. Justin had gone back to LA, Peggy to Minnesota, and Roisin was beset by the unpredictability of life with a toddler. The rest of my friends would be railing over three bottles of wine about the Arab Spring or the economic crisis in Europe. Since they were all liberals, heated discussion with forceful opinions would rage, and by the end of the night everyone would be in agreement, largely because they had been from the start. I had nothing new to add to the news reports. My news involved the spontaneous arrival of discarnate spirits. I could see that story sinking like the Greek economy. I could see their muted response while they pondered whether that was something I'd actually said, and then decide it hadn't been. If I were to admit what I'd experienced to most of my friends, the backlash would be fierce. The more rational would think me crazy; no doubt, I'd lose a lot of respect in their eyes. Still, except for Peter's Reiki group, I was pretty isolated. I needed to meet people who shared my experiences or who had knowledge that would enhance my understanding. I needed to meet like-minded people, and I definitely needed a good teacher.

A church or center like Rev. Cutler's in Virginia seemed like a good idea. The one Spiritualist church I found in the City only offered séances on Sunday. A séance sounded interesting. I imagined evocative evenings in fashionable Victorian parlors, where the well-to-do, such as Mary Todd, Sir Arthur Conan Doyle, and Queen Victoria, gathered around tables in dark rooms. I imagined a mysterious medium in lace and silk calling out to the spirit world, asking for the son or husband or mother of someone present to join them in their darkened room that smelled of incense and was shrouded in mystery and shadows. The Victorians were wowed and titillated by their brush with immortality; they were fascinated with the prospect of eternal life. Leading thinkers busied themselves with paranormal investigations and existential questioning. Specialist newspapers were filled with accounts of table rappings and tippings and levitation. Sadly, these darkened rooms were also a breeding ground for fraud and extortion and crooks who preyed on human frailty, which gave the pursuit of truth and legitimate mediums, present and future, a bad name.

In all likelihood, the séance in the Spiritualist church in the City was nothing like a Victorian parlor. Still, it didn't appeal to me. As a society, we had reached a new level of sophistication. The space age had given us a new understanding of the cosmos and our place in it. We were in the quantum information age and on the brink of quantum computing. Quantum reality forced us to question the nature of everything we took to be real and question the very existence of absolute, objective truth. It made us see the world as weird, spooky, uncertain, and marvelous. We had made huge advances in neuroscience and developed new theories of consciousness. In medicine, we had resuscitation techniques that brought people back to life after much longer periods than had been possible before, which offered a tome of research on near-death experiences, much of which couldn't be explained in material terms. In short, we had evolved. So, while speaking to disembodied spirits in the dark sounded like a terrific if not dramatic experience, I wanted to get away from theatrics and superstition. I was struggling to come to terms with mediumship at all. If I were to do it well, I needed to find a supportive and progressive community and use whatever ability I had to help people, explore my own existential questions, and live in a state of interbeing and common purpose with Johann.

A search on Meetup found a six-week class series on psychic and mediumship development starting at the Manhattan Metaphysical group. It was to be held at a dance studio on West 30th, directly opposite the Edgar Cayce Center. I signed up right away. Since it called itself a metaphysical group, I presumed it would also be concerned with the fundamental nature of reality and questions of what is real, which meant they might have some great answers.

A picture of Bambi flashed into my mind, clear and swift, the way of all visual communications from Johann.

Bambi? Why Bambi? Am I a fawn to the slaughter?

He didn't respond with his usual levity, which made me uneasy. After all, Bambi ran into a lot of problems before he reached his happy ending.

The dance studio was small, but its large north-west facing windows captured the evening sun that reflected on the bright white walls and varnished floor, which made it seem light and spacious. Semi-sheer curtains fell across wall-to-wall mirrors and cupboards hid green cleaning supplies that left a residue of eucalyptus and lemon dancing on the air.

"Come in, take a seat," Tina said.

She was an interesting character, Tina. She busied herself with organization, which gave her an air of authority, but I sensed underneath that she wasn't too comfortable in her own skin. Her bio didn't say much except that she had been a working medium for over ten years and taught classes at various centers in the tristate area. I didn't know what to look for in a teacher at the time, so I really didn't know if this was a good place to start.

I sat on the empty folding chair in the middle of a group of eight — six women and two men — and smiled to the few who looked my way. Tina took a roll call: Bradley, a gay man who could pass for Nathan Lane if he had more humor and less hubris; Diana, a friendly woman in her fifties whose skin hung off her thin frame, making her look much older than her years; Lucas, a thirty-something gay man, who rarely raised his head as if he didn't want to be pulled from his inward gaze to suffer the violence of the outside world; two women who came together and sat together, Emily and Kate, who seemed open to new experiences; Carla, a twenty-something drama queen, who already had to change chairs and take an emergency call; Hannah, another middle-aged woman who sat firm-faced and tight-lipped, nodding occasionally as if she knew something the rest of us didn't; and me, who had formed snap impressions of everyone, just, I suspected, as had they. Their experience ranged from Bradley's and Hannah's five or so years to everyone else's one or two, except for me who, at that time, had only a collection of spontaneous incidences.

Tina explained that each evening for the next six weeks would be structured to include meditation, psychic exercises to get information about the living, and mediumship exercises to communicate with the departed. This would mean learning to use our clairvoyance, clairsentience, and clairaudience, or our ability to psychically see, sense, and hear. Since discarnate spirits use these senses to communicate, she said, we would parlay those abilities into spirit communication in the second half of each class. Tina didn't include reading and study or place any emphasis on personal development or self-healing as Rev. Cutler had done, which surprised me. It seemed that would be necessary to do this work without issues and shadows. Hadn't Silver Birch said, "We strive to get as close as we can, but our proximity is dependent upon your atmosphere, your growth, your evolution"?

We partnered up to do "divination exercises," which was what Tina called them. I was with Diana. She was kind, and I liked her. We had to read the colors of each other's auras or energy field and interpret them. It was fun once I stopped trying to squint to see her aura and sense it intuitively instead. Baby blue. Definitely. And a little yellow. Soft spoken and gracious I interpreted, a good communicator, slow to argue, quick to placate, but sometimes felt overwhelmed or disempowered by others thinking she was a pushover because she didn't push back. She understood. She saw red and purple in me, pulled between the physical and spiritual worlds, she said, and conflicted between my rational mind and my need for spiritual growth. We giggled back there in our corner after learning that we could understand each other by looking into our invisible energy fields — the same energy field, I realized, I had been expanding to feel Johann's embrace.

We switched partners and did the exercise a few more times with varying success. I noticed the chemistry was different with different people and that their own openness and self-awareness played a role in whether the information was right or not. It was easier to get practical details when sitting with Emily and hard to get beyond vague feelings with Lucas. I saw lots of color with Carla. It was much like any interpersonal dynamic. We gravitate to different people in our regular five-sense world too. We understand some better than others. I assumed this would be the case with discarnate spirits; presumably, we could understand or misunderstand them too.

After a ten-minute break, Tina told us to pair up to work with spirit communication. Hannah plopped herself down in front of me. She shuffled to the edge of her chair and leaned toward me.

"Okay," she said. "I have a young man here. He's tall. He's very close to you. Is this your brother?"

"No."

"Is it a romantic relationship?"

"Yes."

"Yes, I thought so."

She just said brother.

"Did he live by the ocean."

"Eh ... sort of. On the East River."

"I also feel a heart condition with him."

"Yes."

"Was he very sociable?"

"Yes."

"Yes," she said. "I can see that."

She was staring at me intently, as if she were searching for answers in my expressions. She was also asking a lot of questions, and I was giving her quite a bit of information.

Are you really communicating with her?

"He has a lot of love for you," she said.

She sat back in her chair.

"How long has he been in spirit?" she asked.

"Less than a year."

I was hoping she had something positive to tell me as Iris had done.

"Ah," she said. "He wants you to move on."

"What?"

"They find new loves in the spirit world, you know, so he has a new love and has moved on and you should too," she said.

"That can't be right," I said.

"Sweetie, they try to tell us this, but we don't listen. You're holding him back with your grief. He's stuck here because he has to take care of you. I've seen it all before."

"Where are you getting this from?" I asked. "He's gone to extraordinary lengths to show me how our relationship can continue, and he's given me a new purpose in my life."

"That's how you see it, sweetie. He's trying to move you forward, but it's by yourself not with him. You need to let him go before you harm him."

"Harm him?"

"He has a new relationship there, but you're not letting him go to be happy."

I should have known better than to believe what I was hearing, but she was like a rat picking at a scab. Some deep-seated fear was sparked in me. Could I be holding him back and harming him with my neediness? And what of this new love? Why would he tell me he loved me forever and then find a new love? No, this made no sense.

Hannah sat there with a smug know-it-all smile that I had a sudden yearning to slap.

"Is your husband alive?" I asked Hannah.

"Yes," she said.

"Do you think he would leave you after less than a year in spirit form?"

"I don't know," she said.

"How long have you been married?"

"Twenty-three years."

"And you don't know whether he would want to continue a relationship with you?"

"I don't think it's healthy to keep in touch that often," she said, shifting the focus off herself.

"We used to send each other text messages all day when he was in physical form," I said. "That's what sharing thoughts on and off all day is like. It's like sending little texts to touch each other's mind. That doesn't hold anyone back."

"It's still harmful."

"Says who?"

"Listen," she said. "I'm sure your husband will stay until you don't need him anymore."

"I'm sure yours will too," I said.

I was abrasive and angry. Reactive. It was Nadia all over again. I thought I had grown since then. Why was I triggered like this?

Liebling, why is she saying this?

If he responded, I couldn't hear. I was unsettled, disturbed, in no place to be receptive.

Tina told us to switch for one last practice session. I don't know how I ended up with Bradley, but I did. Aside from hauling around about sixty extra pounds and his questionable dress sense for a man his age, he looked perfectly normal, but his haughtiness made me uneasy. Then again, I was feeling uneasy in general since my exchange with Hannah. He rubbed the palm of his hands in circles for some reason and closed his eyes. I didn't know why he kept his eyes closed. Maybe it helped him focus. Maybe people found it mysterious.

"I have a young man here. He went to spirit early. Do you understand?"

"Yes," I said.

"I'm being pulled to my chest area," he said, "and I'm having trouble breathing."

"Yes."

"I see him by water."

"Yes."

"He drowned."

"No."

He opened his eyes.

"No?"

"No."

"Well, he wants to say thank you for being there for him in the end."

"What do you mean?"

"He's saying thank you for being with him when he passed to spirit."

"I wasn't there."

"Well that's what he's saying," Bradley said.

"Does he mean emotionally, as in we were together in the relationship sense?"

Liebling, are you communicating with him, or am I helping him make this fit?

"That must be what he means. He's stepping back now."

Bradley seemed annoyed with me. I didn't want to be ungrateful, but I just didn't feel he was connected as Iris had been, and Iris had been in a different country at the time. It was probably best to just let it go, but Bradley had other ideas.

"You need to pray for him," Bradley added with confidence.

"What?"

"He's earthbound."

"What do you mean?"

"How often does he communicate with you?" he asked.

"Every day."

"Yes, he's holding onto something here and is afraid to go into the light. That's why I had trouble connecting with him properly."

Is he blaming you for his poor mediumship?

"That's an awful thing to say to someone. Would you say that?" I asked.

"That's how he feels," Bradley said. "I've seen it before."

"I can feel how he feels," I said, "and he's not afraid or lost or confused."

Bradley's shrug was dismissive, and it irritated me. He was lording his more extensive experience over me.

Why is he saying this about you?

I felt into the space around me for Johann as I had learned to do, but I couldn't see or hear or sense anything from him.

"People communicate from the spirit world all the time to help the people they love. It's not because they're afraid to go into the light," I said. "I got a message from another medium that he loved me forever." I sounded shrill. I was being defensive. Definitely triggered.

"He might love you forever, but that doesn't mean you're supposed to hang on and make him hang on."

"Where are you getting this from?" I asked.

"I've seen it," he said. "Sometimes suicides or people with violent deaths are earthbound because they can't move on because of what happened."

"I communicated with a woman who committed suicide, and she felt healed. She was full of love for her family."

"That's what you think," Bradley shrugged.

"I didn't think it, I *felt* her," I argued. "Besides, if Johann was stuck, he'd tell me."

Why was I still defending myself? Didn't I know Johann better than him, even in spirit form? Talking to this guy was like drinking out of a firehose. He had an answer for everything. I was off-balance, scrambling, unprepared, and annoyed.

"Not if he was in denial," Bradley said. "That's the problem with earthbound spirits. They can be very convincing like your partner, and so you believe them, but they have unfinished business or they get stuck to their home or where they died or they get attached to people."

"Isn't that the plot of *The Entity*?"

"Be snarky if you want," he said. "But let me ask you this: are you hungry or tired after you're in contact him?"

I remembered how famished I usually was after blending with him in the altered state.

"Hungry, sometimes."

"See?"

"See what?"

"He's not moving on."

"Because I'm hungry?"

"Because he's draining your energy."

"I get that hungry after yoga."

He ignored my protestations.

"What are you two talking about?' Emily whispered. "You're making a lot of noise."

"She has an earthbound spirit with her," Bradley said.

"Oh, that's awful," Emily said. "It's tragic when they end up in an unnatural state like that. Come to our spirit rescue circle, we'll help it cross over."

"No ..." But I didn't know how to finish. The room was stifling. Their faces were too close and their voices too loud. I didn't have enough knowledge or experience to argue. Tina was on her phone out in the hallway, wandering around unsteadily on spindly stilettos that could barely support her robust frame, oblivious to the distress her students were causing.

I walked out and went to the bathroom where I held onto the sink, heart racing, and hands shaking, feeling as if I'd suffered onslaught. I had. I was angry that Bradley and Hannah presumed to know more about Johann and our relationship than me. I felt violated by the intrusion, but underneath the anger, I was worried. They had more experience than me. Was there any chance they could be right? Could I have gotten Johann's continued presence wrong?

Are you here? I can't feel you.

No response. I could feel myself sliding into a negative place, confused, fearful, in too dense a space to sense him at all. Hadn't everyone told me to maintain a high vibration? I felt stupid and powerless, shrouded, disturbed even, not by an unsettled spirit but by the troubled thoughts they'd instilled in me. I went back to the room, got my bag, and went home.

An army of diggers were converting the park outside my childhood home into a huge swimming pool. The grass was gone but the trees were left standing so it looked like a bayou with clear water and a tiled bed. Someone called for swimmers to pull up tufts of grass that were pushing through the tiles. I swam down and tugged on a tuft as hard as I could, but it wouldn't give. I was running out of air. I felt the pressure on my face and the pain of spasms in my diaphragm. I was drowning, but I couldn't let go. My lungs forced a painful intake of air. I woke up gasping.

I probably would have slept better had I taken a shower to wash off that encounter before bed, or sat on my cushion and connected with a positive feeling, or just stayed with my own intuitive understanding of the ongoing dance between the physical and spirit worlds, but I didn't know enough at that time to blow it off. Instead, I ruminated on Bradley's and Emily's words, and the longer I did that, the more they festered in my mind. Lower and lower I went. I knew I wouldn't be able to hear Johann in this state, but I tried anyway.

Can you hear me?

Silence.

Are they right? Are you supposed to move on?

The questions sounded absurd in my head and insulting to ask. But I was rattled. I opened my MacBook and scanned the NDE literature again. In almost every case, the dying people saw the light, gravitated toward it, and were met and welcomed by people they knew who had predeceased them. Some patients recalled conversations in the operating room or events outside that happened while they were technically dead, which meant their experiences were not the imaginings of an oxygen-starved brain. In the literature on deathbed visions, case after case reported how the dying saw their loved ones gather around them at the end. Some saw people they had never known. If the family gathers and no one dies alone, I reasoned, how could someone get lost? Did the whole family come all the way to collect them and then forget about them halfway home? Where is home? It seemed absurd to be adding geography to the unseen worlds of discarnate consciousness, as if we're here and it's over there somewhere with a vacuum in between.

I vacillated between anxiety and anger. Bradley had to be wrong. Johann had been kind and caring. He felt happy. He was loving and loved. But every time I arrived at the conclusion that Hannah's or Bradley's theories were complete nonsense, anxiety whispered in the hollows of my head. Each time I asked, *Are you okay?* Each time I got nothing by way of reply. Was he avoiding answering me, was there a truth there that he didn't want to tell, or was it simply impossible to penetrate the weight of my mind at that time?

Still, a chill crept up my spine. Even the remotest possibility of Johann being distressed caused me alarm.

Had I come across anything about earthbound spirits in my reading? Silver Birch never mentioned them, nor had Andrew Jackson Davis, nor anyone else I'd read for that matter.

I needed more information. A Google search on "earthbound spirits" returned almost 400,000 results, terabytes of information on what they were, what caused them, how to help them or get rid of them, but none of these accounts had reliable sources or credible evidence.

In his epic poem, *The Iliad, Homer wrote about spirits hanging about because of unfinished business, which has* permeated modern film and fiction as spirits failing to "move on" until they tie up loose ends and make for a tidier plot than tackling the continuity of love and consciousness across spheres. The concept seemed to have some relationship to the pneuma of Christian Scriptures, where it was used to denote "demon" but was also a common word for "spirit" or in some contexts, simply an "impure spirit." It also sounded a little like the Buddhists' hungry ghosts, terrible creatures who were said to suffer according to their karma until they atoned for their sins. It also sounded like the Hindu concept that people's misfortune isn't caused by their own irresponsibility but by angry ancestors wandering the earth, heaping financial or mental or physical health problems on them until a holy man does a ritual to release them.

The more I read, the more it seemed that all religions had adopted the idea of the hungry ghost in one form or another. It also seemed that "meddling with the dead" was a power issue — either political, intellectual, or emotional. There was the regimentation of religion to keep us in line with the promise of reward or fear of punishment if we transgressed its rules. There was the power of men over women and the extermination of thousands of women in the fifteenth century who dared to exhibit independent thought or communicate directly with the spirit world without the intervention of the priestly caste.

Talking to the dead always seemed to have negative connotations. It was understandable, I supposed. As a race, we gravitate to the negative to survive. Paranoia is our friend, and since our amygdala prefers a known situation, even if it's scary, to an unpredictable one, it make sense that this would also influence theories about the afterlife. This seemed to feed into the problem of group-think and subjective experiences being passed off as absolutisms. In *American Exorcism, Michael Cuneo wrote that after the release of the movie The Exorcist in 1973, churches were besieged with requests for exorcisms. He* saw hundreds of ordinary people throwing themselves onto the floor, writhing, shrieking, or puking to purge themselves of some perversion. However, he saw no spinning heads or levitating beds or demonic scratch marks appearing on their faces; instead, he saw a lot of emotionally troubled people pleading for a personal transformation and freedom from depression, anxiety, addiction, or sexual appetites.

All I could find in everything I read was the earthbound spirit or spirit attachment concept being passed down the line, reinvented or embellished as it went, without sources or studies or attention to its genesis. The only epistemological thought behind it seemed to be "it must be true."

Was it possible to know anything objectively? How could there be any objective truth about the invisible world when no one even knew what was real in the physical world? Even science hadn't come to a reliable conclusion on the nature of consciousness. Was life a continuum of subjective, ineffable experiences, which in turn gave rise to subjective perception and transmission from one to another? As humans, we tend to interpret new evidence as confirmation of pre-existing beliefs. Confirmation bias the psychologists call it. Had I believed in hauntings and earthbound spirits, would I have splashed about holy water and burned sage when Johann appeared instead of coming to understand what was really happening? Would I have interpreted the gentle souls who appeared in my room in childhood as disturbed entities? Given how malleable is perception, I began to realize that mindfulness, self-reflection, and challenging personal biases is critical to intellectual and spiritual humility. These practices were also critical to avoiding absolutisms, to interpreting events to suit preconceptions, to claiming to know objective truth, and to passing dogma off as knowledge as Bradley had done. Most important, they were critical to the principle of doing no harm.

It was almost four in the morning when I stopped reading, and I had arrived back, more or less, at what I believed based on my own experience before I met Bradley or buried myself in this heinous reading. People did not die alone. People were met by those who love them. People in spirit form wanted to share joy and healing and love. And since I'd learned that people continue to grow and heal in spirit form, it stood to reason that they would want to offer an apology for wrongs they'd committed or express the things they couldn't say in physical form; but if the person here believed the superstitions, it was easy to see that they might misconstrue an attempt to express their love or make amends as threatening.

I was saddened how many times people chose belief systems that robbed them of love and healing whether they were in spirit or physical form. I was also saddened that beautiful stories across all religious and literary traditions of ecstatic experiences were overlooked. God spoke to people, angels appeared in dreams, disciples were filled with the Holy Spirit on the Pentecost. There were accounts of ordinary people experiencing religious ecstasy and euphoric altered states of consciousness and the sense of oneness with God, Brahman, the Tao, the Divine, the Source, the First Cause. There were stories everywhere of the perennial connection between love and death that I had experienced. Surely, anyone claiming the ability to mediate between worlds bore the responsibility of being informed and discriminating and self-reflective enough to act in accordance with these principals. At the very least, surely the first responsibility of one to another was to do no harm.

Something St. Paul had written scratched around my mind. I found it in 1 Corinthians 13. "If I speak in the tongues of men and of angels, but have not love, I am a noisy gong or a clanging cymbal," he wrote. "And if I have prophetic powers, and understand all mysteries and all knowledge, and if I have all faith, so as to remove mountains, but have not love, I am nothing."

Bradley had been the noisy gong and clanging cymbal. There was no love or common sense in what he said. How much better it would have been had he been aware that his beliefs were just his opinion, an interpretation of experiences colored by myth, instead of beating the bereaved with his ego's need to control through absolutisms.

Are you here?

Did I feel Johann caress my eyes? I was so exhausted, I couldn't tell. I put my iPad down and settled into an uneasy sleep.

The dirt walkway up to the mansion wound around a perfectly still black pond that held a mirror to the sky and the Japanese maples and weeping willows hanging overhead. This place had nothing of the peace of a Japanese garden. There were no birds or breeze, and something sinister lay beneath the water. I leaned over to look in. A dense nest of weeds and roots began moving. I stepped back in fright. Two men approached. Government men of some sort. One leaned over the pond. A root shot out of the water, wrapped around his neck, and dragged him in. The other guy and I watched until he was pulled under and his air bubbles stopped breaking the surface.

Hannah appeared beside me. "He met someone else," she said.

Something shrieked.

I woke in fright, not to a message from Johann, which I'd hoped for, but to my phone ringing on my nightstand.

"Come over quick, please!" Roisin said.

"What time is it?"

"It's six-thirty," she said.

"What's wrong?" I asked.

"There's something in my house."

"Call the cops."

"Not that kind of something, an invisible kind of something," she said.

"If it's invisible, how can you tell?"

"Because Sean just took his first step, so I clapped, and I put my hands out to pick him up, but he turned to the space beside me and put his hands up to thin air like he wanted someone I couldn't see to pick him up."

"What do you want me to do?"

"Come over. Find out who's here," she said.

"I'm not a ghostbuster."

"Come on. It won't take long."

"Okay. I'll be there in a few."

I didn't know if I could help her. I hadn't slept much. I felt depleted and my energy was heavy from the volume of reading I'd done on fear and superstition.

Roisin was clutching Sean at the kitchen window by the fire escape when I arrived.

"It's in the living room," she said.

"You think it stayed in the living room when you ran in here?"

"Just go," she said.

I had never initiated contact with a person in spirit form. Until now, they had come to me. I hoped whoever was there would be able and willing to make themselves known to me, despite my gloomy mood. I stepped into the living room and heard one crisp word, delivered with such force that it punched through my anxiety and into my mind.

Martha.

Memories of my Auntie Martha filled my mind, but it couldn't have been my Auntie Martha because she was alive. Nothing else came, except for a subtle feeling of excitement. Was this as Silver Birch had said — one word loaded with preconceptions and associations, only this time not working to confuse the message but working to deliver it?

I went back to the kitchen, hoping I'd understood the woman correctly.

"Nothing?" Roisin asked.

"It's a woman. I think she's your aunt. She's in her late fifties, or she was when she died. She has dark hair, a big voice, and a big personality, and she's about your size and weight," I said. "Do you know her?"

"That's my Aunt Joanie," she said. "How did you get all that so quickly?"

"She said Martha and that's what my Aunt Martha is like."

"Wow, brilliant," she said.

She was elated at first, then grew perplexed.

"Is something wrong?" I asked.

"We had a huge row just before she died. I never spoke to her again. It was really bad because we'd been really close."

She put Sean in his highchair.

"It was almost five years ago," she said. "I can't even remember what that stupid argument was about, but I feel like shit every time I think of her. Even if I remember something nice, the next thing I remember is that argument and her dying and never being able to make up. I thought she'd still be mad at me."

"No, she's not mad," I said. "She felt happy actually. Definitely beyond determined to get that through to me."

"Brilliant," she said. "That's a relief."

She put the kettle on and put out two mugs for tea.

"Why is she here?" she asked.

"Not sure. Maybe she wanted to see the baby take his first step," I said, "since he could see her. Apparently, babies see people in spirit form all the time."

"Jesus, that's brilliant," she said.

"Why were you spooked?" I asked. "You've been listening to me talking about this stuff for months."

"I know," she said. "Probably old wives' tales. It's a bit creepy when it happens to you. You know, there's someone behind you that you can't see. It could be anyone. I was imagining all kinds of bad things. Stupid, isn't it?"

"No," I said. "I've been dealing with that sort of stuff for days. I feel like I've been dragged through a hedge backwards."

"Why? What happened?" she asked.

"Someone in a class told me that Johann was lost and afraid to let go."

"Wow," she said. "Is that true?"

"No," I said. "Well, I don't think so."

"Did you ask him?"

"Yes."

"And?"

"He hasn't answered yet," I said. "They said he met someone else."

"Well, that's just ridiculous," she said.

I sipped my tea.

"Don't tell me you believe that—after all you've been through?"

"No. I don't know. I don't know what to believe," I said.

"Why are you bothering with these people? You just gave me a message from my auntie. You don't need classes, surely."

"I don't think you can just roll out of bed into it," I said. "It's like playing an instrument. You can have great musical potential, but you still have to learn to play. Besides, there's a lot of responsibility, you know. I don't want to unwittingly batter someone with biases or issues. Bereaved people are fragile. I don't want to make anyone feel worse. I've already borne the brunt of that."

"Sounds like it," she said.

"Besides," I went on, "I can only do this because of Johann, so it's important for me to do right by him."

"True," she said.

We sat in silence drinking our tea. Roisin reflecting on Aunt Joanie's visit, happy they were on good terms again and that she was watching over the baby.

"It's brilliant, isn't it?" she said.

"Yes," I said. "Brilliant."

Standing on West 30th in the rain without an umbrella, debating whether it was wise or productive to go back for week two of six, wasn't a smart move. Then again, going back to that class at all wasn't a smart move. I hadn't heard from Johann all week as I'd churned and mulled. But I was loathed to let Bradley and Hannah chase me away.

An old, grey Volvo with Peter Goldbeck at the wheel splashed up to the sidewalk and parked. He rolled down the window.

"Why are you standing there in the rain?" he asked.

"I'm debating whether to go back to a mediumship class I started last week," I said.

"That good, eh?"

"Not great. Are you going to the center?"

"Yeah, I have a healing group tonight. You're welcome to come."

"I might."

I lingered, then turned on my tail and walked into the center for Reiki instead.

It was busy when I stepped out of the elevator. Peter was trying to organize a small room to accommodate the seven or eight people in his private healing group.

"Bertie, Marianne, ah, Karen you're here. Anyone else here for Reiki, follow me," Peter said, clearing a path through the crowd and carrying us along in a current behind him.

This was perfect. I needed to get away from the noise. People with extrasensory abilities and no common sense were hurting my head. I'd barely come out of the closet, and I already wanted to crawl back in.

Our little group sat down to share Reiki — that is, give and receive Reiki healing for ourselves and for those in need around the world. After about twenty minutes of healing meditation, Peter brought us back to the room for what he called a "Reiki mind journey."

"Whatever baggage you're still hanging onto, put it down. You won't need it where you're going," he said. "Okay everyone, settle in and buckle up, we're gonna turn up the frequency."

While we relaxed back into our chairs, with our feet on the floor and our hands on our lap, and all the tension seeping out of us, Peter's voice brought us out of our physical awareness and deep into our imagination, guiding us along paths and then into a world of sound and color and the abstract sense of being free in the ki or chi. I could hear his words, but I wasn't retaining them. They were gliding over me, sweeping me into some part of my subconscious or some part of the altered state I'd never been.

"You've arrived," he said. "Open your mind to see where you are."

I arrived on a white gas planet and stood in the midst of a dense haze.

"Someone is approaching you," Peter said. "Speak to them."

At first, I sensed Johann draw close, but just when I expected to see him, something unexpected happened instead. A large blue fish leaped out of the mist and hung in midair in front of my face as if it were as curious about me as I it before diving back into the gas. It didn't speak, neither did I. What do you say to a blue fish on a gas planet?

A few minutes later, Peter brought us back the way we came, through the colors, the sounds, and back into the room. Then he asked us to open our eyes, have a stretch, and share.

Bertie had a reunion with an old friend long passed. The other two women found themselves in different types of bright, peaceful, otherworldly environments. I shared my encounter with the fish. They laughed, a good-natured laugh. None of it seemed to make any sense, but at least it gave my heaving brain a rest.

On the way home, as I waited on the deserted subway platform for the G, my tiny spark of light began to fade. No matter how hard I tried to ignore them, Hannah's words were festering in my mind. I hadn't heard from Johann since that awful class, and I was worried. It seemed ludicrous given all we had been through that he would just up and meet someone else, but I felt like a Jersey cow, lumbering along, failing to keep up. Was I too slow and too dull?

Is there someone new offering you more than me?

Silence.

Back home, I was exhausted but couldn't sleep. I scrolled through Netflix and came across *Into the Universe with Stephen Hawking*. After the week I'd had, a bit of science and reason sounded like a much-needed respite. Thirty minutes into the episode on aliens, Hawking talked about life forms that might exist on different worlds. In an animated sequence, he showed a creamy gas planet that looked just like the one I'd seen in my mind journey. I got off the sofa and crawled close to the TV, just in time to see a large, blue jellyfish appear out of the gas and float at eye-level on the screen where my large blue fish had been.

"What on earth ...?"

Is this a message from you?

Ja, meine süße.

It's you! You're here. You can hear me. I can hear you!

I only understood the "ja" in the crisp, rapid thought he placed in my head, but that was enough.

You haven't run off with someone else.

I felt his laughter tingle up my spine.

You've no idea of how relieved I am to feel you. Well, yes, actually, you do. But what's this message? You're giving me a message related to science somehow. I don't understand it.

His answer hit me in that sudden knowing sort of way, as if the thought in his mind were simultaneously in mine.

Reason! That's it. Right? Look to reason and not superstition.

I felt him surround me, filling me with that comfort, the feeling of completeness that only he could provide. I'd finally made it home to him after a long, miserable journey.

What I don't understand is why did you let me go through all of this? I asked. *Why didn't you warn me away from those people?*

Soon.

Another infuriatingly cryptic one-word answer that would likely make sense later.

Before I fell asleep, I sent Peter a text about how I'd shared that imaginary fish on a gas planet with Stephen Hawking.

"Stay afloat," he texted back. "Don't let the scary folks get you down."

I needed a new teacher. I searched the Spiritualists' National Union website again on the off-chance that, although it was based in the UK, it might have recommendations for teachers or centers in the U.S. It listed an affiliated church forty miles away, across the East River, through Manhattan, and out one of the tunnels into northern New Jersey. Battling through New York City traffic would make it feel like a four-hundred-mile drive, but that weekend, it was offering a workshop with a healer called Tom Cratsley who had traveled down from the Lily Dale Spiritualist community in Upstate New York. He was a minister who studied religion and psychology at Harvard Divinity School and had been working as a counselor and healer for over thirty-five years. A day of healing sounded like just the ticket.

That weekend, I got up early, gassed up the car, and set out. Johann was singing a song in my head.

... the finest years ...

The tune was familiar, and I could make out some of the lyrics. It was an old seventies song that I couldn't quite place.

Once I turned onto Route 4 off the George Washington Bridge and had navigated through the rat's nest of exits and interstates. I turned on the radio to hear Bread singing, "You gave my life to me / Set me free, set me free / The finest years I ever knew / Were all the years I had with you ..."

Lovely, Liebling, thank you!

I wasn't just thrilled to hear the message in the lyrics and know he was with me listening to them on this drive to rural New Jersey, I was thrilled that he was happy. That meant, I had to be going in the right direction.

The Journey Within Spiritualist church was a wooden building that stood in a small town surrounded by woodlands and lakes — blissful after the bedlam of Brooklyn and city traffic. The creaky stairs led to stained glass doors and into a bright chapel with rows of chairs in cream covers and white walls decorated with angels and wreaths of pink roses. I was early, and it was empty. A low om vibrated from hidden speakers with mesmerizing effect, like an invitation to put worries and ego down and breathe easily. I sat there for a few minutes, peacefully, washing off the madness and exhaustion of recent weeks until a swinging door and chatter announced the arrival of the students.

Outside in the hall, the pastor, Reverend Janet, was welcoming people with high spirits and great ardor while the church secretary checked people in at a small table. Janet was a powerful figure with a large physique and a commanding voice. I read that she'd been communicating with spirits since childhood and had spent five years as a Roman Catholic nun before leaving the convent to set up her own mediumship practice and this church.

In the chapel, she welcomed us and introduced Tom. For all his marvelous credentials, Tom was a humble character with a rosy face who carried himself with the refreshing air of a person more interested in being of service than feeding his own ego.

We were a small group, and we started off by sitting in silent meditation and setting positive intention. Once we settled in, Tom guided us into the power to attune to healing energy and invite it to flow to us. This created a sensation that was subtly different than meditation or sitting alone in the power had been. After some time, he asked us to allow the energy that was flowing to us to flow through us to others in the room. It was a powerful sensation, and it caused more expansive body distortions than I'd experienced on my cushion. They reached well up to the ceiling and around the room. It was marvelous to feel free of the boundaries of my ego and my small physical form. I could feel the healing restoring my reserves that had been depleted in recent weeks. Even more marvelous was the power I could feel from Johann in this place.

Liebling, my goodness, I feel you so strongly here.

We worked with the energy in different ways for the rest of the morning. By lunchtime, there was a definite shift in the room. It was still and beneficent. It was extraordinary how ten people in a room could affect a space so profoundly and be affected by it in return. If we could always be this positive and connected, I thought, all rooms would feel like this.

I went to the local diner for lunch. When I got back, I heard Janet belly laughing in an office just off the hall.

"Who's she talking to?" I asked a student from my group.

"That's Colin Bates," she said. "He's a tutor from the Arthur Findlay College in England. He's teaching a mediumship intensive here next week."

"Are you doing it?" I asked.

"No, it's full," she said. "I tried to register too late. I was really disappointed. He's a great teacher. He's been teaching for more than thirty years. All over the world."

Colin was a flamboyant character, quick to smile and exuberant in his greetings that he delivered to passersby in a lively English accent. Together there, sitting in the office with the door open, they had a considerable amount of experience of mediumship, the afterlife, and the human condition. I couldn't pass up that opportunity to ask the questions I'd spent so many hours researching.

The church secretary inched past me to bring them coffee from the local Dunkin' Donuts.

"Thanks, Patty," Janet said.

I knocked on the open door.

"Can I help you?" Janet asked.

"Yes," I said. "Sorry to interrupt, but I'd love to ask you a few questions? My fiancé died recently, and I had some bad experiences with some student mediums recently. I'd love to get your opinion on some issues I ran into."

"Come on in," Colin said.

"They said he was earthbound," I said, squeezing into a chair crammed into the corner.

"What do you consider to be earthbound?" Colin asked. "Many people consider a ghost to be an earthbound spirit, but a ghost isn't a spirit at all. A ghost is an echo of the past. It's like a memory in time."

He sipped his coffee.

"I was invited to a house one weekend that the new owners said had a very bad feeling," he went on. "A young couple had just moved in with their children. As soon as I walked in the door, there was a feeling of oppression within the house. There was only one room that didn't feel oppressive. That room had been redecorated and painted, the windows were changed, everything was redone, and it was fine. I sat down in another room and moved into the quiet, and immediately what came to my awareness was the old owners. I asked the couple, 'Did you meet the people you bought the house from? Were they very depressive?' He said 'Yes, they were,' and they'd lived there for twenty years. You see, the echo of their own emotion was still in the house. It wasn't a spirit; it was the energy of what had been. You can actually test this by going into a place where there's been a battle or something bad has happened. The resonance will be there. It's an echo of the past."

"It's like the ghost hunters that go into a house," Janet said. "They say they encounter the energy of someone who was murdered there, and then they claim a spirit is stuck there. Well, maybe they just walked into that house and reexperienced psychically what happened there. But that's just the energy, there's no spirit there. If spirits got stuck," she added. "there'd have to be an incompetent God."

That made sense. It also made sense that we leave a mark on our space. I'd been aware of the energy of places since childhood, whether there'd been an argument or whether it was happy. But what about the bunk shaking in the Girl Guides house? That wasn't an echo.

"I don't know the history of the place, so it could be something historically connected to the house," Janet said, "but a lot of us that are mediumistic have experiences during our childhood when the ancestors are walking with you or trying to tell you that you're mediumistic and you can hear them. You just weren't ready for it at that point."

She started tidying up the table.

"People also use the idea of earthbound spirits or spirit attachments to excuse bad behavior," Janet went on. "Terrible stuff happens all the time on the planet because of free will or mental illness, but individuals are responsible for that, not the spirit world."

"And what about people who die by suicide?" I asked.

"I think everybody, regardless of how they lived, are welcome home as a soul," Janet said. "But I think when you get there, there's an evaluation of your life, like a review of what you've done to people and the damage you've done and how you acted against your own soul on the planet. But I think God understands that some people don't see the value of their life. I don't encourage it as a way out," she added. "I encourage people to finish their lives because when you get to the next level, you still have to figure out what you can do next to grow. Everything is about progression of the soul."

This reminded me of something I'd read about the early Christian church before the Nicene Creed — the standard statement of belief

— was adopted. The theologian Origen, who was considered the greatest genius the early church ever produced, rejected the idea of hell and believed souls return to earth for the education they need for their progress toward heaven, where everyone eventually ended up.

"So, you're saying if you don't do the work here, you have to do it there "I said.

"You have to do it there," she said.

"So, if it's all about progression of the soul, can we impede their progress or harm them somehow?" I asked. "I've come across people who say that they can't move on if we don't."

"You can't stop people from moving forward," Colin said. "And you can't conjure up the dead either. When you have eternal love, nothing will stop your thoughts of your loved one or their thoughts of you, so the connection continues. Grief is always there, but as years pass, we learn to place it in a different part of us. But no, I don't believe you can hold anyone back. Their love and their need to still be a part of our lives is very real. It's a very natural phenomenon. There can be questions unanswered or things undone. It can be unspoken words, like 'I love you,' 'I'm sorry,' it can be 'I have regrets.' But the communication continues. It is an eternal progression."

"And the light?" I asked. "This means I couldn't keep Johann out of the light?"

"He's already in the light," Colin added simply. "We are all in the light. We are never out of the light because we cannot be where God is not."

Liebling, how simple is that?

I could have stayed there all day talking about metaphysical and existential beliefs, about the unseen world, morals, ethics, personal responsibility, the power of mediumship to heal, but Tom called us back into class. After all the intellectual gymnastics and soul searching I'd done in recent weeks to sift through the rights and wrongs and supposed complexities of the relationship between the physical and spirit world, the message ended up being simple: love endures.

The second period of healing class went as blissfully as the first. We continued to practice in pairs, and then we each had an opportunity to sit with Tom for individual healing.

I had only just sat down in the chair opposite him when he opened his eyes.

"Are you aware that there's a young man with you?" he asked. "A tall man?"

"Yes," I said.

"You have a very strong bond," he said. "You are growing and learning together. You're helping him, and he's helping you."

"Thank you," I said.

"But it's more than that," he said. "You also have a shared purpose here. You're helping people through the veil, and that's part of the soul's evolution for both of you. Does that make sense?"

"Yes, it does, Tom, thank you. It makes a lot of sense."

Tom's words stayed with me the whole way home. I was too elated to care about traffic congestion. I felt revitalized in body and mind. I'd finally found people evolved in their thinking who adopted a more sophisticated understanding of the planes of existence and aligned with my own reason and intuition.

Glyn Edwards said that mediumship wasn't just about giving messages, it was about embodying and sharing with others the attributes of love and tolerance that those in spirit form showed us. I'd learned that the spirit world exists on a high vibration and to reach it honestly and ethically, we needed to embody those attributes ourselves. I'd also learned that whether we're in physical or spirit form, we had a choice to progress across planes. I also knew now, without a doubt, that Johann and I would always be together in the light.

I drove down the FDR and across the Queensboro Bridge toward home. By the time I parked in Greenpoint, I understood why it was important that events played out as they did. He always accused me of having to find things out for myself: "You listen to no one," he used to say, "and then you make up your own mind."

I get why you didn't warn me away from Bradley and Hannah. Without that experience, I wouldn't have done all that research. I wouldn't have questioned belief systems, and I wouldn't have understood how people form prejudices about the world unseen and project them onto others. And I may not have found the church. I certainly wouldn't have found it today when Tom and Colin were there.

I felt his kisses dance around my eyes, his happiness filling me, and a single word.

Ja.

He popped the image of Bambi into my head again.

You're right. I laughed. *I was like Bambi. Things got worse before they got better. But they did get better. And you helped me along the way.*

Release

Every true love and friendship is a story of unexpected transformation.
If we are the same person before and after we loved,
that means we haven't loved enough.

Elif Shafak

I felt optimistic. I'd been running on fumes and was reenergized. My first steps hadn't been stellar, but I now realized it was just as important to learn the way things aren't as it was to learn the way things are. I'd learned the importance of self-care and maintaining a positive space, a higher vibration, the very conditions Silver Birch said facilitated how close those in spirit could draw.

I sent an email to Janet enquiring about development classes, asking if there were any prerequisites and reminding her that while I seemed to have some natural ability, I had no formal training worth mentioning, which was the case at that time. She emailed back to say her Monday night classes would be starting again in a few weeks, and I was welcome to join.

I have a good feeling about this Liebling, don't you?

He inserted an image into my mind of two white, anatomically perfect figures, drawn mid-stride like images on an Egyptian tomb against a bright pink background, which I'd come to associate with unconditional love. The man was facing one way and the woman the other, but they were joined at the hand and foot. It was beautiful and soothing and reassured me that, no matter where we were, our bond endured.

Over breakfast, I listened to Glyn Edward's MP3 again. His voice had enormous power to uplift. He talked about taking a commonsense approach to mediumship and undertaking it seriously and intelligently. He talked about being seen as well-adjusted people so as to have the respect of humanity for the work undertaken for the spirit. When he spoke like this in his old-fashioned English accent about meaning and purpose, he encouraged me to focus on the bigger picture, the overarching message that this work was about embracing life by embodying the kindness of the spirit world and sharing that with other people. How different life would be if everyone felt the unconditional love of the spirit world and knew that death is only the birth of the soul into a new and delightful life in which we continue to evolve. Even without the faculty of mediumship, that message gave life meaning.

Yes, today I was optimistic. I saw new beauty and purpose in life with my beloved.

A pencil sketch of a bunch of grapes filled my mind as I woke. *Morning.*

I had a gloriously long sleep and felt great that day. I had my usual cold-to-lukewarm shower courtesy of Zybi, but I didn't complain. I didn't want to give him a reason to raise the rent. The rents in the neighborhood were starting to rocket the way they had done when I lived in an artist's loft in DUMBO. Developers raised rents so high, we were all pushed out, scattering like rats into cheaper areas. Over the years, I'd been gentrified out of every dump on the Brooklyn waterfront. I didn't want to antagonize Zybi and get pushed out of here too. I couldn't afford the going rate anymore, and I didn't want to leave the neighborhood into which all my memories of Johann were etched.

I took my tea, pencils, and journal to McGolrick Park to sketch the grapes. On my way to the benches, I noticed a chalk outline on the ground by the pavilion that looked like a cluster of circles. On closer inspection, I saw it was a bunch of grapes with two words written in white chalk underneath: *Herzlichen Glückwunsch.* A Google search told me the words were German for "Congratulations," and a snippet gave an example of *Herzlichen Glückwunsch Zum Geburtstag,* which meant "Happy Birthday."

Whose birthday is it?

Wait.
Wait for what?
Silence.

Back home, I checked my Facebook feed, but no one was receiving accolades or birthday greetings. Then, in the "People You May Know" list on the sidebar, I saw his mother's name. I clicked through. It showed her photo on a new page with only a handful of posts showing the date she joined, some people she'd become friends with, and one life event, her birthday, which was the following week.

The message is for your mother! Do you want me to wish her a happy birthday for you?

Johann rarely talked about his mother and had seen her even less. As a child, he lived with his father. As an adult, he moved to another city and then to the U.S. He and his mother drifted over time and distance so that hardly any, if any at all, relationship survived. Shortly before he died, she got a computer and sent him an email. It was a promising new beginning given the amount of issues they had to resolve, but he died before they could truly become reacquainted and before any healing could happen for either of them.

"Still meeting at Grumpies?" I'd texted him one day.
"Yes."
"Are you on your way?"
"In the bathroom. Talking to my mother."
"You're talking to your mother?"
"Yes."
"On the toilet?"
"No."
At Grumpies, I pressed him for details.
"How did it go?"
"What?"
"Talking to your mother?"
"The way all conversations go when someone finds God late in life."
"Your mother found God?"
"Yes."
"What happened?
"Old age probably. What do you want?"
"I want to know what happened with your mother."
"No, I mean what do you want?" he said pointing to the board.

That was how conversations ended when he, for his own private reasons, didn't want to peer into the past.

On the day he died, I hadn't known how to reach her. I searched the web and looked up German online telephone directories but had no luck. In the end, I had to let it go and hope that she had been told gently. I couldn't imagine the pain of finding a son and losing him again just as their relationship had begun to heal and renew.

What should I do?

Write.

I wasn't sure what to write, so I kept it short. I explained who I was and apologized that I hadn't known how to contact her on the day he died. I assured her that he was loved and had been happy. I told her that one of the last things he said to me was "the only women in my life are you and my mother." I hoped that would offer some consolation. Then, I signed off by wishing her a happy birthday.

Is that okay? If she responds, I'll write her a longer note.

He felt calm, so I assumed it was.

Although I did this for him, I hoped she'd write back for me too. I no longer had any contact with his young son, which meant she was the only remaining connection to him in the physical world. How lovely it would be to know her. How lovely it would be to talk to someone who also loved him and grieved him and had hopes and dreams and memories to share.

That evening, I decided to walk down to the river, where we'd spent so many hours together. I felt closer to him there, closer to the past there at least. I arrived to find the pier under construction and surrounded by a wire fence sporting "No Trespassing" and "Trespassers Will Be Prosecuted" signs. Someone had cut a big hole in the fence and, judging by the bent-back edges, a lot of people had been climbing through. This was Brooklyn. No one paid attention to signs.

A security guard in an ill-fitting uniform appeared when I was halfway through.

"You cannot go there," he said in a thick African accent, probably not long off the boat from Ghana or Nigeria.

I flashed my press pass.

"I'm doing a story on the waterfront developments," I said.

The poor fellow didn't know what to do. Brand new in a boring job in a big city, he must have thought a press pass was an official ID that automatically granted the bearer freedom of the city. He let me pass.

In the middle of the pier, I had just sat down in the fresh breeze to listen to the soothing ripples of the East River and watch the sun set over the Manhattan skyline when a siren squealed down the block. At the end of Kent Street, two cops were standing behind open car doors. One waved me back. I passed the African guy on my way. He was nervous.

"Can you read?" one officer said. "What you're doing is criminal trespass."

He was a tall, blond cop with deep furrows and crevices running down his cheeks. This guy was mean. The other cop stood behind the door of the car, hand on revolver. I'd seen this years before when I was pulled over in a high-risk stop in LA in the early hours of the morning. I was working in TV at the time and was driving home from a late call when I saw red and blue lights flash in my rearview mirror. I pulled over, took out my driver's license, and had just reached to my glove compartment for my registration when the megaphone came on and a cop bellowed. "Step out of the car. Put your hands on your head. Step onto the sidewalk." Next thing I knew, I was standing with my face pressed into a wire fence, hands on my head, with one cop patting me down for weapons and the other searching the car. When they realized I was a twenty-five-year-old just off the boat from Ireland, they explained the definition of idiocy: me speeding at 2:00 a.m. in Downtown LA and reaching into the glove compartment for a would-be gun. I'd also run a stop sign, which was a moving violation, but they let it go and sent me on my way. These Brooklyn cops weren't as nice as the LAPD in Downtown LA in the middle of the night. That said something.

"Do you have ID?" the blonde cop asked me.

I handed him my driver's license and the PBA card Meera had given me. The other cop got into the car to check it. Then blonde cop turned on the African guy.

"What's your boss gonna say when he hears you can't do your job."

The African guy was so petrified, he forgot how to speak English. He stood there ringing his hands and muttering something in an African dialect and backed away in fright. It was a pathetic power trip on the part of the cop. This poor guy was easy to scare.

"It's not his fault," I said. "I showed him my press pass and told him I had permission. He's not American. He didn't know it wasn't a permit. Can't you give him a break?"

The cop turned on me as if he wanted to punch me.

"Go back to your post," he snapped at the guy. "You wait there."

He got into the car and left me standing on Kent Street for twenty minutes — a ridiculous amount of time to run a background check and likely intended to show me who was in charge. The African guy went back to his post, conflicted, as though he didn't know whether to thank me for defending him or hate me for almost getting him fired.

Any way you can get me out of this, Liebling?

The car door opened.

"We're not taking you down to the precinct," he said handing me my driver's license, PBA card, and a summons. "You're lucky. You got a court date. Don't miss it."

I stopped by Roisin's on the way home and complained about the state of the neighborhood. The developers were ruining the place, building on every patch of land, overpopulating the area, and driving up rents. The artists who made it the great neighborhood it once was were long gone. The character had changed completely.

"Are you thinking of moving?" she asked.

"Where would I go?"

"A lot of people are going to Bushwick," she said.

"I don't want to go to Bushwick. I want to take classes in New Jersey. The last thing I need to do is move farther east to Bushwick."

I wasn't being entirely truthful. I did want to get to New Jersey, that was true, and I was fed up with the neighborhood and Zybi and the cold water and the parking lot outside my ground-floor window, but all my memories of the way things had been were here. I didn't want to let them go.

Two weeks later, my court date came up. I trekked to Center Street in Manhattan at a ridiculously early hour to stand before the judge in an old forty-story hulking building. At 9:00 a.m., the doors opened, and within five minutes, the place was packed. The high ceilings and marble floors amplified every clicking heel and every argument at every window of every irate petty criminal in the place. I went to one window and queued. I was directed to another window and queued. Then I was sent into the courtroom and told to sit in a wooden pew with a hundred or so other people and queue.

I was third to be called before the judge. A stony-faced court assistant took my paperwork, shuffled it along to the next employee and then the next without a word until it landed in front of the judge. I was nervous. I hadn't worked for a long time and my bank account was anemic. I doubted I could afford the fine, and I didn't want to go to jail for inability to pay.

"How do you plead?" asked the judge.

"Guilty," I said.

He scribbled something on my papers.

"I am moving this to an adjournment in contemplation of dismissal. This means the charge will be dismissed if you do not engage in additional criminal conduct or other acts prohibited by this court for the next six months. That is the condition of this adjournment. Do you understand?"

"Yes."

"You can go."

That was it. I tumbled out of the building, liberated from the mayhem and noise, without an arrest or a fine. I thought of Meera and Nonny, her late grandmother, the reason I had the PBA card that averted an arrest in the first place.

Thank you, Nonny. You just kept me out of jail.

A couple of weeks later, I woke up to a nice email in German from Johann's mother. "*Liebe Karen, Herzlichen dank* für Ihre lieben *worte. Ich kann nicht Englisch sprechen* ..." it started. I ran it through the Google translator. She thanked me for my letter and apologized for her delay in responding, explaining that it took her some time to read it because she spoke no English and had to translate it word by word with a dictionary. She had loads of questions: What had happened? Had he been taking care of himself? What kind of life had he? Her questions read like the desperate effort of a disconsolate mother trying to share the years lost to her when he was alive on the planet and grieve the years that would never come.

I spent the next few days writing her a long letter about his life, his job, his home, our plans, how much he loved his young son, and how much I loved him. I told her he was smart and popular. I shared how he loved parties and art openings, holidays, watching movies, long walks, and lazy afternoons. I told her that we laughed and argued, that he was complicated, often difficult, and sometimes critical but had a kind heart. I loved telling her about him.

Johann had said she found God, which meant she would likely believe in heaven, but if I told her what he'd shown me, she might think me crazy and him unsettled or disturbed. Without knowing her better and without being able to speak German, it would be hard to gauge what she understood, where she stood, or how receptive she'd be. The only way I could help her without inadvertently doing harm, I realized, was to answer her questions. I asked her gently in the end if she thought our loved ones continued to walk with us.

If she says yes, I'll broach the subject. If she says no, I'll have to leave it up to you, okay?

In a single moment, I felt positivity radiate from him inside me and one word whispered in my mind: *Ja.*

In the end, all I wrote was that he believed the owner of the local bike shop had a good death because he spent his last day doing something he loved, and that's how Johann's last day had also been. I hoped that would offer her some comfort. For the first time since his passing, I realized this email was forcing me to form coherent sentences about his death. It was imposing order onto my disordered thoughts and showing me that on some level I'd been haunting our old hangouts and harboring what ifs: what we could have or should have or would have done differently had we known. The longer this letter to his mother became, the more I realized I needed to release my regrets, because this was the only way life could be now. I felt stupid arriving at this awareness so late, but that's the purpose of a eulogy I supposed, and this was my eulogy, the belated conclusion to the way things had been.

I was sharing a lot of details about his life, which would ordinarily make him uncomfortable. I thought I felt a twinge of discomfort, but that could have been my projection or my expectation based on the way he'd been. Things were different now. We were both letting go of our outworn patterns that no longer served us.

We are, aren't we?

Silence.

Aren't we?

Still no answer, which was the sort of treatment I'd always get when he couldn't give me the answer I wanted to hear and didn't want to start an argument.

Don't do that. I am *letting go of stuff I don't need.*

I edited the email again until it was perfect — aside from being in English. It needed a translator who could capture its nuances. I emailed Iris, the German woman who gave me the message from Johann in the online class, and asked her for help. She said she'd be happy to translate. A week later, she emailed it back, and I sent it on with a photo of Johann and me.

I thought I was doing this to help you, but connecting with your mother and writing a eulogy has helped me in a way I didn't even know I needed.

I was excited. Classes were starting back at the church in New Jersey that night. Not only would this help me take care of my side of this path we were walking together, I assumed it would also enhance our communication and our ability to blend with each other.

I left two hours before it started to give myself plenty of time to traverse the city. I set up my GPS, gassed up the car, and zipped over the Pulaski Bridge to the Queensboro Bridge and ran smack into the middle of rush hour. I crept onto the FDR, then inched across the GW Bridge. By the time I passed Fort Lee in New Jersey, it was already 6:50 p.m. Further on, traffic was at a complete standstill. By the time I clambered up the wooden stairs to the church, I was hassled, sweaty, and ridiculously late. I peered through the stained-glass doors to see everyone sitting in rows. Janet waved me in. The practice period was over, and they were asking her questions about their experiences during the exercises. Half an hour later, the class was over, and I lumbered toward home, with a parting word from Janet to arrive next time on time.

A week had passed since I sent Iris's translation to Johann's mother, and I'd heard nothing back. At first, I was delighted to be able to help. Then, I worried that I may have upset her. Now, I was convinced I'd offended her and was filled with remorse.

Liebling, can you help?

He must have helped because three days later, a long email arrived from her with baby photos of him attached. *"Herzlichen dank* für *deinen großen, lieben brief,"* she wrote. I ran it through the translator to read, "Thank you for your long, lovely letter." She expressed gratitude for sharing my story because she had struggled alone with his passing. "I am so happy that he had a chance to experience your love, but of course I am so sad that you didn't have a future together. It is such a shame." She went on to tell me that he was a clever child who made insightful observations but would only ever do what interested him. "He had many clever questions and comments, and he had enormous artistic talent," she wrote. "He was also a very sensitive child. Once, when he was very young, he covered some baby birds with my over glove because it was raining."

Aw Liebling, how sweet is that?

I poured over the rest of her letter. To my question about continued relationships with loved ones, she simply said she'd have to think about it, which I knew was her polite way of saying "no" and probably her way of being sensitive to my grief. She signed off with affection, hoping I wasn't sad, hoping I could find some joy in life, and telling me to contact her if there was anything she could do to help.

This was probably the happiest I'd been since Johann sent me a kaleidoscope of butterflies in Virginia. I read her email three times, trying to match the English translation with the original German as if I could squeeze more words out of it that way. She would have been my mother-in-law, so I'd lost that relationship too when he died. I hadn't realized the extent to which that mattered to me until now. But now I had it back, and I was thrilled. I was also thrilled that he had let go of whatever resentments he'd been holding toward her and took steps to heal the relationship in the only way he could. In the end, he brought the three of us together, and we were all a little happier now.

"Oh, my God," Roisin said when I told her how he sheltered the baby birds from the rain. "That's too cute!"

I could feel him cringing and cursing me for sharing the story.

We think other people's baby stories are cute but rarely do we think so of our own. Who hasn't been mortified by parents telling people embarrassing baby stories of silly things we did before we had sense or self-consciousness? But I couldn't help myself. I was so happy to connect with his mother and hear precious pieces of his childhood that I had to tell someone, and Roisin was the only mutual friend I trusted enough to understand.

In the early hours of the following morning, I woke with a jolt to find a mouse's ass in my mind. Not just any mouse. It had a long tail with colored stripes.

What on earth is that?

I turned on the light and picked up my journal and pencils to sketch it. I was coloring the tail when I realized what it was — one of my mother's stories from when I was three years old. We had a mouse problem in our old place in Dublin. I was watching TV one evening when a mouse darted under the TV table so fast it was almost a blur. I ran to my mother on my little legs in such a fright and kept opening and closing my mouth to explain but no words would come out. Finally, I pointed back to the area under the TV table and said, "A mouse!" Then stretching my arms wide, I apparently cried, "His tail is this long, and it's different colors." I assumed later that the blur was caused by the speed of the mouse and registered in my little brain as a long tail. I didn't remember colored stripes, but that must have been the way Johann interpreted the colors I thought I saw. Why I thought it was different colors, I'd no idea. Shock maybe, but my mother thought this was too funny not to tell over and over. In each retelling, she mimicked me gaping and gasping and unable to speak, and I came to hate, really hate, that story. Now, decades later, Johann had gone fishing in my memories until he found an embarrassing baby story of mine to offer up as payback for sharing his.

I felt him laughing.

Okay, no more. I promise.

The little exchange over the birds and the mouse reminded me of how open my mind was to everyone in spirit form. Roisin's Aunt Joanie was able to pluck a reference from my mind to communicate a lot of information about herself. Presumably, by being willing to mediate between planes, it was understood that full access was granted to my consciousness to facilitate the communication of information.

I was curious about the nature of consciousness. I tried to read current studies, but they boggled my mind. I watched an interview with Professor Stuart Hameroff from the University of Arizona, who proposed controversially that our knowledge and memories, what we consider our self or consciousness, was stored as quantum information in the brain in microtubules, which, upon the death of the brain, leaked out into the universe and remained entangled and able to communicate at a distance; quantum entanglement, a fundamental property of quantum mechanics. I couldn't understand his theory and certainly wasn't qualified to critique it, but NDE studies lent it credence by showing that information continued to be acquired after the brain was dead. Mediumship showed that information was organized and communicated intelligently by and to incarnate and discarnate consciousness, which seemed to suggest that consciousness was like a stream containing all minds and all thoughts into which we all dipped.

Coming to understand the afterlife was helping me to understand something I'd never quite grasped in undergrad philosophy when we studied the Vedic texts, the Upanishads in particular. I was beginning to grasp the concept of the atman, the self or individual soul, and the Brahman, the absolute, eternal, transcendent, cosmic soul, as inseparable principles. Everything in the universe is contained within the Brahman with which the atman could communicate and fuse. Why a quantum physicist such as Erwin Schrödinger was interested in Vedanta made sense now, as did his comment, "This life of yours which you are living is not merely a piece of this entire existence, but is in a certain sense the whole …" The Vedic texts anticipated the physics of the modern world. We exist, at least at this stage of our soul's evolution, as individual consciousness blending in the bliss of the one boundless wave of an all-pervading consciousness.

After the ordeal of trying to get across New York City in rush hour the previous Monday night, I left at 4:30 p.m. to get ahead of the traffic and give myself three hours to traverse fifty miles to New Jersey. Unfortunately, it was another disaster. Traffic on the Queensboro crept and the FDR trickled. After almost an hour of breathing in noxious fumes and trying to tune out the cacophony of horns honking at cars that had nowhere to go, the traffic guy on 1010 WINS radio said there was an accident up ahead and FDR north from East 96th Street was at a standstill. Take an alternate route he advised. Too late. I was hemmed in and nowhere near an exit. I made it ten blocks in the next thirty minutes. The next traffic report said a truck had broken down on the GW. Take an alternate route he advised. By the time I got to Harlem, it was already 6:30 p.m. I wouldn't make it anywhere close to on time. I crept to the next exit and went home, disheartened. Joining the church group was looking less and less possible. I'd either have to drive out early and spend the whole day hanging around in rural New Jersey or resign myself to its occasional weekend workshops and take online classes in between.

I know it's not ideal. But what other solution do I have?
Think.
I am thinking! I protested, but I knew I must have been overlooking an obvious fix.

Zybi was talking to a neighbor in the street when I got home. I tried to slip past him. I was tired and cranky and had a splitting headache and wanted to be left alone. I checked my mail. A credit card payment hadn't been made. I must have overdrawn my checking account. I hadn't looked at my accounts in months, and I hadn't written a story since Johann died, so the coffers were almost empty. I needed to get back to work, but the truth was, I'd lost interest in politics and geopolitics. I loved the fourth estate and the great investigative stories that changed the world: Seymour Hersh on the My Lai massacre, the Pentagon Papers, and the Watergate scandal, Wilfred Burchett in Hiroshima, Robert Parry exposing the Iran-Contra scandal. But the days of major media funding months of research and investigation were growing dim. We had citizen journalism, but that was teetering on opinion and unsourced blogs and corporate-driven publicity campaigns passing as news. I wished we could get back to the days where Bernstein and Woodward could break a story that would topple the government. We needed truth, that was the purpose of journalism, but it was becoming a luxury few editors and most reporters couldn't afford. Frankly, neither could I.

I devoted the next day to finding and pitching spirituality stories. I wanted to write about the issues that mattered to me now: understanding our connection to each other — physical and non-physical. Becoming aware of continued existence had helped me feel more fulfilled and purposeful. It changed me, and I knew if we could all awaken to our true nature, the human race and the planet would be in much better shape.

I scanned the religion and spirituality newsfeeds, hoping for a story that I could parlay into a paying feature article or an op-ed that would pay the rent. Most news centered on mainstream religions and amounted more or less to the politics of the Church. Concepts of the afterlife was a niche market not seriously entertained by the major religions or the religious columns of mainstream news and magazines. Any publications that did focus on this area seemed more interested in near death experiences, out of body experiences, or "channeling" descriptions of the afterlife from a supposed enlightened spirit through an entranced medium — in other words, their interest was in life in the afterlife. I wanted to write about what the absence of death could teach us about this life, and how it removed our primal, existential fear, which would allow us respond to others with compassion and loving kindness even in times of crisis. The Buddhist and yoga magazines were filled with these subjects, but not when they were wrapped up in notions of communicating with discarnate loved ones in the afterlife. I seemed to have fallen into a niche within a niche.

Finding a way forward in this arena was going to take a while, if there were a way forward at all. By lunchtime, it looked like I'd only one option: to go backward. I spent the rest of the day catching up on political events and pitching analyses, features, and op-eds to editors I knew. I emailed my regular editors for stringer assignments, but at the end of the day, all I had by return email was a collection of explanations for why my old editors weren't hiring freelancers anymore. The Internet killed the stringer, I was told. Newspaper sales were down, budgets were tight, and the amount of content that needed to be generated every hour to keep updating websites meant they could only afford to pay fifty dollars for a story. The problem with fifty-dollar stories, one editor admitted, was quality. For that rate, stringers had to churn stories out in under an hour. Good journalism, searching, researching, verifying, and writing history doesn't come cheap. Stringers could rarely deliver, so it was better for the editor to just pull stories from newswires like Reuters or the AP.

I was stymied. It seemed I couldn't go forward or backward.

I called Ralph, another New York journo I met in Baghdad to see how he was managing. He wrote for the *New York Times* and *Bloomberg* and some other major media outlets. He was struggling too, but he picked up some teaching and a bit of editing to keep afloat. He offered to send me some editing work, part-time and mind-numbing was how he described it, but the pay was decent, and I could work from home. I accepted, gratefully.

Even with some part-time, work-from-home in the offing, I still needed to come up with a chunk of quick cash to replenish my anemic bank account and pay off those bills. I was wandering my apartment wondering what options I had, if any, when I stopped in front of my wall-to-wall bookcases filled with my beloved books, all of which I'd read and never would again. I looked around at the original art hanging on my walls, the angry, dramatic, and chaotic art from local artists that suited my mindset back when I bought it. I looked in my wardrobe, which was stuffed with designer clothes, including Betsy Johnson and Vivienne Westwood, which were bought by the old me and not worn in almost a year. The living room was dominated by a large TV screen and a barely used stereo and DVD player. Drawers were filled with an assortment of almost new electronics. This place and everything in it was a relic of the person I used to be.

What do you think? Should I just sell the lot?

He embraced me with a feeling of freedom, a strange sensation that flowed through me, removing pressure, anxiety, and worry, leaving me feeling buoyant and exhilarated. It felt as if he were saying "Finally, you're getting it!"

The whole next week was spent photographing and listing clothes, shoes, jewelry, electronics, artwork, and collectors books on Amazon, Craigslist, and eBay. Collectors books were packed in boxes and hauled to Strand Books in Union Square. It was hard to stand there on 12th and

Broadway, listening to the manager total up the value of my treasures. I began to feel sorry for myself and lamented the circumstances that brought me to this place. Why was I so mawkish? There was no better place to leave the boxes of human thought I'd collected over the years than here.

When I got home, I lingered a moment in front of my lovely but now empty bookcases. Then I photographed them, listed them on Craigslist, and offloaded them the next day.

Over the next two weeks, I sold everything I didn't want or need. It was fantastic to wake up each day to less stuff, less weight, and more space. Anything I didn't sell, I sent to charity. I scrubbed the place clean. I closed the blinds to soften the sunlight and hide the parking lot outside. By the time I finished, the energy of the apartment had shifted dramatically. It was spacious and airy. It was the closest to Zen I'd felt since I'd been in the Zendo.

"You could put a crazy person in here, and they'd calm down," Roisin said.

It did feel noticeably calmer. I could breathe. I could pay the bills. I was no longer focused on what I lacked.

This is good, right Liebling? I've let go of everything I don't need.
Nein.
What do you mean "no"? What else is there?

The words came so fast, I couldn't hear his whole reply, but it came with a knowing that I'd something more to release, something I couldn't hear because I didn't want to hear it.

BANG.

A pounding on the door woke me with a jolt. I reached for the clock — 7:10 a.m. I'd only been asleep three hours because of the racket of trucks grinding along McGuinness.

"Go away. It's the middle of the night," I shouted.

BANG.

This had to be Zybi.

"Dammit," I mumbled, pulling on a bathrobe and shuffling to the door.

"I'm sleeping Zybi," I said, opening the door. "I'll come up later."

"Here," he said, handing me the lease. "Sign and bring back."

I was closing the door with lease in hand when I noticed the rent increase was $500.

"Are you kidding?" I said.

"No," he said. "Everything more money now. Heat, water, electricity."

Some Polish friend of his in the neighborhood must have told him the neighborhood was gentrifying and he could get a lot more money. Zybi loved money.

"You can't do that," I said.

"I can."

He could. The apartment wasn't rent stabilized, which meant it wasn't regulated by the city's tenant laws, which meant he could charge whatever someone was willing to pay.

"How about $200," I said.

"$500," he said.

I didn't want to move, but this small, noisy place wasn't worth another $500.

"Forget it," I said. "I'll leave."

Zybi went upstairs for his breakfast, onion pierogies and cabbage rolls by the smell of it. He was happy. Whether I stayed or left, he'd be better off. Bloody Zybi.

For the rest of the day, I mulled over my options. Moving would be expensive: movers, brokers fees, deposits. That was even if I could find a place. I had one month to find a new apartment in this city. It would be a time-consuming, head-wrecking, finance-sucking nightmare. In this neighborhood, I'd be lucky to find a shoebox. I didn't want to go farther into Brooklyn or into the outer reaches of Queens. That would take me east, even further away from the church. I needed to go west, but west was Manhattan, which was cost prohibitive. Mostly, though, I wanted to stay where I was. I didn't want to be pushed out of the place I'd lived with Johann. I didn't want to be ejected from the bricks into which our history was etched.

If you have a miracle up your sleeve, Liebling, I could use it now.

That night, I went to sleep miserable and woke up shortly after dawn to find he had put in my mind a shiny, three-dimensional heart on a map of the North Bronx in my mind.

You want me to move to the Bronx? You can't be serious!

I hadn't been to the Bronx since my first summer in New York back in the nineties. It was jam packed with monstrous buildings housing hundreds of families, bugs, and rodents. Drivers stuck signs in their car windows that read "No Radio" to stop people breaking them, and you couldn't ride the subway after dark. The Bronx, especially the South Bronx, had a notorious reputation.

To be honest, there was another reason I didn't want to go up there. I was sick of change. I was sick of being dislodged and disconnected. I couldn't go back, not to where I worked, not to where I lived, not to the life I had, not to the person I used to be. Plato said the things that change most are the things that are least real. But my life, Johann, my home, my work felt real to me. I had moved on in all sorts of ways, the way people tell you do, but not this way. I couldn't let go of the remnants of our life as it has been.

That's an awfully long way up Liebling. Please don't tell me to look there.

I didn't want to be an ingrate, but I hoped it was just an "I love you" message and not the location of my new home. I searched the listings just to make sure. But he was right. There was an apartment on the spot where his heart had been. I knew he was looking out for me when he did that, but living at the edge of the Bronx? There would be nothing familiar there, no waterfront, no Grumpies, no idle afternoons watching the rain fall, or coffee with friends, or walks in the park. That was part of who we were. I couldn't let that go.

I checked the MTA map for public transportation. There was no subway stop up there. The subway only peaked its way across the Harlem River and into the south end of the neighborhood, which was nowhere near walking distance from the heart on the map. Being off the subway in New York City is a different life. It's hard to understand the logistics of the city without living here. It's not like anywhere else. It's dense, frenetic, aggressive. People converge on Midtown and Lower Manhattan, not the boroughs, and definitely not the outer reaches of a borough without a subway stop. It had easy access to the GW Bridge and New Jersey, but I'd have to do a two- or three-hour round-trip commute just to have coffee with someone downtown. I couldn't imagine being more isolated than in that place. Johann knew New York. Why would he put me all the way up there?

I might as well move to Albany as live there.

I was a child throwing a tantrum.

Maybe there's another apartment in the south end near the last subway stop?

I searched. I could feel him, quietly watching me chasing my tail as he always did, waiting for me to tire out and realize he was right all along.

There was nothing. I looked at his marker again, sulked and gave in and called the management company. The apartment was still available, the woman said, and I could see it that day. Renting from management directly would save thousands in brokers fees, which was a little silver in the lining at least, but I was still less than thrilled. I took down the address, hung up, and mapped it. The map located it at the south end of the neighborhood by the subway where I'd just searched and found nothing. I called back.

"Yes, that's right," the woman at the management company said. "Oh, I see. Sorry, the address we posted on Craigslist is wrong. No, it's not up by Yonkers, it's down by the subway. Do you still want to see it?"

"Yes," I said. "I'm on my way."

I hopped in my car and made the long, hot drive out of Brooklyn, around Manhattan, and into the Bronx to see what the area was like. As soon as I pulled off the I-287 into the south end of the neighborhood, I knew I'd love it. It was like a sleepy village where expat Irish converged and the rest of the city forgot. There were little rows of shops and the odd café and bar. The nearby Van Cortlandt Park was huge, and it had riding stables, a lake, and hiking trails. The apartment was large, bright, newly refurbished. It was the top floor, so there would be no more Zybis thundering across the ceiling at dawn. What's more, because it was listed incorrectly, anyone who wanted to live in this area hadn't bothered to go see it. I'd no competition. It was just sitting there, waiting for someone like me to be nudged along. When I signed the lease that afternoon, I learned the place was rent stabilized, regulated by the city, so the landlord couldn't rack up the rent.

Johann had struck gold.

How on earth did you know the apartment was actually in the right place but listed in the wrong place? And stabilized? How can you see these things?

I'd no idea how he did this, but I was delighted. He knew what I needed even when I didn't. He walked with me when I was stressed and helped even when I thought I knew better.

Two weeks later, in the very early hours, the movers came and got me out of Brooklyn. It wasn't a great day to move; it was overcast and raining heavily, but by the time I'd moved in, the rain had stopped. I spent the day unpacking and organizing my large, fresh, new apartment. I opened the windows out onto the park. No trucks, or honking horns, or jackhammers, or carbon monoxide, or people milling and jostling through the streets. There was only space and quiet, rustling trees, birds chirping, and the fresh forest air calming the landscape after the storm. This was perfect. It was far enough away but not too far. I had a train to all things cosmopolitan and trails to nature and connectedness. Ten minutes away was the bridge to the church and the opportunity to advance my training. Why had I held onto our old stomping grounds for so long when our new stomping grounds were here, everywhere, everywhere in this world and the next?

I love it, Liebling. Thank you!

Master Hanh said that joy and happiness arise from letting go. "Please sit down and take an inventory of your life," he said. "There are things you've been hanging on to that really are not useful and deprive you of your freedom. Find the courage to let them go."

I'd let go. With a lot of help. Finally.

Home

I merged so completely with love, and was so fused,
that I became love, and love became me.

Jalal-ud-Din Rumi

The lake was full of geese and ducks. Four swans glided by. Yeats's poem, the "Wild Swans at Coole" set in the west of Ireland came to mind, and I remembered how as a student I lamented that one swan was alone, widowed maybe, since swans mate for life. Today, I wasn't sorrowful. The park in the early morning was glorious. The air was cool, but the grass was dry, and the traffic on the Henry Hudson was a dull and distant hum. Clouds hung lightly in the sky. It wouldn't rain. I passed a man at an easel, painting the woodlands. A pigeon sat on top of his canvas, tipping forward slightly as if to get a better look. The man held his brush mid-air as if he were afraid to scare the bird away by lunging toward it with a dab of paint.

"You have a fan," I said.

"So I do," he laughed.

No sooner had I sat down on the rocks beside the lake than a motley flock paddled toward me, the geese the vanguard and the ducks bringing up the rear. They knew people meant food. I tore off pieces of my breakfast sandwich, and they left the water one by one and crowded around for a snack. Something hopped out of a hole, dashed past, and disappeared into a bush. A chipmunk. Nifty little thing. Squirrels were everywhere, and lots of birds: pigeons obviously, and sparrows, red-winged blackbirds, coal tits, and what could be larks. I recognized the beige feathers of mourning doves and the red bellies of American robins, but there were others I didn't know. A bird soared in the sky. There must be hawks and owls in the denser woodland farther north. As a Girl Guide, I knew lots of birds by sight, but that information had long ago fallen out of my head. I needed to get a book. Still, the pecking order was clear. The birds gave the squirrels a wide berth, but the squirrels were chased off by the geese. The speedy sparrows could snatch a crumb and be gone before anyone realized. The chipmunks darted in and out concerned only about their own affairs. The swans glided to the edge of the water, regal, expecting the human to come to them.

Once the flock finished my breakfast, they slipped away into the lake or into the trees.

I crossed my legs, steadied myself on the grass, and settled in to meditate on this space. It was soporific, the coolness of water droplets on my face, the chirp and splash of the birds in the lake, the rustle of leaves in the rising and falling of the wind. Usually, after a period of meditation, my lower legs went numb and my only thought was whether I'd sat long enough, but not today. Today, I didn't want to stop. Instead of wiggling feeling back into my feet, I extended my subtle body and sat for a period — I don't know how long — in the power. I asked for healing to flow to me from the spirit planes and then through me to every person, creature, and part of nature in need. I wondered if that were too broad a request or if I should choose who needed healing most, until I realized there were no limits. The more I let go of the notion of scarcity, the more my heart opened to receive and give, and the more my physical body awareness fell away and the formlessness of subtle energy body swelled and undulated like an unseen wave in the invisible energy of the park. I never felt so expansive or so connected.

Johann, are you here? Can you feel this?

The familiarity of his essence enveloped me. At first, I felt the expansion of my own subtle body, the blending of his, the familiar and wondrous sense of presence and completeness. Static electricity danced lightly across my face like kisses, sending delightful shivers across my skin. I felt lighter, fuller, the weight of what I'd come to know as me — ego, desires, fears, tears — all of it dissolved. A bolt of energy tingled up my spine, causing my whole body to shudder. I wanted more. I wanted to be free of my physical form so that I could truly experience the intensity that I knew was possible were I uninhibited by physicality. I focused more on expanding my subtle body, trying harder, pushing harder to achieve formlessness,

but the energy dropped. I was frustrated. I'd come so close to reaching a new level of intensity and instead I dropped back into skin and bones.
I wish I could really be there with you.
Surrender.

My phone beeped on the walk home.

"Hi Missus, how's the Bronx?" Roisin wrote. "Miss you."

"Miss you too. Come visit."

"I will. Still hearing from himself?"

"Yes. Daily."

"How's it going?"

"Fantastic."

"Any developments?"

"Learning to blend energy. It's magical."

"Really? Do tell."

"It's like a cosmic orgasm. Almost."

"Better than sex?"

"It makes sex feel like a back scratch."

"Well ... Don't want to disparage Des, but I'd settle for a good back scratch sometimes."

I laughed.

"Gotta run. Promise to visit soon," she signed off.

I was waiting for the walk signal on Broadway when I overheard two men talking nearby.

"Hey Joey, how's it going?" said the first.

"I'm heading to Gerry's Hardware," said the second. "Have a rat in my kitchen."

"Yeah, it's the weather. I caught a couple of mice too," said the first.

"It's a rat," said the second.

"Gerry's has those glue traps for mice," said the first.

"It's a rat!"

"They're about this size," said the first, holding his hands a few inches apart.

"That?" said the second as he spread his arms wide. "I need one this size to catch that freaking thing."

It was an unintentionally funny exchange, but given that much of what we hear is colored by our own experiences and perception, if we listen at all, I realized it was truly amazing that anyone on the planet ever engaged in the same conversation. The odds seemed really stacked against those in spirit form getting past our mental chatter and preconceived notions.

I was increasingly fascinated by the workings of the brain. In its need to make sense of things, it would rather be wrong than experience the discomfort of uncertainty. I'd seen how, within moments of receiving an image or sound, my brain jumped to draw on a frame of reference to make sense of it.

What a challenge it must be for you too.

I understood now why he layered so much information into an image or sound or feeling and why one detail held an entire story. It felt as if I was dreaming his dream and sharing his story in allusions and images, sounds and feelings, and the associations in between.

That's why you're so pithy in your communication and why you pack more meaning into images, sounds, and feelings than just the images, sounds, and feelings. You convey the greatest amount of information with the least amount of effort while I'm in that receptive state. Right?

Gut gelernt.

'Good learning.' Is that what you said? Thank you, Liebling.

Between the work in class and my early morning meditations, I experienced a huge increase in sensitivity. My beloved felt so strong around me that he felt even more present and more intimately connected to me than he ever had in physical form. I barely turned my thoughts to him before I felt the largeness of his essence touching mine.

After a few weeks off, class started back at the church, which meant my Monday nights involved heading out of the Bronx, over the GW, and arriving in New Jersey on time and with relative ease. We worked in small groups. I was with Maxine, a quirky looking woman who looked like she spent her days in arts and crafts and jewelry making; Vanessa, a pretty woman with a mop of curls who was finding her mediumistic feet; Patricia, a stick-thin woman who had been communicating with spirits her whole life; and Dina, a petite extrovert with an updo.

To get used to stepping in and out of flow more easily, we were to make a connection with someone in spirit form, share specific details to prove who it was, then share their message, and we were to do this in five minutes.

"She wants us in the spirit world like a ferret up a drain pipe," Dina said.

I noticed my morning practice of blending with Johann must have helped me reach the altered state more quickly when communicating with strangers for strangers. It was becoming easier to simply step into the flow of consciousness between worlds and facilitate the heart and mind of one touching the heart and mind of the other. I had only to send out a thought when I felt a presence.

That night, it was a man in his forties with a dark beard.

"He's a brother. Your brother Patricia, I believe."

"That sounds like him so far," Patricia said.

Her brother inflated his head to look like Mr. Mackey from South Park.

"He was a teacher, very smart, and he has an odd sense of humor," I said.

She nodded.

"I don't think anyone got his jokes," I added.

"They didn't."

"He's letting me know that you weren't smart enough to get his jokes."

"That's what he said."

"But he's realized now that they were really lousy jokes, and he's sorry for saying you weren't smart for all those years because he sees now how it made you feel bad about yourself."

"Yes, that's true."

"He's very sorry." I said. "He wants you to know that you are smart, and you shouldn't believe anything negative about yourself."

"Ah. Nice to know." She laughed. "Thank you. Much appreciated."

Thank you, brother.

"There's a middle-aged woman here with me who wants to talk to you," Maxine said. "She has thick, dark hair and glasses and she chews on the ends. Karen, do you recognize her?"

"Not yet," I said.

"She's a teacher too," Maxine said.

I racked my brains. What teacher could this be?

"There's a white fence around her house."

My goodness, Miss Byrnes? Is that you?

"Yes, she was my English teacher in high school. I didn't know she'd passed."

"She's come to give you some encouragement," Maxine said. "She wants you to go back to college."

I was elated to hear from Miss Byrnes. In my teens, when I was drinking and getting high, she persuaded me to go to college. She was the only teacher I ever had who cared, and I went a long way on her few words of encouragement back then. But go back to college now? I thought Maxine may have gotten a memory and a message confused, but I let it go.

"I can't believe she remembers me," I said. "It was so long ago, that's brilliant. Thanks Max."

Thank you, Miss Byrnes.

I turned to Vanessa and saw the image of a young woman pushing a navy-blue stroller. It looked like my baby stroller, so I knew she was referencing it to tell me she was the baby's mother. I couldn't see into the stroller to know if the baby was with her in spirit form, but I sensed it was, and my heart sank.

"Vanessa," I said. "I have a young woman here with me, late teens or twenty. She's tall and pretty. She has shiny brown hair, cropped, and big brown eyes. She doesn't feel directly related to you, possibly a friend. Do you recognize her?"

"Yes."

"She's pushing a stroller, so I know she had a baby ..." I stopped. I didn't want to speak what she was sharing. "... and my sense is the baby is with her there."

"Yes, it's Mary. She was my friend's daughter," Vanessa said. "She choked on her own vomit in childbirth, and the baby died too."

My whole being lurched. I knew those in spirit were in the presence of love, but for her to go from nine months of joyful expectation, to excitement as she rushed to the delivery room, to the death of both in the same moment was an assault on the nerves. I wanted to say something to Vanessa by way of comfort. What wouldn't sound trite? And for whose comfort? I was getting in the way and preventing her from sharing the thoughts and feelings she wanted to share. I needed to surrender my ego, needs, and desires and focus on feeling how she felt and sharing what she needed to share, not mitigate my own discomfort with platitudes.

An urge came over me to curl up into a fetal position and never stretch out again.

"The baby was a girl."

"Yes."

"This will sound strange Vanessa, but the baby knew she was never meant to straighten up. She was never meant to walk in this world. Her purpose wasn't here," I said. "She was supposed to grow up in the spirit world. I can't prove it, but that's how she feels."

"I understand."

"They want to serve people."

"Yes, that's right," Vanessa said. "Mary wanted to be a social worker."

"She's expressing that they're together in the spirit world, and they have a purpose there helping children who arrive early. She wants you to stop thinking of this as a tragedy. Can you tell your friend? My sense from her is that she needs to hear that they're together and they're okay."

"Yes, I will. She does need to hear it. That's lovely. Really lovely. Thank you."

"Thanks, Vanessa."

Thank you, Mary.

I thought about Mary and her baby long after she left me. I assumed the baby appeared as a baby because that's how she'd be recognized, but they would both have grown in the spirit world. Hadn't Rev. Janet said everything was about the evolution of the soul and what people didn't get a chance to do here, they could do in there? I was saddened by Mary's tragedy and consoled by her grace. Her fate had been heartbreaking, yet she focused on serving others. There was only a single thread in the tapestry of the baby's physical presence and yet she too had grown into a richness of life and purpose. Grace, they say, comes violently. What violence had been theirs, but my goodness, what grace.

"I'm male. I feel handsome."

Dina had interrupted my thoughts with her strange way of speaking in the first person.

"I have something here in my chest. I'm finding it hard to breathe. I have a bicycle. I'm visual. I absorb everything I see. You understand?"

I nodded.

"I am right beside you," she said, pressing her hands together to emphasize her point, "and I mean right beside you, like I can't get close enough to you. I long for you. I watch you all the time."

"I understand," I said.

"But not in a creepy way," she added.

"I know what you mean."

We laughed.

I felt a brush of a feather across my forehead.

"He pushes your hair off your forehead, like in the movie *The Way We Were*. Did you see that? Streisand and Redford?"

"No, I haven't seen it," I said, putting my hand to my forehead.

"Great movie. They loved each other but couldn't be together. Anyway, I keep getting a feeling that he's still with you, but you could be closer. Do you understand?"

"I don't know how we could be closer."

"That's what he's sharing with me. He's a lovely man, isn't he?" she said, squeezing her shoulders up to her ears.

"That he is," I said.

I drove home happy each night after those classes, but never more so than that night when my beloved showed up. That night had been revelatory. I laughed with a brother and shared the tragedy of a teenager and her grace. I'd been remembered by my favorite schoolteacher who'd helped steer the course of my life. I was awed by the enduring bonds we create in life. I began to see that these enduring bonds weren't just about little messages, they were about healing, growth, and continued support. I was reminded that I was inseparable from my beloved and he from me. It wasn't mystical or supernatural. It was the most natural expression of love there could be.

Later that week, I woke to hear Johann's whisper in my mind.

Mod ... or ...

I couldn't make it out. I dozed for a while, and when I woke again, he was showing me plump red lips over the wavy symbol for water.

Lips over water?

A search on the term returned *En los labios del agua,* translated as *On the lips of the water,* a book by Mexican writer Alberto Ruy-Sanchez. It was described as a long love letter from the protagonist to his beloved and the quest that takes him to different lands where he discovers that his desire to reach her transcends distance and time. Unfortunately, there was no English translation of this book, so I could learn no more, but there was a translation of another of Ruy-Sanchez's books, *Mogador: The Names of the Air.*

Mogador! That's what I couldn't make out.

The New York Public Library had a copy, so I reserved it online and hopped on the subway to 42nd Street. I sensed there was something interesting here to find. One reviewer had described Ruy-Sanchez as "a painter of dreams, who manages to fuse the most unblemished sensuality with the most transparent spirituality." That sounded right up my street.

I pushed through the packed tourists and up the steps of the library on Fifth and clacked my way across marble floors to the general research section of the Schwarzman Building. The silence was a relief after the crowded trek through the throng of Times Square. I picked up my book and spent the early afternoon under the skyscape mural in the Rose Room. It was magical, the smell of old books and the cold floor and cool air.

Mogador was set in an imaginary, walled city off the coast of Morocco and told the story of Fatma who is coming of age and seized by desire.

The neighbors blame the change in her on a strange spiritual presence. One thinks she's been possessed by the soul of a dead person who visits her in sleep or dreams. Fatma later has an intimate encounter in a bathhouse with a young woman, Kadiya, who later disappears. Fatma searches the streets in vain for her beloved and finally becomes resigned to connecting with her in a place where she is neither completely awake nor asleep. In this state of semi-sleep, she finds that everything in her room is inhabited by Kadiya's presence. Everything contains depths within it where all things are connected and nothing exists in isolation. Ruy-Sanchez's language was exotic and erotic, but it was essentially a love story of one spirit calling out to another and dreaming, as Fatma says, "your dream of me in my dreams."

You want me to dream my dream of you in your dreams? Or dream your dream of me in mine?

I rode the subway home with this conundrum. Then, in the middle of the night, I had a flash of inspiration: her semi-sleep sounded like an altered state.

Is that what you mean? Stop trying to force it and let it flow like a dream?

Ja.

The next morning, I climbed through the thicket until I came upon a secluded rocky outcrop overlooking the lake and sat down to surrender my monkey mind to the peace of nature. I focused on my breath until the chirping and rustling and rippling lake faded and my mind came to a single-pointed focus in the moment. I felt the power of my subtle body, the power of my spirit, expand beyond my dense physical form until I felt that body distortion and the liberation of approaching formlessness. I brought my attention to the moment and let everything else go, letting my mind alight on the sounds, smells, images of the moment and then the next moment, allowing the world around me, visible and invisible, pass by as if another's dream and I merely the observer.

After a few minutes, I felt Johann step into the space with me. Instead of trying to grasp at greater intimacy, I merely observed the energy build around me and surrendered my sense of self to the moment. As always, in this space with him, I felt more complete, both boundless and connected, and loved unconditionally. With that awareness came a glorious sense of peace and perfection. The static electricity of his presence quivered across my skin, pressure built at my tailbone and sent bursts of rapturous energy tingling up my spine and through the crown of my head. I was on the verge of slipping out of my physical body to meet him in the glorious, ecstatic formlessness. I reached for more. Instead, I slipped out of my subtle body and back into my brain and bones.

Dammit!

I had grasped instead of surrendering. Still, for the moments it lasted, it was sheer bliss, further and deeper into the euphoria of oneness than I'd ever before experienced.

That was glorious Liebling.

I was sitting there wiggling feeling back into my feet, delighted with myself, when he whispered two crisp words.

Minimum intimacy.

Seriously Liebling, that was minimum intimacy?

He popped an image into my mind of Pooh and Piglet sitting on a branch with hands on heads. I googled the image on my phone and found it with a caption: "Don't rush it. Take time, think, think, think."

That night before bed I read some of the writings of Ram Dass, master of LSD and yogic-induced altered states of consciousness.

"Stop pushing against the more dense forms," he wrote. "You're constantly bringing spirit down into form, and you're constantly, as a form, moving toward spirit, or the formless ... experience your life as that, as moving in and out of all these planes all the time."

Ram Dass had spoken like a Zen koan, simple and impossible, in the ever stranger language of my life.

My mother called. An unannounced transatlantic call from my mother never boded well.

"Karen, it's Mam. I have a bit of bad news for you."

"Who died?"

"Your Auntie Terry isn't well."

"What do you mean not well?"

Terry was my godmother, my father's younger sister, and my favorite aunt. She and my mother met at fifteen and had been best friends ever since. I had evocative black and white photos of the two of them cycling in the Irish countryside or dolled up on O'Connell Street in Dublin in pencil skirts and winklepickers for a night on the town. Terry introduced my parents and was my mother's bridesmaid. Pretty in pale pink. She was the image of Nana McCarthy, both of them with delicate features and pretty smiles. People said I resembled her, but I never saw it. They were both talented knitwear designers and dressmakers. Nana made my first communion dress and Terry my debutant or prom dress. They made me feel beautiful when I was young. Nana was tough as old boots; she had to be to raise nine children and run two clothing factories and deal with a husband who was fond of the sauce. Terry was young at heart, animated, and free spirited. She never forgot my birthday. At my parents' house in Dublin, I had a collection of jewelry from gifts of birthdays past.

"She has stage four cancer of the esophagus," my mother said. She was inhaling the words lest the story become true if they escaped on her breath. I scrambled to weigh them.

"How bad is it?" I asked. "Can they treat it?"

"She's in an induced coma."

"I don't understand. They just found it and it was that advanced?"

"We've known for five months."

"Five months? Why didn't you tell me?"

"I thought she'd get better."

My mother's terror was measured in denial. She'd likely been saying the rosary daily or had given up one of the meager treats she ever afforded herself to bargain with God for His intervention. She had Hodgkin's lymphoma when I was an undergrad, which was beaten after six arduous months of chemotherapy and the humiliation of sickness. But esophageal cancer and Hodgkin's were different beasts, and she knew it.

"Can they do anything?'

"Well, yes, there is good news." Her frightened voice lightened. "They said if they could operate, she has a fifty-fifty chance, and the doctor just said her vitals were strong, so he booked a theater for Monday morning at 8:00 a.m. I didn't want to tell you until we had some good news."

"Okay, okay, good," I said. "That's something."

My heart went out to my mother. She was rarely given to tears. Her default emotion was anger, the only power she knew, due largely to growing up with an alcoholic father who sold everything, even her pet dog for booze. I hoped Terry wasn't suffering, but my mother was, that much I knew.

"Should I come home?" I asked.

"No, you're grand. Stay where you are. We'll see how she is after the surgery on Monday."

I woke up to Johann filling my mind with a red heart with little, white wings and some words: *Süße, dir gehört mein herz*, which I translated to mean, "Love, you own my heart." There was no better way to start my day than with his expression of love, and I needed to feel loved, especially that day when I was so worried for Terry and my mother.

There was a workshop at the church that weekend, but I didn't want to go. I really wanted to sit by the phone. But that served no purpose. In the end, I dragged myself out of bed, and got ready to go — better to be close to the spirit plane than sitting around my apartment waiting for news that wouldn't come until the surgeons arrived on Monday.

Every student I worked with that day said there was an old woman with them, offering me pearls, but they gave me nothing else clear enough to identify the giver. I skipped most exercises. I really hadn't the energy to work.

In the afternoon, I paired with Lorraine.

"Righto," Lorraine said, rubbing her spindly hands together with vigor and shuffling in her seat. "Let's see who we have here. I have ... hmm ... I dunno. I just hear a sewing machine."

That could have been Nana. She'd always had the sewing machine on the go.

"Okay, it's an old lady, very small woman, do you know who I mean?"

"My grandmother was small, but she wasn't old. She did sew."

"She feels very old," Lorraine said. "She's giving you a pearl. Do you know why a pearl is significant to her?"

"No, I don't, sorry."

"Wait, it's not a pearl, it's a string of pearl drops I think."

"Yes!" The memory sprang to mind. "That's my communion dress! My grandmother made it and stitched a row of pearl drops across the front. I forgot about that."

"She's worried," Lorraine said. "She's nursing a sick person. Do you understand?"

"Yes!"

"She doesn't have time to talk now. She's totally focused on the sick person, but she wants you to know she's helping them."

"Thank you, Lorraine," I said. "I understand."

On the drive home, I thanked Nana for being there. I was optimistic now that all would be well on Monday. I imagined my mother calling to tell me the surgery was a success. I imagined the lilt in her voice and her joy. I followed this notion around my mind for forty miles until I almost rear-ended an SUV on the GW and my fantasy was arrested by a sudden, sharp, sinking feeling.

Nana, are you there to help her to get well or to bring her home?
I was exhausted when I got back to the Bronx that night, but I ate lightly
and sat in the power on my cushion, mustering whatever energy I could
to send healing to my aunt in her hospital bed. Before I was finished,
more static electricity than I'd ever experienced was crackling across
my face, my arms, all over my bare skin, and making my hair stand on
end. It couldn't be Johann. There was no need for him to generate this
much energy to make his presence known. Something else was going on.

At 2:30 a.m., I woke with a jolt. There was a presence in the pitch-
dark room.

Nana! It's you! Why are you here?

A young woman was with her.

Who is with you, Nana?

It hit me. In a split second. As if one of them told me, not with a
word or a visual, but by putting the thought in my head so that it was
conceived and received simultaneously.

Oh my God! It's Terry. Auntie Terry! You're here. You feel fantastic.

She felt younger than her years, beautiful, vibrant, and so happy. I
burst into tears, not from sadness but as a spontaneous release of the
intensity of her feelings that overwhelmed my physical form. I had
been so worried about her suffering, but she was happy and fabulous
and with Nana. I was delighted for them and thrilled to share the bliss
of their new existence.

Then they were gone.

I should have been sad to learn she died, but I couldn't be sad when I felt
her joy. I grabbed my phone, expecting to see a missed call from my mother
to tell me Auntie Terry was dead, but there was nothing. Why hadn't she
called? She'd think it strange to get a call from me at this hour. If I told her
why, she would think my visitation ludicrous, a bad dream, something I
ate, dismissing it the way she did my childhood encounters. Still, I dialed.

"Hi Mam."

"Oh, Karen, what time is it there? Why are you calling so early?"

"I couldn't sleep. Is there any news on Auntie Terry?"

"No, no, everything the same. Her surgery is tomorrow morning."

Terry was still alive? How had she visited me in the radiance of spirit
form when she was on life support in intensive care and scheduled for
surgery the next morning? There was no point in telling my mother about
her visit now. I was too confused, and she'd definitely think it nonsense.

"Okay," I said. "Call if you hear anything. Doesn't matter what time
it is."

I went back to bed puzzled.

After a few hours of fitful sleep, I showered and dressed and drove out to the second day of my weekend workshop. My delight at the previous night's visit gave way to doubt. They had been so clear. What had I gotten wrong?

The rhythmic gasp of the respirator and the beeping of machines was how this woman started her story on the second day of my workshop. We had been told to invite someone along to share the moment of their transition either to help themselves or help their loved one still here. Everything felt different in the workshop that day. I felt hypersensitive, everything was intense. I'd partnered with Kelly, a middle-aged woman with a well-mannered exterior that belied the formidable strength packed into her small stature. As soon as I sat before her, I felt the presence of a woman who died in a hospital bed, in the ICU by the sound of it, just like Auntie Terry. I didn't want to be this close to something I didn't want to imagine that day.

"I have a woman here Kelly, who feels like an aunt, no, a great-aunt possibly. She's in a hospital. She has lines in her hands and two or three drips hanging by her bed. She's covered in electrodes that are sending the weak electrical impulses from her heart to monitors. There's a clothespin on her finger that's measuring her feeble pulse. She has been here a long time." I paused. "You know who she is?"

"Yes, my great-aunt Jane."

"Okay, thanks Kelly. It must be late evening because she's showing me that the sky is cobalt blue. A nurse sitting is at a station to the left with her back to Jane. She's writing on papers under a dim light that shines from below a shelf. It's focused, so it doesn't disturb anyone else. There's a clock overhead, I think. She can hear the rasp of the respirator and the silence between beeps because she's sharing the sounds with me. This room is measuring time to death in beeps and gasps. And she knows it. She's close to going, but there is no one there. There are no family or friends around her bed. She's dying alone."

"Yes," Kelly said. "That's how it was — the ICU with the nurses' station — and she was alone. It was awful. I was on my way, but I got there too late."

"There was someone there," I said. "She's giving me the sense that someone is coming and her mood is lifting. She feels excited."

I waited for her to show me the arrival.

"She must have been a religious woman."

"Yes, very" Kelly said.

"I can't see who's here, and this may sound strange, but it feels like a saint or a spiritual figure."

"I would understand that."

"She knows where she's going. She's showing me an old man in a brown robe with a bushy beard. He's come to help her. Do you know him?"

"I don't think so," she said.

"He reminds me of Padre Pio," I said.

"Oh yes, she prayed to Padre Pio," Kelly said.

"She's elated to see him. She wants to get free of her body to go with him."

Jane stopped showing me the ICU. She showed me nothing else from the physical world. All I could feel was her joy.

"I can't see past that Kelly. I assume that the alarm went off when her heart stopped and nurses ran to her bed, but she's not showing me any of that. She wants you to know she had a perfect transition. She wasn't alone, so she doesn't want you to feel guilty for not getting there on time."

"Thank you," Kelly said. She relaxed back in her chair. "It's a relief to know she wasn't alone. I've felt bad about that ever since she died."

I wondered if the rawness of Terry's situation that day made it easier for Jane to access my memories, which were freshly forming and easily used to convey the nuances of her own passing. I thought about how incongruous was our morbid fear of death. Jane's passing felt like she had just been born into the fullness of life.

As I fell to sleep that night, my beloved put a small, pink heart in my mind, a tiny whisper of his undying love and the support of his presence. Then, silently, he wrapped me in the warmth and comfort of his essence.

Thank you for being here, Liebling. I'd be lost without you.

Shortly after 8:00 a.m. the next morning, my mother called.

"I have bad news, Karen." Her voice was broken, her heart too. "The doctor came in this morning and said Terry had taken a turn and was too weak to operate, so he canceled the surgery."

"What will they do now?"

"Nothing. They're going to turn the machine off when everyone gets to the hospital."

"Aw, Mam. How are you coping?"

"What can you do?" she said. "She's in God's hands now."

We sat in silence on the phone for a minute or so, my mother grieving her best friend, me trying to understand what happened.

"Did it just happen?"

"What?"

"The turn?"

"No, it was around half seven yesterday morning. The hospital called your uncle, but he didn't tell us until this morning when the surgeon came in and saw her."

That meant Auntie Terry took the turn at around 2:30 a.m. Eastern Standard Time on Sunday morning, the time she and Nana woke me up. That must have been the moment she died, the moment she left her physical form behind. It would have been evident had she not been on life support. Should I tell my mother, the woman who prayed to the saints on a regular basis, but believed those who communed with the dead to be delusional? She never put much stock in my childhood conversations with blank spaces; she wrote them off as imaginary friends, which is why I never told her about the events of the last year. She was also easily angered, and today, with her nerves frayed and her heart broken, she'd snap. No, this wasn't the time to mention the incident the night before, especially since Terry was still considered, by the medical profession at least, to be alive in her physical form.

"She'll be home soon," I said. "With Nana."

"Please God," she said.

"Do you want me to come home for the funeral?"

"No, there's no point. There's nothing you can do."

All day, I replayed the events as they unfolded since Friday and my conversations with my mother, Terry, Nana, Jane. Maybe, when their grief was a little less raw and their nerves less overwrought, when I could sit in front of them and gauge their receptivity, I could tell them Terry felt glorious and that she didn't die alone.

Still, when I settled down enough to sleep that night, I fretted that I hadn't done enough. I didn't know what else to do in a situation where hearts were broken and where my story of the afterlife would be ill-timed and ill-received.

Johann put a little heart into my mind with a whisper.

You did good work.

Thank you, my love. That means so much to me.

The following Sunday, I wrapped myself in fleece, took my tea and the *New York Times*, climbed into the thicket, and sat on a rock under the yellow trees to read. There were cafés in the neighborhood and benches in the park, but I needed quiet and peace.

Mona Simpson's eulogy for her brother Steve Jobs who had died two weeks before appeared in the opinion section. She shared memories of his life, his capacity for wonderment, his lack of cynicism, his belief that love happened all the time, everywhere. At his moment of death, he looked at those around his bed, his sister, children, life partner, and then looked over their shoulders and said — she wrote with emphasis — "OH WOW. OH WOW. OH WOW."

I wouldn't have understood that the year before. I would have attributed that to a flood of endorphins or the loss of oxygen to the eye. But now, I'd seen glimmers of the "oh wow" when I woke up to messages of endearment and navigated my day and my way — knowing I wasn't alone — that help was at hand and that love was truly eternal. I'd seen it in how lovers and families and children reunite, how pets remember, how suicides heal, how people in spirit find purpose and how they have infinite capacity for love and forgiveness and intimacy. I'd seen it in the joy and remorse that had been shared with me from the world of spirit: the need to express words left unsaid, the need to recall memories shared, the need to show that bonds endure, and the simplest need of all to say, "I did not die. I am here, and I love you."

Mona Simpson wrote that in the end we die *in medias res*, in the middle of a story. I knew now that death is in medias res. Death is the middle of our story. I knew, not from faith but from experience, that the rest of our existence is lived out in formlessness, not in some far-off place, over there, up there, or down a tunnel of light. If the physicists who devised string theory or membrane theory can say there are ten or eleven dimensions existing around us along with the three we perceive, was it so hard to believe that the afterlife is right here in the same stream of consciousness shared by the spirit and physical worlds, where every day unspoken words and intuitive feelings are silently expressed between the living and the living and the living and the so-called dead? I knew now that in the collective consciousness, the discarnate were only ever a thought away from us and us from them. How many times had I thought of Johann and felt him respond? Wasn't it just as likely that he had thought of me, and I felt his thoughts, and I responded? I wondered how many times in a day we think we are thinking about our loved ones, when they are actually thinking of us.

The wind grew sharp. I could feel the chill in my spine. I clambered down the rock face and along the trail back to the city streets. I passed a mother trying to strap her screaming child into a stroller. He was arching his back and kicking and protesting as much as he could to avoid being tied down. I wondered if he ever saw the spirits of his ancestors the way children who had recently come out of spirit and into physical form did. The veil is thin for those on the cusp of entering and those on the cusp of leaving this life. I wondered if his mother dismissed them as imaginary friends as had mine had done.

Johann had opened this door, and now I wanted to do more. I wanted to receive and share more than just details for those in the spirit world. I wanted to be able to share their memories of life past and witness their continued existence. I wanted to show that they participate in their loved ones' physical lives, aware of their challenges, and offering to help. I wanted to be able to tell their story — the story they wanted to tell. I wanted to comfort the bereaved the way Johann's presence comforted me: the comfort he offered by connecting me with his mother, the love and compassion he offered when Auntie Terry died, the fear of death he'd taken away, the hope he'd given me, the sense of purpose, and above all, his unconditional love.

I wanted to blend with him in the formlessness, in the state of interbeing, like Fatma's dream, but I was still Pooh in the tree, holding my head in my hands and trying to think.

Liebling, show me what to do.

The next morning, I woke to find in my mind the image of a large building with a big arrow pointing to one of its mullioned windows. It had something of Hogwarts about it. I'd no idea what Johann meant, but it hit me later when I was foraging in the fridge for lunch.

The college! He hadn't shown me Hogwarts, he'd shown me the sprawling Jacobean country estate of the Arthur Findlay College for the advancement of Spiritualism and the psychic sciences. This must have been what Miss Byrnes meant too when she talked about going back to college. I pulled up its website, read its history, and poured over the classes it offered. Glyn Edwards had a course starting soon, which was designed, it said, to raise the standard of mediumship, strengthen our ability to blend with the spirit world, and improve the evidence in our communication with those in spirit form. That course could not have been more perfect. After all this time, listening to and trying to emulate Glyn Edwards, here was a chance to train with him. I sent an enquiry and was told by return email that the course was full, but I was waitlisted.

I don't know if I'm ready for this Liebling, but if you and Miss Byrnes think I am, then there'll have to be a cancelation.

A few days later, there was, and so I registered. I booked a flight to London, along with a short-hop flight from London to Dublin afterward so I could have that long chat with my mother about the night Auntie Terry and Nana came by. I put my car in storage and left apartment keys with a neighbor so she could water my plants. Then I packed my bags and crossed the ocean to my new adventure.

After a transatlantic redeye and a very early arrival, I took a short train ride through the English countryside to Stansted Mountfitchet, a sleepy village with small Tudor-style buildings and narrow, winding roads. I walked the ten minutes from the station to the village center and realized I was lost.

"Excuse me," I said to an elderly man in a flat cap and wellies. "Do you know the way to the Arthur Findlay College?"

"Never heard of it."

"I think it's also called Stansted Hall?"

"Oh, you mean Spooky Hall? You go down that road there and take a left into the gatehouse and then follow the road for a mile."

"Thanks," I said, but he'd already marched on with his day.

At the gatehouse, I found the road was a long dirt path through grassy fields that stretched into the morning mist. To my left, horses grazed; to my right, a graveyard was presided over by an old church, parts of which looked like they'd been standing since the Dark Ages. I hiked my bag onto my back and navigated a mile of mud and puddles until I came to a wooden kissing gate at the edge of the college grounds. Beyond, towered the mid-nineteenth-century estate house, the latest incarnation of a structure that had stood in one form or another since the fourteenth century. I'd read that its current incarnation as a Jacobean-styled hall with large, clean windows, round-arch arcades, parapets, tall chimney stacks and landscaped gardens was the result of a complete rebuild in the 1870s, possibly by an Irish architect. In 1923, it was bought by Scottish philanthropist and Spiritualist, Arthur Findlay, who, upon his death, deeded it to the Spiritualists' National Union to create a residential college for the training of competent mediums. And now, this morning, standing at the front door, which was exactly as Johann had shown, I was the latest arrival in a long line of spiritual seekers.

I was early, and the college hadn't roused. Check-in wasn't until three and interviews for tutor assignments weren't until five. The sky was cloudy but not heavy. From the dampness hanging in the air, I could tell it had already rained. I crunched over the white pebble walkway around the building and into the gardens. I crossed the sprawling lawn toward the golden canopy of trees just visible in the mist. The flowers had withdrawn to bulbs and the birds to their nests as nature turned inward. I sat underneath a huge tree, easily twenty feet in circumference, and was absorbed into its history. The land was so quiet, I could feel the earth throb.

A man rounded the trunk. The groundskeeper by the look of him.

"Morning," he said.

"Morning."

"Mind yourself there," he said. "It's a bit slippery around here after the rain."

I knew that accent.

"You're Irish," I said.

"Cork man I am. Yourself?"

"Dublin, but I've lived in New York a long time."

"First time here?" he asked.

"Yep. Brand new."

"Ah, you'll love it," he said, stomping some tufts into the ground and moving on. "I'll see you around so."

For the next half hour, I listened to the wood pigeons' coo and the thrushes' chirp and watched the vapor of my breath drift into the mist until my eyelids closed, and I dozed into the rhythm of life in winter. Whether it was my hours of lakeside meditation or the power of decades of mediums converging on this place to commune with the world of spirit, I didn't know, but in the threshold of consciousness, the half-dream state, I felt my breath dancing gently with the pulse of the earth, following an easy pace, connecting me to the spirits and secrets and wishes of ages.

And my wish.

I want to be with you.

I longed for him and for the intimacy that he intimated was possible in spirit form, the spiritual union that came from a height and depth I couldn't yet fathom.

His physical image appeared in my mind, close and clear, filling me with joy. I traced his forehead and lips and placed my hand over his heart. My skin quivered under his touch, sending waves of euphoria through my body. Pressure built at the base of my spine and began to flow and throb to my hara, the seat of consciousness from where we can achieve one pointedness and mental and emotional stability. Energy surged though my being, tingling through my spine, tantalizing my nerve ends. I breathed into the sensation, fully present with it. From there, the energy flowed to my solar plexus and then my heart. I gasped and pulled back. It was far too intense.

Then came his whisper.

Surrender.

I relaxed again and breathed into the moment and then the next, feeling only my love for him, not grasping or reaching, just allowing my subtle body to expand to touch the power of this place. Formlessness came more easily here, first wide and then high, as if my head were at the top of the tree while my feet were drifting to the end of the lawn and dissolving into oblivion. My breath dispersed into infinite space, where the creaking bough and cloudy sky whispered to me to step into the limitless, immortal beauty of all things. I felt free of the worries of the physical world, free, as if there were nothing in life that the spirit in nature couldn't heal. By just being present, by embracing formlessness — releasing into it, surrendering to it — the anxiety of separateness began to fade, and I began to glimpse, just slightly, the exhilaration that could be experienced in oneness with him, oneness with all things.

Be here, he whispered.

Yes, I said. *Yes.*

I felt a wave of unconditional love, love for just existing, love that didn't have to be earned, love that placed no importance on my shortcomings, failings, or imperfections. Love for no reason and with no agenda. I was embraced by his unconditional acceptance, universal acceptance. I felt his energy flowing in me again, throbbing, building, dropping, and building again, moving faster and more easily the more I surrendered. I melted into the flow, meeting him there, blending atom to atom and surrendering little by little to boundlessness somewhere outside — no, within the essence of all things. We were no bodies here. There were no trees or language, no worries, no façade or secrets, no shame or ego, no past or future, no conflict or restlessness, no them and us, him and me, just everything in nothingness, invisible, ineffable, intangible, indefinable, as we were absorbed into each other, unfolding into cosmic consciousness like notes in the allegro of a symphony played in pitch-perfect unison. I was him. He was me. Separate and the same. Limitless. Rapturous. Uncontainable. Free-floating in bliss, the bliss of each other, the bliss of the universe. I saw it, was it, felt it: the flowing, undulating, absorbing, overwhelming waves of love, beauty, belonging, unity. Then total surrender … and … ecstasy …

Chirp.
Crunch.
Whistle of wind.
Dampness on face.
Grass beneath my fingers.
I was back. Just me under a tree, alone, and ordinary.

Although neither alone nor ordinary. The colors of the garden were more saturated, the drizzle on my face was softer, the winter air was crisper, and the songs of birds were sweeter. Euphoria flowed through my body and spirit. I felt my beloved in the wholeness of my heart. I saw him in the glimmers of sunshine and in the rain. He had shown me the glory of home, and it brought new wonder to life.

Excited chatter pierced the stillness. Pebbles crunched under feet. The distant buzz of the bell and slam of the door announced the arrival of a hundred students eager to meet Glyn Edwards and his team of tutors. It was time to rise. The page was turning on a new chapter.

Liebling, it's beginning. Shall we?

About the Author

~~~

K aren Frances McCarthy is a published author, public speaker, and progressive, Spiritualist medium. Formerly a major media political journalist and war correspondent, she now focuses on writing and speaking about spirituality, existential beliefs, and the philosophy of religion, including belief systems surrounding death, dying, and the afterlife. She is an exponent of writing for mindfulness and spiritual transformation and contributes to a number of media outlets on subjects including spirituality, metaphysics, healing, and bereavement.

Her first book, *The Other Irish* (Sterling, New York, 2011) was supported by Ireland's Department of Foreign Affairs as part of Ireland's cross-border peace process; for this work, she was named one of the top Irish female broadcasters who have made an international impact. In television, she produced *The Crystal Cave* and *Alchemy: The Art of Spiritual Transformation* for Deepak Chopra.

She holds three Certificates of Recognition in mediumship, spiritual healing, and public speaking from the Spiritualist National Union, governing body of the Arthur Findlay College in London where she trained. She has a private mediumship and healing practice with clients around the globe, and teaches in the USA, Ireland, and online. She is currently researching a PhD on contemporary ghost literature at ARU in Cambridge, UK, and is working on a new non-fiction book about the weird world of science and spirituality.

Lightning Source UK Ltd.
Milton Keynes UK
UKHW011049281120
374218UK00002B/304

9 781786 771292